PLAYWRITING

FROM FORMULA TO FORM

A GUIDE TO WRITING A PLAY

WILLIAM MISSOURI DOWNS
University of Wyoming

LOU ANNE WRIGHT
University of Wyoming

PLAYWRITING
FROM FORMULA TO FORM

A GUIDE TO WRITING A PLAY

HARCOURT BRACE COLLEGE PUBLISHERS

Fort Worth Philadelphia San Diego New York Orlando Austin San Antonio
Toronto Montreal London Sydney Tokyo

Publisher: **Christopher P. Klein**
Acquisitions Editor: **Barbara Rosenberg**
Product Manager: **Patricia Murphree**
Project Editor: **Matt Ball**
Art Director: **Garry Harman**
Production Manager: **Diane Gray**

ISBN: 0-15-503861-3
Library of Congress Catalog Card Number: 97-72178

Address for orders:
Harcourt Brace College Publishers
6277 Sea Harbor Drive
Orlando, FL 32887-6777
1-800-782-4479

Address for editorial correspondence:
Harcourt Brace College Publishers
301 Commerce Street, Suite 3700
Fort Worth, TX 76102

Web site address:
http://www.hbcollege.com

Printed in the United States of America

Harcourt Brace & Company will provide complimentary supplements or supplement packages to those adopters qualified under our adoption policy. Please contact your sales representative to learn how you qualify. If as an adopter or potential user you receive supplements you do not need, please return them to your sales representative or send them to: Attn: Returns Department, Troy Warehouse, 465 South Lincoln Drive, Troy, MO 63379.

7 8 9 0 1 2 3 4 5 6   067   9 8 7 6 5 4 3 2 1

TO OUR WRITING TEACHERS

Lew Hunter
Milan Stitt
Stirling Sulliphant
Lanford Wilson
Richard Walter
Rod Marriott
Hal Ackerman
and James Livingston

SPECIAL THANKS TO

David Hall

Lew and Pamela Hunter, Rebecca Hilliker, Oliver Walter, Erik Ramsey, Caroline Rule, Laura Vass, Katherine Kirkaldie, Scott Pardue, Glen Merzer, Pat Gabridge, Robin Russin, Tom Shadyac, Dana Singer, Linda Eisenstein, William and Doris Streib, James and Billie Wright, Andy Bryson, Joe Gregg and the Center for Teaching Excellence, Cliff Marks and Jeannie Holland, Shozo Sato, Rick and Laura Hall, The Circle Rep Theatre, U.C.L.A. Film School, Peter Grego, Linda de Vries, Michael Barnes, Roger Held and Mark Damen and the Utah Playfest, Jo Weinstein and the Mill Mountain Theatre, Rich Burk for saving that first play, Milan Stitt for starting it all, and the student playwrights of the University of Wyoming.

Also, special thanks to the folks at Harcourt Brace College Publishers: Barbara Rosenberg, acquisitions editor; Matt Ball, project editor; Garry Harman, art director; and Diane Gray, production manager.

And thanks to Lisa Dillman, a Chicago playwright, for her expert proofreading.

PREFACE

Art is not nature's creation—it is man's. . . . The rearrangement of nature is achieved through technique—known in drama as form, or structure. Each art has its own technique based upon fundamental principles.

Dean & Carra

Being a playwright is not a birthright. There are no child prodigies in playwriting. Seldom do playwrights find a strong, mature voice before their middle to late twenties. Whether you have the talent to become a playwright is out of your control, and as a result unimportant. What you can do is master technique, structure, and the practical side of the art.

"Most playwrights go wrong on the fifth word," according to Meredith Willson, author of The Music Man. "When you start a play and type 'Act One, Scene One,' your writing is every bit as good as Arthur Miller or Eugene O'Neill. It's that fifth word where beginners start to go wrong." This book is devoted to technique, structure, and those lessons all playwrights must master in order to reveal their talent and write that fifth word.

It was the last day of Playwriting 101. For weeks I had lectured on the fundamental principles and techniques for writing good plays. Class exercises had covered the secrets of developing strong characters, believable dialogue, and powerful stories. I'd painstakingly discussed everything from format to production. There was nothing left to say. It was time for the students to go home, face the silence of the empty page, and write. As the class slowly filed out, one usually quiet student raised her hand and asked tentatively, "Yeah, but how do you write a play?"

There's the rub. If there were such a thing as a how-to book on playwriting, it would be like those self-help books on plumbing. It might show you how to fix a broken faucet, but it wouldn't make you a plumber. A playwriting how-to book would allow you to borrow someone else's techniques and formulas, but it couldn't make you a playwright. That's not all bad. All playwrights learn from the past, have gone though a period of apprenticeship, and acquired knowledge of structure and technique. This book is about structure and technique.

Structure is how a play logically fits together. It's the arrangement and interconnection of story and character. Structure can follow a precise formulaic blueprint or a loose method, but either way it is a design. Techniques are the practices, devices, even tricks playwrights use to construct believable characters, sharp dialogue, and strong stories. Mastering structure and technique gives the playwright a range of options and the freedom to be creative.

Creativity, technique, and structure are all interrelated. Without technique, your creativity is limited; without creativity, your structure turns into pure formula. As creativity is the one element in the equation that cannot be taught, the goal of this book is to demystify the elements that can. This is a down-to-earth, practical guide and as close to a how-to or self-help book as is possible. It will solve many of your writing problems, but it can't make you a playwright (or a plumber for that matter).

Beginning and intermediate playwrights fall into several categories. First, there are the ones who rebel against structure and technique. These writers reject the mechanics of writing. They worry that structure and technique are only a list of platitudes that limit their creativity and result in manufactured, fill-in-the-blank, formula plots. These writers strike out to invent a "new tradition," only to discover, in the end, their pages of deep emotions and private thoughts, don't play to an audience. Confounded by this lack of appreciation, they defend their failure by thinking of themselves as ahead of their time. More often than not, the problem isn't their advanced ideas, but a lack of good structure and technique. If you're going to rebel against formula, first find out what it is. This book will identify formula and teach you how to follow or avoid it.

Many new writers imitate their favorite playwrights. University playwriting classes are filled with young Wilsons, Mamets, and Becketts who have consciously or unconsciously substituted someone else's design in their own work. There is nothing wrong with this. Many famous dramatists began by aping other writers. Shakespeare and Ibsen, for example, were imitative at first, but eventually found their own voices. We imitate because the empty page is hard to face. We imitate for security, as a safeguard against false starts and half-finished plays. This book contains methods to help writers find their own voices and develop unique styles.

Some would-be writers can't write unless they feel "in the mood." As callous as it sounds, this is only an excuse. Writers write whether they're in the mood or not. They depend on their technique to support them until the creative impulse comes. This book gives you techniques to become more creative, or at the very least, put you "in the mood."

Some students aren't ready to jump into that first script. For those who feel safer mastering technique through exercises, some chapters contain drills and activities designed to limber up the writer. Like a pianist flexing her fingers by playing scales before a concert, these exercises are designed to help the playwright practice the basics.

Many find playwriting an isolated art. Often it's difficult to judge where your talents stand in relation to others. Reading published, professional plays is good, but it doesn't allow students to study plays written by playwrights of their own age and level. To help break the isolation, we include three student-written plays: (1) a strong undergraduate play that came in second at a regional American College Theater Festival (ACTF) one-act play competition, (2) a script that won its student author acceptance to graduate school and took first place at a regional ACTF festival, and (3) a national winner of the American College Theatre Festival.

Still other playwrights finish a script, but don't know how to market it. Even with an agent, playwrights can't sit back and hope the critical world beats a path to their doors; they must win contests, lure producers, and self-promote. Proper script format, a good synopsis, cover letter, and résumé are paramount. Too often theatres reject scripts that don't look professional. In these chapters we cover the basics of self-promotion and how to appear professional. It's also difficult to understand how your play is judged by various contests and theatres, and so we include the evaluation sheets typically used by producing organizations and contests.

Some playwrights succeed in getting a production but can't make the difficult transition from solo artist to member of an artistic ensemble. A playwright must work with actors, designers, and directors. This book looks at all it takes to become a playwright, from the first scratchy notes to closing night.

Next are the writers who transfer to playwriting from other genres, only to find it a rocky transition. Experienced journalists, screenwriters, poets, novelists, and short story writers often stumble when they attempt to write their first play. Keats, Shelley, Byron, and Wordsworth were all great writers who tried but couldn't adapt their writing skills to the practical limitations of the stage. Others write from a cinematic background, creating something closer to a movie than a play. This fault lies mostly in students raised on the staccato style of sitcoms and the silver screen. They hide their inability to write sustained dialogue by using blackouts and brief scenes, none long enough to allow true depth. Although they share many common areas, playwriting differs from all other forms of creative writing. It has a unique scope, purpose, and medium and must be mastered as an individual art. This book will help you make the transition and curb cinematic thinking and teach you to write comfortably within the limited world of playwriting.

For playwrights interested in screenwriting, my partner and I include a chapter on writing for television and movies. This chapter concentrates on the differences between playwriting and screenwriting in terms of technique, structure, agents, unions, and environment. We include advice on how to break into the industry, how to pitch, and how to properly format your screenplay, teleplay, and even sitcom. This chapter is unique in that we look at screenwriting from a playwright's point of view.

Finally, there are the single-script playwrights. They write one script; it never gets produced, or it is panned, so they give up. Grounded by this lack of success, these writers question their talent. They attempt to justify failure by saying, "Playwrights are born, not made." They're wrong. Their talents will be realized only if they go back to the basics, study technique, structure, and the practical lessons of their art.

This book is dedicated to the belief that playwrights are made, not born.

Lou Anne Wright

William Missouri Downs holds an M.F.A. in acting from the University of Illinois and an M.F.A. in screenwriting from U.C.L.A. He was trained in playwriting under Lanford Wilson and Milan Stitt at the Circle Repertory Theatre in New York. Bill has authored nearly a dozen plays, including *Jewish Sports Heroes and Texas Intellectuals, Imitating Life, Dead White Males, Innocent Thoughts,* and *Kabuki Faust.* He has won numerous writing awards, among them the National Playwrights Award and the Jack Nicholson Award for screenwriting. Bill's plays have been produced all over the world, including the Kennedy Center, the Berkeley Repertory, The Civic Opera House in downtown Chicago, The Fine Arts Center in Durban, South Africa, and The International Theatre Festival in Israel. In Hollywood, Bill wrote for such NBC sitcoms as *My Two Dads, Amen,* and *The Fresh Prince of Bel Air.* He also sold the movie *Executive Privilege* to Tri-star.

Lou Anne Wright holds an MFA in Voice, Speech and Dialects from the National Theatre Conservatory. She wrote the play *Kabuki Medea* which won the Jefferson Award for Best Production in Chicago and the Bay Area Critics Award for Best Production in San Francisco. The play was also produced at the Kennedy Center in Washington DC as a part of the AT&T Arts Festival. Her screenwriting credits include the film adaptation of Eudora Welty's *The Hitch-Hikers,* which featured Patty Duke and Richard Hatch (and for which she was nominated for the Directors Guild of America's Lillian Gish award).

Together
Both Bill and Lou Anne teach at the University of Wyoming. Their students have won numerous awards including two regional and one national award for best student-written play from the American College Theatre Association. University of Wyoming playwrights have taken first place in the Rocky Mountain Theatre Association's playwriting contest three years in a row.

CONTENTS

INTRODUCTION

Two weeks after I sold my first screenplay, I was summoned to the boardroom of Imagine Films. Their brass and glass offices are located nineteen stories above the streets of Century City, a modern row of sky-scrapers that occupies the now de-

> *The writer's problem is to describe things which other people are too busy to describe.*
>
> James Baldwin

molished historic back lot of Twentieth Century Fox. Several producers were pitching ideas that I was to incorporate in the rewrite.

"What if we used the warehouse scene from the first *Beverly Hills Cop?*" pitched a producer wearing a tie with a picture of a fish on it. Agreement from the other fish ties. The secretary wrote it down with a big smiley face in the margin.

"And what if we adjusted the classroom scene from the first *Indiana Jones?*" said the trout in the corner. This earned two smiley faces from the secretary.

My own notepad was empty. I was an hour into my first Hollywood note session and I was totally lost. I began to question what I was doing there. I was nothing more than a playwright who was tired of royalty checks bouncing. Having had my fill of suffering for my art (that is, eating TV dinners and living in a mobile home), I had chucked it all and moved to soggy California to write for the entertainment industry. I longed for the one thing all playwrights desire: to earn a living as a writer.

"I don't think it works that our hero is a CIA agent," the swordfish at the watercooler added. "Let's make him something people can identify with. A pickle salesman worked in *Crossing Delancey!*" This was worth two-and-a-half smiley faces. Personally, I couldn't understand how any of these suggestions were going to work in *my* movie, a modern screen version of *Captains*

Courageous (the Jules Verne novel that was turned into a Spencer Tracy movie classic). But I figured that while in Rome I could damn well be a Roman, so I piped up with, "What if we used the breastfeeding scene from *Paint Your Wagon?*" A pause. A Pinter pause.[i] *Paint Your Wagon* had always been one of my favorite movies, even Clint Eastwood's solo number. Silence! I felt compelled to explain to the large, unblinking eyes around me, "You see, our hero, lost in the woods for a month, discovers a cabin, inside is a woman breastfeeding a baby, and . . ." My voice drifted off. Nothing but big, blank stares. I turned to the secretary for help, but apparently I didn't rate a smiley face. For the rest of the day I pretended to take notes and kept my mouth shut.

After the meeting, I followed one of the producers to the parking deck, where I begged him to tell me what was wrong with my idea. At least what I pitched had tied into the story. He leaned against his Range Rover, put a fatherly arm on my shoulder and said, "Bill, *Paint Your Wagon* lost money."

I walked home, around the Beverly Hills Country Club, along the condos of Wilshire Boulevard, and past the derelicts of Santa Monica. I had finally sold a screenplay, and I felt like hell. After my rewrite, the script was given to another writer, who rewrote my rewrites, and then another who rewrote both of us. Eventually, the movie was never made. That screenplay is gathering dust on a shelf somewhere in Century City, locked away from the California sun.

That night I admonished myself for feeling rejected. After all, the check was good, there was a new car in the driveway, and I was looking straight down the barrel of a loaded future. During the next few years I wrote only what I thought would sell. This mistake drove me to sitcoms.

A year later, I was a staff writer on an NBC show, *My Two Dads*, a silly sitcom about a girl who had two fathers. For every story aired, the staff writers would pitch dozens of rejects. One morning I drove through the studio gate, confident that I had an idea and it was a winner. My pitch revolved around the character of the daughter, who, while digging through some old boxes in the basement of the apartment complex, discovers an incriminating newspaper article. The article states that the two fathers' best friend, an ornery federal judge who lived next door, has a felony arrest in her past. The newspaper would be old and tattered, and the fathers couldn't read why the magistrate was arrested, but the information would be enough to send the sitcom family into a panic. The episode would be centered on the "comic escapades" of the fathers trying to get the truth out of the old judge and, in the end, making the hard decision to "do the right thing." In the climactic last scene, in front of the inquiry board, they would discover that the judge had indeed been arrested in 1963. The place: Selma, Alabama. The charge: participating in a civil rights march. NBC loved the idea, except, of course, "the Selma, Alabama, thing."

---

[i] A long meaningful pause named for playwright Harold Pinter.

"Why does it have to be a civil rights march? Do we really want to open a can of worms? That tells people it's okay to break some laws," one producer pointed out.

"Exactly," I said.

"This is a family show. Make it that the daughter discovers the judge's ex-husband!"

If you fight the networks in Hollywood you'll find yourself without a job, so I wrote the episode switching the "Selma, Alabama, thing" for an ex-husband. I made the ex an inauspicious man and just as ornery as the judge. NBC loved the script, except, of course, the "ex-husband thing."

"By creating an ex who's a foil for the judge, you make a negative statement about some marriages."

"Exactly."

"This is a family show. Change it so that the ex-husband is sorry and wants forgiveness."

I went home and rewrote. In the end, the episode that aired was the story of a sad man who made the biggest mistake of his life the day he divorced the judge. In the last scene the judge forgave her ex, love triumphed, and we faded to black with the new/old lovers dancing on the roof of the building while the pseudo-family sang *I Love You Truly*. It was a major achievement. It had taken hundreds of hours to write, rewrite, rehearse, tape, and edit. The cost? Nearly a half million dollars per episode, but from the network's point of view, all the money and hard work paid off, for we had succeeded in airing another episode of *My Two Dads* that said absolutely nothing. It made no useful statements, had no moral, and didn't insult anyone, not even the Klan. But the check was good.

Every episode of a sitcom I wrote had one of two themes: either, "If we just stick together everything will be fine," or, "Be yourself." I was proud when one of my episodes managed both themes simultaneously. Then, one day I tuned in to an episode of *The Fresh Prince of Bel Air* I had written, only to discover I didn't recognize it. I watched the whole episode, desperate to find one joke, one line, one comma of mine. I had been totally rewritten by the staff writers. My name was still on it, yet there was nothing left. But the check was good.

As the credits rolled, a friend called to tell me he had just seen it and thought it was my best work yet. I smiled, swallowed hard, and said, "Thanks." I knew then that I had lost my creative self. I no longer had an individual style. I had nothing to say, and therefore, I was no longer a writer. I had given up my first love, playwriting, to become a pure formula hack.

This book is the result of lessons learned when I left Hollywood, divorced myself from The Business, and set out to rediscover the art of writing plays.

William Downs

Chapter 1

THE IDEA

Georges Polti, in his book *The Thirty-Six Dramatic Situations* (1921), claimed that there are a limited number of human emotions and therefore a limited number of story ideas. All plays, novels, and short stories, he said, were variations of only thirty-six plots. They included categories such as "Fatal Imprudence," "Daring Enterprise," and "Murderous Adultery." According to him, there are no new ideas. William Wallace Cook also attempted to categorize plots in *Plotto* (1928).[1] His book was supposed to help the writer construct a plot by stringing together hundreds of possible "interchangeable clauses." Some playwrights seek out these scarce old volumes in the hope that they will free dormant creativity and give the playwright the one thing all writers long for, that rarest of all commodities, *an original idea*.

> *Right now it's only a notion, but I think I can get money to make it into a concept and then later turn it into an idea.*
>
> Woody Allen (from *Annie Hall*)

There may be no new ideas. If not, then the only originality comes from the life and unique point of view of an individual writer. A playwright is an interpreter of life. In the process of interpretation, a playwright states his or her unique truth about how life is or should be. To do this, a playwright must have a philosophy. More than just an opinion, a philosophy is a logically definable point of view. Philosophy results from an investigation of the causes and laws underlying reality. If a playwright has a distinct point of view, then the number

---

[1] *The Thirty-Six Dramatic Situations* was recently reprinted by The Writer, Inc. ISBN 0-87116-109-5. *Plotto* had only one printing and can be difficult to find, but a new book and computer program that are similar are available through *Plot Unlimited,* 1(800) 833-PLOT.

of possible stories is unlimited. Look to yourself, to your philosophies, and you'll find an original idea.

GERMINAL AND HALF IDEAS

A play begins with a germinal idea. It can come from a newspaper article, a factual event, a poem, or a photo, but it's more likely to spring from a personal story, a fancy, or an intimate experience. Playwrights are inspired by haunting memories, dreams and nightmares, harbored resentments, unfinished business, or a social injustice. Anything that stimulates the playwright's personal point of view is a good germinal idea. Yet, not all ideas can become plays. To become a play, an idea must have two strong characteristics. First, it must be the spark that ignites months of brainstorming, long hours of reflection, and countless nights of creative writing. Second, it must be stageable.

Not all ideas are stageable. A *half-idea* is a notion that lacks the necessary elements needed to evolve into a play. At first the idea sounds promising, but when the playwright begins development and writing, his vision comes up short. Half-ideas never work because they lack the necessary elements of drama. Some of these elements include character, plot, action, conflict/crisis, unity, and truth. Half-ideas can also lack clarity or proper scope, suffer from cinematic thinking, or spring from story ideas outside the writer's knowledge.

CHARACTER

In a recent beginning playwriting class, twelve students were asked to write a short paragraph stating (or *pitching*) their play ideas. The following are those students' ideas. Most are half-ideas.

Playwright #1
Working Title: *The Forgotten*

The play I want to write is inspired by the fall of Saigon in 1976. The last helicopter left the roof of the U.S. embassy only hours before the North Vietnamese entered the compound. What the Americans didn't know is that they had accidentally left four marines on the roof of the building. Back on the ship, their absence was not detected for over two hours. I think I can make a strong statement about America's involvement in war. In the end, of course, they're rescued, but for two hours they wouldn't know, so there'd be much inherent conflict.

This is certainly an interesting idea, but at this point it's a half-idea because there are no **characters.** Who are these four marines? What happens on the roof of the embassy will depend on their personalities, their wants, and desires. A good idea has at least a basic concept of who the main characters are. Until the student has at least a vague notion of who his story's characters are, he doesn't have a full idea. As it turned out, this student had never spoken with a marine, never been in the armed forces, and had quite of bit of research to do before he could improve the idea.

PLOT

Playwright #2

Working Title: *A Hard Act to Follow*

I want to write about my grandfather, a man who lived to be over a hundred. He had a hard life, lost three children at birth, and had been widowed twice, but he never seemed to let the world get him down and so he was a source of hope and inspiration for my whole family. He had a gold tooth and was missing a finger, which he claimed he lost to a bear. We never believed it. By writing about the last years of his life, I think I can make a statement about not taking life too seriously. Something about enjoying the time we've got.

Again, this is a half-idea. The playwright has the beginnings of a character, but what's the story? What happens in the play? What does the grandfather *do?* These are the elements of **plot.** You don't have to have the whole story worked out, but a good idea contains at least a hint of what transpires in the play, of what the character ultimately wants (the "objective"), and what or who is stopping him or her from getting it. This grandfather story could work as a short story, but as a play, it's a half-idea until it has some semblance of action.

ACTION

To a playwright, **action** means more than just physical movement; the action of the play includes the human acts, conflicts, and thoughts that move a story forward. Action is the continuous, progressive development, growth, and change in the story and characters. Action is dramatic movement; it's what the characters *do*. Even if they have no physical action, they will express mental action through dialogue. In the broadest sense, action is the movement of the story, but it can also be as small as a character's thoughts (as long as those thoughts develop, progress, and cause a new action). David Ball in his book *Backwards & Forwards* states, "Action occurs when something happens that makes or permits something else to happen." In this way, Hamlet's "To be or not to be" soliloquy is full of action even though little activity occurs on the stage. Plays such as Chekhov's *The Cherry Orchard* or Beckett's *Waiting For Godot* may appear static, but they are full of action. A play cannot contain character without action or action without character. They are inseparable. Characters define the actions; the action of a play becomes possible only when it's motivated by believable characters. A scene, sentence, or word lacking action will make a play static.

CONFLICT/CRISIS

Playwright #3

Working Title: *My Kind of Heaven*

I want to write about real people and real lives. In particular, my childhood. I came from a loving family. I think people have forgotten that there are loving, dare I say, perfect families out there. I want to tell the story of a vacation my family took when I was twelve. We did everything, camped at Yellowstone, met new and interesting people, saw wonderful sights, and drew together as a family. In the end, we reaffirmed our love for one another.

This idea has characters (though the playwright didn't go into much detail) and some action, but it's still a half-idea because it lacks the third element of a play— **conflict/crisis.** Conflict and crisis form the core of drama. Just as action is more than physical movement, conflict can be more than conflict between only two people. A play can be full of a character's *internal conflicts*. Crisis is the one element that makes a play unique from all other forms of storytelling. Because all plays operate under a time constraint, they can examine only the critical moments in characters' lives. "Drama may be called the art of crises," said drama critic William Archer. We can write about those elements of life that do not contain conflict and crisis, the parts that aren't about an immediate dilemma or entanglement, but not in the form of a play. No one wants to see a play about what UCLA writing professor Richard Walter calls, "The land of the happy people."

UNITY

Playwright #4

Working Title: *Cry for the Moon*

I want to write about a woman who travels across country in a minivan. She's running away from a horrible relationship. Married three times, her husband was a truck driver who loved to get drunk and beat up women. The policewoman who arrested the wife-beater was a good person. She didn't want to make the arrest but instead wanted to teach him how to control his temper. The policewoman was kicked off the force because she cared too much. The policewoman's son Max never recovered from his mother being unemployed and so he grew up to be a bum. One day the son became so depressed about his grades that he jumped off a bridge. It's a sad ending but sometimes life is sad.

This idea has characters, there's action, plenty of opportunities for conflict and crisis, but it's still a half-idea because it lacks **unity.**

Discussions of unity in a play date back at least to Aristotle, about twenty-three hundred years ago, in his book *Poetics*. Aristotle proposed the *unity of action,* a cohesiveness that brings all the elements of a play—the conflicts, the crisis, the characters, and the action—to bear on a single subject or *spine.*

This playwright's idea begins with a woman who runs away from an abusive husband, and then we never hear what happens to her. The story wanders and therefore lacks unity. This idea might work for a novel, but definitely not a play.

TRUTH

Playwright #5

Working Title: *Innocent Revenge*

This play is about a man who was mad at his wife and wanted to kill her. He got a baseball bat and waited in Central Park for her to pass by. When she did, he hit her; she fell and impaled herself on a park bench. My story is about the trial and how the man is really innocent. In the end, the jury agrees, because the park bench is what killed the woman, not the husband. He leaves the courtroom, starts his life over, and this time he gets it right.

What's wrong with this idea? It has all the elements of a play but it's lacking something. It lacks **truth.** The audience's experiences make the action of the play hard for them to believe, improbable, even illogical. What jury would find the park bench and not the husband responsible for the death? The only possible justification is that the playwright wants to make some sort of statement about our screwed up judicial system, but he doesn't say that. The story is a contrivance. A good playwright seeks out the truth and shares it with an audience. A play has no meaning except in relation to an audience. This idea contains no truth and is, therefore, a half-idea.

WHAT IS A GOOD IDEA?

At their most basic, all plays are about characters, what they do ("action"), and the conflicts and crises that result. All of these are formed into a unity or spine (sometimes called a *root-action*). This is combined with plot and truth to make the beginning of a play. Your idea should have at least an inkling of each element before you go any further. Experienced playwrights automatically fulfill these four requirements, but a beginning playwright must seriously consider his or her idea before starting down the long path of development. You don't want to write for weeks or months only to find that your basic foundation is flawed.

Ask yourself if your idea has character, plot, action, conflict/crisis, truth, and unity. If it lacks any of the five, then it's a half-idea, and you need to either fix it or discard it.

Playwright #6

Working Title: *Fathers & Daughters*

This is a play about the archetypal father-daughter relationship. I believe that mothers do not teach girls to be women, but through their rewards and punishments, fathers do. We seem to look to the other sexes to reaffirm our own. I want to write about a daughter who is incomplete. Her father is a macho man who in his heart is afraid of women because he doesn't understand them, and the daughter has trouble valuing her own femininity. When the daughter discovers that her father is dying she comes home to confront him and try to get from him the one thing all women need—the knowledge that being a woman is not less than being a man.

The sixth time is a charm. What is the action? The daughter coming home to confront her father. More exact actions are needed, but it's a beginning. Who are the characters? The macho father and feminist daughter. What is the conflict? This occurs as the father and daughter work out their differing opinions. What is the crisis? The daughter must act now because the father is dying. What is the unity? The action revolves around a homecoming shortly before the father's death. Is there truth? That's hard to assess at this point, but it doesn't ring false. So far each element is only partially worked out, but the core of all the elements exists. It's a beginning, and a good one.

Many young playwrights yearn to reinvent what a play is, but too often their definitions become broad or incomprehensible and render the word *play* meaningless. This happened recently in an introduction-to-theatre class. The students were attempting to define "art." In the end, they determined that a painting, the mountains, a tree, and a person were all works of art. Art was everywhere and everything. By defining art this way, they had succeeded in making the word "art" meaningless. If a word means everything, then it means nothing. The same is true with a play.

Dialogue and characters alone do not make a play. Anyone can write ten pages of narrative and call it a novel. What's hard is to understand and apply the fundamentals and still be creative. If ever an exception was made to the need for character, action, conflict/crisis, truth, and unity, then the play was either incomprehensible or "broke new ground" and was immediately forgotten. In short, it's impossible to write a play without these elements, so why try?

Most good ideas start off as half-ideas. Rarely does a brilliant play pop, fully worked out, into the writer's head. Ideas come in fits and starts, and each one has an incubation period. Eventually, if a playwright thinks about the missing elements, stays with the idea, and takes it down its logical path, there will come the beginnings of a good play.

L A C K   O F   C L A R I T Y

Because an idea has the basic elements doesn't necessarily mean that the playwright is ready to write.

Playwright #7

Working Title: *Dancing in Dark Cells*

My concept involves the manifestations of the bleaker goals and aspirations of man. An exploration of how we extrapolate the truth upon the steel traps of false souls; the materialistic actualizations of two main conventionalists, both of whom remain close despite the demagnetized roles of society and anticlimactic roles of the media. I explore the duality of the human condition as opposed to the singularity of our hostility; a single set of which may gain ascendancy over the commonplace "mortal coil."

Between them, the authors of this book have three MFAs, have witnessed theatre the world over, have studied with the masters, attended every type of performance (including cricket matches), and we still haven't the vaguest idea of what this student is trying to say. A good playwright is a master communicator. If you can't communicate your ideas, you're not ready to write. If the only way you can become profound is to be abstract, then you're falling into the "just go for it" syndrome. The major symptom of this syndrome, often assumed by young actors, directors, and other theatre people, is that you can, without training, move with instinct and inspiration. Unless you're a psychic, sheer instinct gives you no advantage. Besides, instinct comes not as a birthright, but from years of practicing an art. Inspiration is important, but it is not enough. Jean Vilar, the French actor, said, "Inspiration, a necessary evil, provides, in theatre as in architecture, only a rough sketch for a masterpiece which must be built." To build a play you must have technique.

The goal of playwright #7 is to mystify his intentions. He is covering for a lack of technique. In his own words, this playwright should go back to the proverbial drawing board with the intention of manifesting his conceptualizations with greater overlying duality (that is, demagnetize his idea).

S C O P E

Playwright #8

Working Title: *In the West*

I have always wanted to tell the story of the cowboys. From the first explorers to Custer's last stand, to the last real cowboys of Alaska. This play would deal with the Indian question, the devastation of the buffalo herds, the coming of the Iron Horse, and depletion of our national resources. There would be scenes depicting the Donner party, the outlaws, and the simple sheep rancher. There is a statement here about part of the American character that I think we've lost.

This is not a half-idea. It has tons of conflict/crisis, plenty of characters, plenty of action, and the unity of the story is the West. No, it's not a half-idea; it's dozens of ideas.

A play is a limited form of storytelling; it's bound by certain restrictions. This history of the West might fit into the confines of a massive outdoor drama, but even then it would only give a shallow look at each of its many episodes. Its *scope* is too big for a play. On the other hand, it might make a great novel or miniseries.

By definition, a play has a narrow scope. It generally concerns itself with a limited number of characters and only a few hours in those characters' lives (although the hours may be spread over many years). Even epic theater, a form of drama popularized by Bertolt Brecht, who turned plays into sagas, is limited when compared to a movie or novel. A poem is often the most limited in scope, while a novel can be infinite. A play falls closer to a poem than a novel. Figure 1.1 compares width of scope in various writing forms.

Scope means more than just choosing a story that's small enough to fit within the confines of a play. A playwright is an artist who creatively selects and compresses the important parts of life into a simple, heightened work of art. The Roman poet Horace (65–8 B.C.) said, "Whatever you write, make it simple and unified." This western history play could be written, but it would be better to start with a more specific idea. The playwright can still make his point about the American West by concentrating on and telling a tenth of the story he originally wanted to tell.

Faced with the problem of scope, this student playwright changed stories and wrote a one-act in which a family reunion becomes a nightmare. The son escapes from a mental institution, the father announces he has AIDS and attempts suicide but fails, the daughter attempts suicide and succeeds, while the mother reveals a dark family secret and has a heart attack. All of this happened within the course of thirty-five pages! One page of dialogue, on average, equals roughly one minute to one minute fifteen seconds of stage time, so we can guess that this play, if staged, would have been less than forty minutes long! The student had certainly succeeded in selecting and compressing, but he had

Figure 1.1

A Scale of Scope

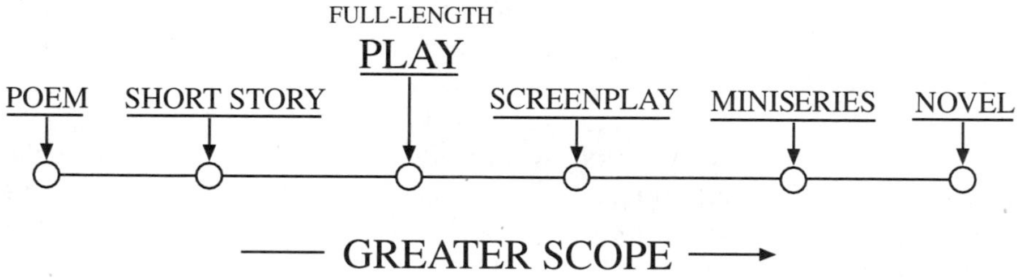

| POEM | SHORT STORY | FULL-LENGTH PLAY | SCREENPLAY | MINISERIES | NOVEL |

⟶ GREATER SCOPE ⟶

taken it too far. Selection and compression doesn't mean cramming events into a short space (except for farce); it means choosing only a few important events in the characters' lives and fully exploring the emotions and conflicts involved.

CINEMATIC THINKING

Playwright #9

Working Title: *The First Annual Historic Bar Tour*

This is a play about a group of professionals who take a tour of the historic bars of Chicago. The characters are all like lawyers, doctors, and are quite proper. At the first bar they play superior games with each other but then they begin getting drunk. As they go from one bar to another, they get drunker and drunker and begin telling each other what they really think. By the last bar, total social order will have broken down as they will fall in love with each other's spouses and slap fights break out between the most sophisticated. I see them telling the bus driver how to drive. Stopping at a gym to laugh at the fat people, turning green from swimming in the Chicago River, and being pulled over by the police. I think it would make a good comedy that would show the fundamental hypocrisy of people.

The fault here is **cinematic thinking.** The writer sees the story as a movie, not a play. The frequent jumps in time and location as the tour moves from bar to bus to gym and back to bar will be difficult to stage. Movies and television can use an almost unlimited number of sets and characters, but the theatre is limited not only by the physical requirements of the stage but by cost. This playwright's idea, even if the sets were simple and suggestive, would still lean in the direction of cinematic thinking.

We attended a reading of a play at UCLA in which the playwright's final stage direction read, "Sam walks out the door, we hear the sound of him getting into his car, and through the window we see his taillights drive off and fade into the distance." This is a perfect example of cinematic thinking. This playwright is seeing the end of his play as a movie and not a play. How could a director possibly stage taillights fading into the distance? Yes, it can be done, but the cost and headaches for the technical director will not be worth the effect. The producer would be more likely to consider the play not worth the effort required to produce it, which would mean no production. Successful playwrights concentrate on the language and the psychological action of a few characters and a limited amount of time. Broadway produces some massive pageant dramas and huge spectacles, but they are rare. For every *Miss Saigon,* where a helicopter lands on stage, there are a thousand small plays that stay within the physical and economic limitation of most theatres.

Ask yourself, would your idea work better as a movie? As you imagine the story, are you seeing close-ups and camera angles? Do you see the action taking place in real life rather than on a stage? If the answer to any of these is "yes," then you may be guilty of cinematic thinking.

Jerzy Grotowski, director of the Polish Laboratory Theatre, called for a "Poor Theatre." A theatre that eliminated technological aids and concentrated on the actor–audience relationship. You can take away the costumes, scenery, makeup, lighting, and sound but you cannot eliminate the actor. Write for the actor. Limit yourself to the confines of the poor theatre and you will find true freedom (and probably more productions).

NONREALISTIC PLAYS

Playwright #10

Working Title: *Burnt Leaves*

I want to work with levels and contrasting images to express my feeling. It's absurd to understand another's "condition"; we are all alone. Actors will improvise with my script to develop the idea. This play will not follow the usual "cause and effect" of a realistic play, but will present a juxtaposition of real life and symbols of our inability to talk to one another.

This idea for a nonrealistic play may fulfill all the elements needed, and could be wonderful theatre, but it's not the subject of this book. A beginning playwright, like a beginning painter, should learn the basics of realism first. Many of the great painters started with realism. Picasso and Chagall mastered realistic techniques before they moved into the avant-garde styles. There are many good books (for example, *Theatre of the Absurd* by Martin Esslin) that cover nonrealistic theatre, but you should learn to play the scales before you play a concerto, and learn concerto form before you play jazz. If nothing else, mastering realistic techniques will make you a better nonrealistic writer.

WRITE ABOUT WHAT YOU KNOW

Playwright #11

Working Title: *Black as Snow*

I have this idea about a black family who moves into an all white town. It's based on a story I heard about a black doctor who moved into a house in the Upper Peninsula of Michigan, a predominantly white part of the United States. Even though this small town desperately needed a doctor, they drove him and his family out. We always hear about how well America is coping with racism and how progressive legislation has become, but it still exists and is still pervasive. This play would show how the black family deals with the hatred as the father's medical practice goes bankrupt and the family falls apart.

This is a good idea for a play. It has conflict/crisis, unity, action, and the beginnings of character. Its scope is well within the confines of the play, and there is truth. Now the question is, can the playwright write it?

There is an old adage in writing, *write about what you know*. If you're writing about what you know, you're not just writing about your own life, but about the emotions and characters you personally understand, situations you can grasp, and the kind of story you want to write. In this case, does this student understand the problems and feelings associated with discrimination? This playwright was a Korean exchange student in the United States for a year's study. Could she understand and write about the feelings of a black family in the midst of a white majority?

As it turned out, she was born and raised in Japan but considered an "alien" by the Japanese government. Even though her family had lived in Japan for three generations, she was denied Japanese citizenship because of her Korean ancestry. All of her life she was treated as a second-class member of her society, and so she did know a great deal about discrimination. She still had much research to do about the black experience, but she had the memories, empathy, and anger that might allow her to write the play. Perhaps writing her own story about growing up Korean in Japan would be easier, but sometimes a writer needs to make a story less personal by putting some distance between herself and the subject.

Even if your idea is not a half-idea, other problems can be identified before you begin writing. Playwright #12's pitch is not a half-idea, but it is still flawed.

FLAVOR-OF-THE-MONTH PLAYS

Playwright #12

Working Title: *Above Suspicion*

This is the story of a famous athlete who is on trial for murder. It's a lot like the O.J. Simpson story, only I'm going to make it a hockey player. I think the idea is very topical and will attract a lot of interest. The conflicts would come from his relationship with his lawyer, missing his children and a final verdict.

When asked why he wanted to write this story the student answered, "It's topical." He went on to say, "If you want to write for Broadway you'd best find out what Broadway is producing and write something like it." The problem is, by the time you finish your "Broadway play," Broadway will be producing something different. The key is to write what you need to write, what you want to write, and with a little luck perhaps Broadway will look your way. If it never does, don't worry, writing *your* play is more satisfying than following popular trends. Fashionable plays (sometimes called *flavor-of-the-month plays*) seldom stand the test of time. The truth the playwright seeks must be true today as well as tomorrow. Don't write what is popular, don't write what you think will be successful, don't write what people want to hear. Write only what you need to write or want to write; make it good, communicate, and you'll increase your chances of becoming successful.

W H Y   W R I T E ?

If your idea has the proper scope, unity, action, conflict/crisis, character, and truth, if it's not cinematic and, above all, it's something you know, then you have a good start. Now you ask yourself, does it command your interest? Could you work on it for months or maybe even years without becoming bored?

Playwriting is not as spontaneous as it may first appear; it requires hard work and long hours. Ask yourself why you want to write. If your sole reason is that you need a topic by tomorrow, and any idea will do, you're in trouble. Your interest will surely wane. If you want to write it to make money, you're in even deeper trouble. Few playwrights make a living at their craft. If your sole reason is to express yourself, you're also in trouble. Expressing yourself is just fine, but playwrights must communicate. The playwright whose sole desire is to express himself, who writes only as therapy, ends up with pages of deep personal emotions that mean nothing to anyone but the playwright. Writing is a painful, lonely process that more often than not leads to failure. Why put yourself through it? The only reason to write is because you have to. You have a deep desire to understand and communicate. Writing is like a painful rash; you have to scratch it or be miserable.

N O W   W H A T ?

You have an idea for a play and at least a vague notion of who the characters are, what the action is, and what conflicts and crises might result. The idea has a basic unity and truth, you want to write it, and you are ready to write it. Now what do you do? You develop it by building the characters and structuring the action. Structure can take two paths, *form* and *formula,* which will be discussed in chapter 2.

EXERCISES

A   N O T E   O N   E X E R C I S E S

An exercise by itself doesn't help the playwright as much as applying an exercise to a play or working draft. American poet Robert Frost once said, "I never write exercises, but sometimes I write poems which fail and then I call them exercises."

Exercise #1

If you don't have an idea, write a short paragraph on each of the following. Examine your life for interesting examples of the following:

Haunting memories

Dreams/nightmares

Harbored resentments

Unfinished business

Social injustices

Newspaper articles

Factual events

Poems

Photos

Intimate experiences

All play ideas come from within. What would inspire you to write?

Exercise #2

Write a brief paragraph pitching your play idea, just as the students did in this chapter. Now analyze what you have written. Answer the following questions.

What is the action?

Who are the characters?

What is the conflict?

What is the crisis?

What is the unity?

Is there truth?

Is it a good idea or a half-idea?

Exercise #3

Playwrights want to do more than just tell a personal story, they want to communicate to others. Tell (pitch) your story idea to the class or to a friend. Are they interested? Do they want to know more about the story and characters? Does the idea have clarity?

Exercise #4

Find an empty stage. A small studio theatre would be best. Stand alone on the stage and imagine your play being performed there. Does it fit? Can it be staged? Does it have the proper scope? Is it cinematic?

Chapter 2

FORMULA WRITING

All plays have a structure. *Structure* plots a story's sequence of events or incidents. The characters and actions of real life are raw, in an unorganized state; a play (realistic or unrealistic) structures life into a unified whole. *Plot-structure,* as it is often called, is how a playwright compresses, se-

> *It is the function of all art to give us some perception of an order in life, by imposing order upon it.*
>
> T. S. Eliot

lects, and creates order in a life, and that order provides meaning. Even a play written to prove there is no order to life must be structured to prove its point. Arthur Miller wrote, "The very impulse to write springs from an inner chaos crying for order, for meaning. . . ."

At its most basic, a play's plot-structure is a *formula* that follows predetermined guidelines; at its highest it is *form,* where story takes on a unique structure and logic of its own. To understand the complexities of structuring with form, we must first learn the fundamentals of formula.

FORMULA WRITING

Not all formula writing is bad. For thousands of years playwrights have used formula to write powerful plays. Ancient tragedies, Greek New Comedy, the cycle plays of the Middle Ages, and the French tragedies of the 1600s all followed formulas. The accepted modern formula is so persuasive (and pervasive) that writers often forget it's a formula. Formula is constantly drilled into us, particularly by the media. The first bedtime story you were told as a child most likely followed formula. We're so familiar with the conventions of the modern formula that we tend to treat it as a standard and measure other methods of storytelling as deviations.

Modern formula has three basic qualities. First, it relies on an established, predetermined plot-structure (as all formulas do). Its generic qualities can lead (but not always) to uninteresting plays with predictable outcomes. Second, formula relies on *story* more than *character.* In other words, it changes the characters to fit the story, rather than allowing the story to grow naturally from the characters. Third, it's popular. The typical audience member finds story far more interesting than character. The dominance of story over character is not new. In the long history of the theatre, character usually holds a backseat to story. Aristotle (384–322 B.C.) in *Poetics* said character takes second place. In the modern theatre we like to think character is more important, so formula is universally condemned, even by those playwrights who use it and by audiences who enjoy it.

T H E   S T R U C T U R E   O F   F O R M U L A

To most, formula is simply, "Boy gets girl, boy loses girl, boy wins her back," or "In the beginning you get your hero up a tree, in the middle you throw stones at him, and in the end you let him down." True, these are both formulas, but formula is far more complex than these simple statements reflect. Formula is a detailed outline, a precise blueprint ingrained into our psyches by television and movies. Avoiding formula takes conscious effort, so writers must have an intricate knowledge of formula or they won't be able to eliminate it from their writing (should they choose to do so).

To study formula, let's examine the structures of two very different works that both follow the same basic modern formula. Let's use Shakespeare's *Romeo and Juliet,* a four-hundred-year-old play and, for comparison, the modern Hollywood Rambo movie *First Blood,* an action-adventure flick of a few years back. Shakespeare's *Romeo* and Sylvester Stallone's Rambo (as unlikely as it may seem) do, in fact, share the same exact formulaic structure, just as a grand cathedral and a plain box-like office building can share the same steel skeleton.[1]

To learn the structure of formula (or any structure, for that matter) begin by dividing the story into the basic sections:

BEGINNING

MIDDLE

END

By pinpointing the exact moment one section of the story ends and the next begins, and by defining what components are contained within each section,

---

[1] Cinematic thinking has already been discouraged in this book. We use *Rambo* not as an example of how to write a play but to show how formula can be used to structure contrasting, unrelated stories.

we can discover the mechanics of a story. In other words, we must identify and define when the beginning ends, the middle begins, the middle ends, and the end begins. Confused? Read on; it gets simpler.

THE BEGINNING

The components contained in the beginning of a formula structure are: an event, the basic situation, an introduction of the protagonist and antagonist, a disturbance, a major dramatic question, and a major decision.

Event: Most plays begin with an *event*. An event is a moment of uniqueness or happening in the characters' lives. It can be an unusual incident, special occasion, or crisis. It could be a wedding, a funeral, a homecoming, preparing for a party, or anything that makes this moment a little more special than the normal humdrum of the characters' lives. *Romeo and Juliet* begins with a street brawl between the warring Capulet and Montague gangs. *First Blood* begins with Vietnam vet John Rambo discovering an old friend has died of cancer caused by Agent Orange (a carcinogenic defoliant spray some vets came in contact with during the war in Vietnam).

It's not necessary for a play to begin with an event, but the advantages become clear when you look at who you're writing for. Most playwrights think their audience is, "the general theatre-going public," but they're not the ones who decide if your play will be produced. Your first audience will be producers, directors, and readers.[2] Theatres are bombarded with thousands of plays to read, most of them horrible. Too busy to give a new play the time it may deserve, most readers, directors, and producers speed-read. Beginning your play with an event will grab your reader's attention, because it starts the story with a bang rather than a slow fade in.

On the other hand, slapping an event on the beginning of a play simply to attract the attention of a cynical reader doesn't make for good writing. Some writers go so far as to begin their story at the end, using the climax as the event and then telling the story in flashback. This device seldom works. A good opening event must be germane to the story and not forced or tacked on. The event must be a natural place to begin, central to the plot, and must set up important following events. The best opening events contain the essence of the story.

By beginning *Romeo and Juliet* with the street brawl, Shakespeare starts with an action that is central to the story, full of conflict, and which sets up the forbidden love to follow. Rambo's opening does the same. It's not just some action sequence; it's a tender moment that helps the audience understand John Rambo's coming rage.

---

[2] "Readers" are members of a theatre whose job it is to review incoming scripts and report to management when they find a "good one."

Here are examples of plays and different opening events. Please note: not all of these plays follow formula, but almost all plays, whether formula or not, begin with an event.

Play	Event
Marvin's Room Scott McPherson (1989)	Bessie arrives at the doctor's office. She's not been feeling well.
A Raisin in the Sun Lorraine Hansberry (1955)	The family is excited about a large check that's to arrive in the mail.
An Enemy of the People Henrik Ibsen (1882)	Dr. Stockmann has several friends over for a big dinner to celebrate his new job.
King Lear William Shakespeare (1610)	King Lear divides his kingdom between his daughters.
Medea Euripides (431 B.C.)	Medea has just learned that her husband has been unfaithful.
Oedipus Rex Sophocles (425 B.C.)	A plague has hit the city.

The Protagonist: At the beginning of a play, the audience gives the story a great deal of unearned attention. They're desperate for information, and the script must not disappoint or they'll quickly become bored. The first thing the audience wants to know is, "Who is the protagonist?" The protagonist is the central or chief character who pushes forward the action of the play. It's usually the play's hero, but the character can take many forms. From an obvious hero to a severely flawed soul, the audience must be able to identify and root for that character. If your play doesn't have a clear-cut protagonist (or protagonists— there can be more than one), or if you delay the appearance of the protagonist, the story will appear unfocused.[3] In *First Blood,* John, the protagonist, is the first character introduced. In *Romeo and Juliet* the romantic Romeo is introduced late in the first scene. Juliet is also a protagonist, and her introduction occurs within a few pages of the beginning.

---

[3] A hundred years ago, it was common for playwrights to delay the entrance of the protagonist; this was done because audience members often arrived late to the theatre. This is no longer the norm.

The Basic Situation: Situation can be defined as the state of affairs as the play begins. This includes general information such as time, setting, and location, but it also includes who's who, some background, and character relationships. Often the basic situation has an equilibrium. The lives of the characters have achieved a certain balance—a balance that must be disturbed if there is to be conflict. The basic situation at the beginning of *Romeo and Juliet* finds Romeo depressed because he has been dumped by his girlfriend, Rosaline. The Capulets and Montagues have been feuding for many years, but no one family has an upper hand in the conflict, so there is equilibrium. In *First Blood* we find John Rambo, a warrior without a war. He cannot identify with the country he has worked so hard to defend, and is wandering the great Northwest looking for inner peace. At this point in the story only basic information is needed. You don't want to flood the audience with exposition. Tell only what is needed to get the story going.[4]

Antagonist: An antagonist is what the ancient Greeks called the "opposer of action," the adversary who stands in the way of the protagonist's goals. An antagonist may be a simple villain, a complex character, an element of nature (for example, a storm or a huge whale), or even a part of the protagonist's character (say, alcoholism or self-doubt). The exact conflict between the protagonist and the antagonist need not be spelled out yet, but the audience wants a hint of what the coming conflict *might* be, even though no major conflict yet exists.

In *Romeo and Juliet* the antagonists are set up in the opening street brawl. Within a matter of minutes we know the warring families and Tybalt will be the antagonists. The antagonist in *First Blood* is the police chief. After learning of his friend's death, Rambo wanders into a small town. He's looking for a meal when the city's chief of police lets Rambo know he's not welcome. The cop escorts Rambo to the city limits and tells him to keep walking. The audience knows that the police chief, who represents the country's indifference to Vietnam vets, will be the antagonist. In both cases the major conflict of the story has yet to occur, but the authors hint at what might be coming.

The Disturbance: The next component in formula is a *disturbance*. This is an inciting incident that causes the opening balance to come unglued and gets the main action rolling. When the Montague gang talks Romeo into attending a Capulet party, knowing it could cause trouble, the opening balance is broken. The opposing forces, protagonists and antagonists, are placed into a situation rich with possible conflict. The same is true in *First Blood*. The police chief disturbs Rambo's search for inner peace when he refuses to let Rambo have a meal. The situation is upset and conflict is now possible. Here are some examples of disturbance:

---

[4] For more on exposition see chapter 6.

Play	The Disturbance
Marvin's Room Scott McPherson (1989)	Bessie discovers she has leukemia.
A Raisin in the Sun Lorraine Hansberry (1955)	The Check for $10,000 arrives.
An Enemy of the People Henrik Ibsen (1882)	Dr. Stockmann discovers the local mineral baths are polluted.
King Lear William Shakespeare (1610)	Cordelia does not make a show of the love she has for her father.
Medea Euripides (431 B.C.)	Medea learns that she is to be banished.
Oedipus Rex Sophocles (425 B.C.)	Oedipus learns from the Oracle that the gods have caused the plague.

THE END OF THE BEGINNING

The disturbance causes the basic situation to deteriorate. This deterioration continues until the protagonist must take action. **The beginning of a formula play ends when the protagonist makes a major decision that will result in conflict.** In other words, the disturbance forces the protagonist to take action. This decision also defines what the play is about, it states the protagonist's goal. It's the *core action* of the play. In *Romeo and Juliet,* the beginning ends when the title characters fall in love. It can be argued that they aren't conscious of their decision, but knowing the problems, they don't talk themselves out of it. In *First Blood,* the end of the beginning occurs when John starts to walk away but then stops. He fought for this country, his friends have died for this country, and he can't even get a meal. He decides to walk back into the small town and have dinner. Having dinner may not sound like a "major decision," but after the police chief told him not to show his face there, it becomes a decision (a declaration, if you will) that will lead to great conflicts, complications, and death.

By ending the beginning with the protagonist's major decision, you make your protagonist active. An active protagonist is one who sets out to achieve a difficult goal, must satisfy some deep desire, or is forced to move forward against great odds. Passive protagonists, tossed about by the winds of change, who cannot make decisions, who do not at least try to change their world are unacceptable in drama, because they do not hold an audience's attention.

For example, in Tennessee Williams's *The Glass Menagerie,* the protagonist is Tom and not Laura; Tom takes action while Laura remains passive. **In a play, the protagonist can be a victim only if it results in the protagonist taking action.**

THE MAJOR DRAMATIC QUESTION

The disturbance and the protagonist's decision causes a major dramatic question (sometimes called MDQ). This is the hook that keeps people in the theatre for two hours because they want to know the answers. It's not the overall statement or theme of the play, but a question that causes curiosity and suspense. For example, if the major dramatic question in *Romeo and Juliet* is "Will love triumph over jealousies and hate?" then the theme would be a broader statement about the nature of love.

This section of the beginning, where the disturbance, major decision, and major dramatic question fall, is called the *point of attack.*

POINT OF ATTACK

The point of attack is the moment in the story in which the main fuse is lit, the clouds of conflict appear, and the primary or main action of the story clearly declares itself. If the main action of a play seems to take a long time to get going, it's said to have a late point of attack. If the main action of the play starts within the first few minutes of the beginning, then it has an early point of attack. Both *Romeo* and *First Blood* have early points of attack.

Some formula writers believe that the point of attack should fall about 10 percent of the way into a play. This is called the 10 percent rule. If your play seems to start slowly, if readers are bored early or if the audience seems to rustle in their seats shortly after the beginning, check your point of attack. How many minutes into the play does the disturbance, decision, and major dramatic question take place? When does the main action of the play begin?

Here are some examples of protagonists' decisions that end the beginning of a play. Also listed are the plays' use of early or late point of attack.

Play	Protagonist's decision	Point of Attack
Marvin's Room Scott McPherson (1989)	Bessie decides to communicate with her sister with whom she hasn't gotten along in years.	Early
A Raisin in the Sun Lorraine Hansberry (1955)	Mama decides to give Walter Lee part of the money to invest in a liquor store.	Late
An Enemy of the People Henrik Ibsen (1884)	Dr. Stockmann decides to save the town from the polluted baths.	Late

King Lear William Shakespeare (1610)	King Lear decides *not* to give Cordelia a third of his kingdom.	Very Early
Medea Euripides (431 B.C.)	Medea decides to seek revenge.	Early
Oedipus Rex Sophocles (425 B.C.)	Oedipus sets out to find the cause of the plague.	Early

HOW LONG SHOULD THE BEGINNING BE?

If you know what kind of decision your protagonist makes at the end of the beginning, then you can also predict how long your beginning will be. (This is why it's called a formula; decisions are made without the playwright having to think about it.) If the protagonist makes a morally correct decision, "I will fall in love," "I shall save my father from alcoholism," or "I must catch the killer of my friend," then it's not necessary to have a long beginning. Both Rambo and Romeo make morally correct decisions, so the beginnings are rather short. Romeo falls in love with Juliet by the third scene; Rambo makes the decision to go back and get his meal about four minutes into the movie.

If the protagonist's decision lacks moral fiber, "I'll steal the money," "I shall cheat the boss," "I must take another drink," then the beginning needs to be long enough to make the audience believe that, in a similar situation, they too might make the same decision. For example, in Ibsen's *A Doll House,* Nora decides to lie to her husband about a personal loan she has received. The morality of this decision is questionable, so the play has a longer beginning. On the other hand, if you spend too long with a protagonist who eventually makes a righteous decision, the audience will become bored long before the decision is made. Can you imagine if Romeo and Juliet didn't fall in love until an hour or so into the play?

THE MIDDLE

George Bernard Shaw said, "Anyone can write a good beginning." True, beginnings are easy compared to middles. When a playwright doesn't finish a play because it seemed to fizzle half way through, it's because the idea lacked sufficient *conflicts, crises, obstacles,* and *complications*. Without these elements the protagonist's goals are too quickly met. Conflicts, crises, obstacles, and complications are the roadblocks. They make sure the protagonist's course of action is not clear sailing, for clear sailing is the death of drama. When the protagonist faces no further conflicts, crises, obstacles, and complications, the play is over.

Conflict is what results when a protagonist comes into opposition with an antagonist. It's a clash of wills. The French critic Ferdinand Brunetiere said, "Drama is a representation of the will of man in conflict with the mysterious powers or natural forces which limit and belittle us; it is one of us thrown living upon the stage, there to struggle against fatality, against social law, against one of his fellow mortals, against himself, if need be, against the ambitions, the interests, the prejudices, the folly, the malevolence of those who surround him." In other words, plays are about conflict.

Once, a student writer penned a play with a five page pause in the middle of the story so his two lovers could read poems to one other, run barefoot on the beach (an example of cinematic thinking), and proclaim their love. For five pages all of their problems were solved. When told that this scene lacked conflict and so was not dramatic, the student used the balcony scene from *Romeo and Juliet* as an example—"Nothing more happens in that scene and it's dramatic. If it's good enough for Shakespeare, it's good enough for me." But much more happens in the balcony scene. Yes, the lovers proclaim their love, but it's a forbidden love. They're stealing a brief moment, fearful of being caught. Juliet's family is just beyond the door. If discovered, Romeo could be killed. True, the source of the conflict is not physically present on stage, but it's still present. **Conflict is the life blood of the theatre.**

The student was not convinced. He asked, "Where is the conflict between Othello and Iago? Where is the conflict in *As you Like It?* Where is the conflict in Ibsen's *Ghosts?*" If a scene or play contains no direct conflicts then it must have *crisis.*

The one element that makes a play different from all other forms of storytelling is crisis. William Archer, the Scottish critic, said, "The drama may be called the art of crisis, as fiction is the art of gradual developments." Crisis is the essence of theatre. A scene, a page, a word, a character, a thought without crisis is not dramatic. True, there may be no conflict between Iago and Othello, but their lives are in crisis. The balcony scene may contain little conflict, but it is not lacking in crisis. All plays are about the emergencies, calamities, turning points, entanglements, and difficulties of life. Two lovers running on the beach proclaiming their love, free from any crisis or conflict, is not dramatic and therefore is not a play.

Two elements help a playwright build conflict and crisis. They are obstacle and complication. *Obstacles* are the barriers standing in the way of success. They are hurdles that the protagonist must clear to achieve the goal.

Obstacles must never be a simple string of obstructions that a playwright arbitrarily lines up before the protagonist. Each must be the next logical step and motivated by the events and characters. A play with many obstacles often leans toward farce, while one with fewer more powerful and thoroughly examined obstacles will be more serious. Ferdinand Brunetiere said, "No obstacles, no drama."

A *complication* is an unexpected obstacle. It's an entangling revelation in the protagonist's journey. It can be a discovery or reversal that traps the protagonist. In *Romeo and Juliet,* one of the many complications occurs when Benvolio and Mercutio pick a fight with Tybalt shortly after Romeo's secret marriage to Juliet. Romeo can't fight because Tybalt is now his kinsman. John Rambo's obstacles and complications occur each time the police chief calls for greater support (more police arrive, as well as the National Guard) while John attacks just about everything in sight. We say, give him the meal.

RISING ACTION

A play never rests. Until the final climax, there's always another conflict and crisis, or both. Conflict and crisis cause the characters and story to be in a constant state of flux. This instability is governed by *rising action*. Rising action makes each conflict, crisis, obstacle, and complication more powerful, more dramatic, and more important than those before. In other words, the middle of a play must follow *the path of most resistance*. There may be moments of apparent success, but they always lead to an even greater undoing. The middle of a play is a series of failures for the protagonist. The goal, decided upon by the protagonist at the end of the beginning, must not be realized, at least not yet.

THE END OF THE MIDDLE— THE DARK MOMENT

The middle of a formula play ends when the protagonist totally fails, the quest collapses, the protagonist's shortcomings have tripped her up, and the goal becomes unattainable. This is the *dark moment*. It's the ultimate obstacle—the antagonist has won and the battle appears to be over. In *Romeo and Juliet* the dark moment occurs when Romeo kills Tybalt, Juliet's beloved cousin. Rambo's dark moment is a literal moment of darkness. Pursued by a growing military force, he takes refuge in an abandoned mine. The National Guard uses bazookas to close the entrance, and Rambo is caught in darkness where he will surely suffocate. Here are some examples of plays and their dark moments:

Play	Dark Moment
Marvin's Room Scott McPherson (1989)	Hank says he won't help Bessie by giving her a bone marrow transplant.
A Raisin in the Sun Lorraine Hansberry (1955)	Walter Lee discovers that his friend has run off with his money.
An Enemy of the People Henrik Ibsen (1882)	The town and friends turn against Dr. Stockmann.
King Lear William Shakespeare (1606)	Kicked out of his daughter's castle, Lear rages against the violent storm.
Medea Euripides (431 B.C.)	Medea kills the king and the princess.

Oedipus Rex Sophocles (425 B.C.)	Oedipus learns that he is the cause of the plague.

THE BEGINNING OF THE END — ENLIGHTENMENT

The beginning of the end is *enlightenment*. Enlightenment occurs when the protagonist understands how to defeat the antagonist. Enlightenment can come in many forms: the protagonist may join forces with another, a revelation may shed new light on the problem, or the protagonist, by falling into an emotional abyss, may now be able to see her error.

In *Romeo and Juliet,* the enlightenment is the potion Friar Laurence mixes from his garden. This potion causes Juliet's deep sleep. Her parents think her dead, the arranged wedding is called off, and Juliet is transported to the tomb, where Romeo is to save her. In *First Blood,* John finds an air shaft that leads to the mountaintop and a position of superiority over the armies below.

The enlightenment must not come from out of the blue. Ancient playwrights used to write themselves into a corner and then depend on the character of a god, mechanically lowered onto the stage, to set everything straight. This is called *deus ex machina,* which translates to "a god from a machine." Today the term is used when a playwright fails to logically set up the enlightenment or the ending of a play. If you've ever seen an old melodramatic western, then you understand. It's the dark moment: the wagon train circles, the Indians attack, the settlers run out of bullets, and then, suddenly, enlightenment. The cavalry arrives. This is deus ex machina.

A good enlightenment has two elements. First, it must be something the protagonist could not have understood before enduring the conflicts and trials of the middle. Second, it must be delicately set up earlier in the play. If the set-up is too obvious the audience will get it before the protagonist does and will ask, "Why didn't the protagonist figure this out two hours ago like I did?"

In *Romeo and Juliet,* the enlightenment is set up by Friar Laurence's speech in Act II, Scene 3, showing his vast knowledge of herbs and their effects. In *First Blood* the air shaft is never set up, but it's a logical possibility. Here are some examples of plays and their enlightenments:

Play	Enlightenment
Marvin's Room Scott McPherson (1989)	Hank returns home and agrees to the bone marrow transplant.
A Raisin in the Sun Lorraine Hansberry (1955)	Walter Lee realizes his family's pride is more important than the money.

An Enemy of the People Henrik Ibsen (1883)	Dr. Stockmann discovers the truth is more important than playing society's games.
King Lear William Shakespeare (1606)	King Lear learns of Cordelia's love.
Medea Euripides (431 B.C.)	Medea understands that she must do more to have true justice.
Oedipus Rex Sophocles (425 B.C.)	Oedipus learns that he is the cause of the plague (note that this is the same as the Dark Moment).

CLIMAX

Armed with enlightenment, the protagonist is renewed and ready to defeat the antagonist. The outcome of the play becomes clear, so the pace should increase as the rising action drives toward *climax*. The climax, in a formula play, is defined as the moment the antagonist is defeated. It can also be the final conflict or the point of highest tension. Climax doesn't have to be a violent or horrible moment. It can be quiet, even subtle.

All climaxes contain two important elements. First, the protagonist is never passive but an active participant. Second, the climax is always instigated by the protagonist. The protagonist cannot be a passive being who endures the play's climax, but rather the climax must be a direct result of the protagonist's actions and participation (that is, if your protagonist is offstage during the climax, you've got a problem). In *Romeo and Juliet,* the lovers' suicides mark the defeat of the antagonists (the warring families); in *First Blood,* Rambo finally captures the corrupt police chief.

Here are a list of several plays and their climaxes:

Play	Climax
Marvin's Room Scott McPherson (1989)	Bessie learns that Hank's bone marrow doesn't match hers. He can't save her life.
A Raisin in the Sun Lorraine Hansberry (1955)	Walter Lee throws Karl Lindner, the spokesman for the white community, out of his house.
An Enemy of the People Henrik Ibsen (1884)	Stockmann will not move out of his house. He is going to stay on and teach.

King Lear William Shakespeare (1606)	Cordelia is killed.
Medea Euripides (431 B.C.)	Medea deals her husband the ultimate blow by killing his sons.
Oedipus Rex Sophocles (425 B.C.)	Oedipus blinds himself.

CATHARSIS

After climax is *catharsis*. Catharsis is a final purging of the character's emotions. It's a period of cleansing that hints at what the future might bring. Good writing has two requirements of catharsis. First, it must not linger. Once the climax is over, and the antagonist defeated, the audience wants out. Second, the ending of a play must be consistent with the beginning. Although the ending may not be predictable at the beginning, by the end, in retrospect, the ending must appear to have been inevitable.

In *Romeo and Juliet,* the catharsis occurs when the grief-stricken Montagues and Capulets promise to end their long feud (a scene often cut by directors who don't understand the hopeful ending). In *First Blood,* Rambo's special CIA trainer takes him into custody and will make sure he doesn't stand trial for the trouble he has caused. John feels purged; he has stood up for his rights and made an important statement about how we treat our veterans (if not a very good statement about how we treat our National Guardsmen). Here are some examples of plays and their catharses:

Play	Catharsis
Marvin's Room Scott McPherson (1989)	Hank returns to his family. Bessie learns to accept her fate.
A Raisin in the Sun Lorraine Hansberry (1955)	The family moves out of their flat and into the better neighborhood. There are still hard times ahead but they are ready.
An Enemy of the People Henrik Ibsen (1888)	Stockmann is now alone, but being alone is better than being corrupt.
King Lear William Shakespeare (1606)	King Lear dies but his kingdom is saved.

Medea Euripides (451 B.C.)	Medea leaves to a new life in Athens, while Jason is left to grieve and die.
Oedipus Rex Sophocles (425 B.C.)	The plague is lifted.

Romeo and Juliet and *Rambo,* although having diverse characters and dissimilar stories, follow the same basic formulaic structure. The fundamental elements (event, disturbance, decision, conflict, crisis, obstacles, complication, dark moment, enlightenment, climax, and catharsis) all occur and in the exact same order. Both follow a method of storytelling as old as mankind.

JOSEPH CAMPBELL'S THEORY OF BEGINNING, MIDDLE, AND END

An interesting theory about beginning, middle, and end was published several years ago when Joseph Campbell wrote *The Hero With A Thousand Faces,* in which he examined myths and storytelling throughout the ages. He found that the plot/structure of most myths was similar no matter from what country, culture, or century they came. He discovered a universal formula for storytelling dating back thousands of years. Storytellers from the ancient Greeks to Kenyans to Chinese to Hollywood writers follow the same formula.

Formula is so embedded in our thinking that, even if structural elements are missing, an audience will try to find them. In a story totally devoid of structure, an audience will interpret one moment as a disturbance and another as enlightenment. They'll perceive one character as the protagonist, another as the antagonist, and look for a major decision, climax, and catharsis.

Joseph Campbell split the ancient formula of myth-telling into twelve stages of the "hero's journey." They were:

1. THE ORDINARY WORLD—A myth begins with the hero in his own element.

2. THE CALL TO ADVENTURE—A problem or challenge is presented that will unsettle the ordinary world of the protagonist.

3. THE RELUCTANT HERO—The hero balks at the edge of adventure. The hero faces his fears concerning the unknown.

4. THE WISE OLD MAN—The hero's mentor helps the hero make the right decision, but the hero must undertake the quest alone.

5. INTO THE SPECIAL WORLD—The hero makes the decision to confront the adventure and enters the special world of problems and challenges.

6. TEST, ALLIES, AND ENEMIES—The hero confronts the consequences of his action.

7. THE INMOST CAVE—The hero enters the place of greatest danger.

8. THE SUPREME ORDEAL—The dark moment occurs. The hero must face failure.

9. SEIZING THE SWORD—The hero comes back. With new knowledge or greater understanding, he can now defeat the hostile forces.

10. THE ROAD BACK—The hero returns to the ordinary world, which still contains dangers and problems.

11. RESURRECTION—The hero is reborn, purified.

12. RETURN WITH THE ELIXIR—The hero returns to the ordinary world with the treasure that will heal the world's ills.

Sound familiar? It's exactly the same as a modern formula.

Figure 2.1 maps the structure of standard modern formula (top) and Joseph Campbell's elements of universal myth (bottom). Notice the similarities.

When *The Hero With A Thousand Faces* was published, Hollywood producers were overjoyed. They acted as if they had finally found their bible. Using Campbell's formula, they could make corrections in a story and make it run at "peak performance." Now they could plug any idea into a simple blueprint, without spending time on the blueprint, and come up with a pretty good story. Playwrights were not as thrilled. They knew formula can be a trap. Only if it's handled correctly does it become a viable method of developing a play. The key is creativity. Without creativity, the formula play becomes as boring and predictable as a sitcom.

WORKING OUT A STORY USING FORMULA

Let's take one of our student's ideas and use formula to develop it. *Black as Snow* was playwright #11's working title. Her play idea was about a black doctor and his family who move into a white neighborhood. To develop this idea using formula, you start by asking the standard formula questions and filling in the answers to the structural reference points.

Who is the protagonist? Simple. The black doctor and his family are the heroes. True, there are other possibilities, but this is the most logical. Let's name them the Franks.

Who is the antagonist? More than likely, it's the white families who want to keep the Franks out. Not all the white people will be so closed-minded, so let's find one main family to fill the role. How about the next-door neighbor and community leader, Ms. Burns?

What is the opening event? What special moment in the characters' lives starts the play? There are many possible answers:

1. The black doctor could graduate from medical school.
2. The black family could be moving.
3. The black family could arrive at their new home.
4. The black doctor could be treating his first patient at this new practice.
5. The town might be giving the old white doctor a retirement party.
6. The black family may be rebelling against the father's wish to move north.

Hundreds of events could provide solid beginnings. Too early to make a decision? Then move on to the next element of the formula.

What is the basic situation? This is pretty clear. The doctor wants to move to the Upper Peninsula region of Michigan. We have to justify this, so we'll make him a skiing or hunting enthusiast. Perhaps his son is upset because he had to leave his friends behind, but the daughter is excited about the move and wants to meet new people. Then there is a knock at the door. Ms. Burns, the next-door neighbor, has come over to welcome the new doctor and is shocked. We ask ourselves why she might not know he was black. Perhaps the town put an ad in several major newspapers offering a free house to any doctor who came to the community and the contract was signed before they met him.

What is the disturbance? What gets the action going? If we are to stay with the unity of the action, it must be a racist act:

1. A rock comes through their window.
2. The doctor opens his practice but no one comes.
3. The doctor invites his neighbors over for a housewarming party. When they arrive, he discovers they have banded together into a committee and suggest he and his family leave.
4. The son comes home with a bloody nose and won't tell how it happened.
5. They receive threatening phone calls.

There are dozens more, but the third idea has a nice chance for dramatic conflict. The black family thinks the neighbors are coming over for a housewarming party. When they arrive, they're polite, but after dinner the neighbors tell the black doctor they've made a mistake and they'd prefer it if he and his family found a more "appropriate" place to live. Why is this best? There's an old trick in the theatre, "If you want to make someone cry, first make 'em laugh." Juxtaposing the emotions will create a powerful scene. If you have the neighbors accepting the black family's invitation, being friendly to them, and then telling them to get out, it'll be far more powerful than sending a rock through the window; besides, it leaves room for the all-important rising action.

What is the dramatic question? The simple and obvious question caused by the disturbance is, "Will the family overcome this racist act?"

Figure 2.1

A Comparison of Standard Modern Formula Structure and Joseph Campbell's Elements of Universal Myth

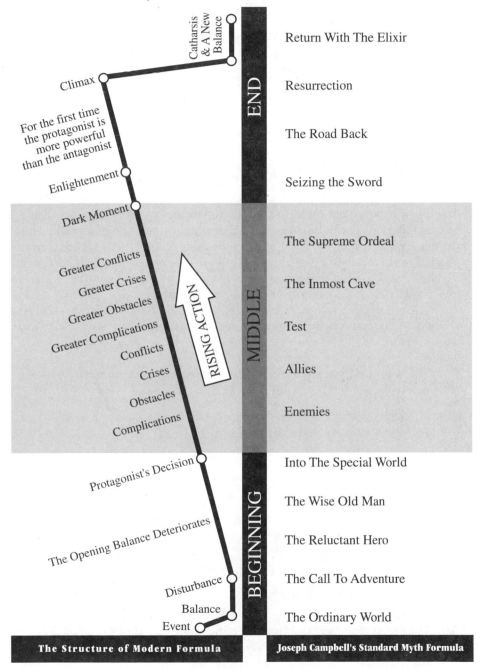

| The Structure of Modern Formula | Joseph Campbell's Standard Myth Formula |

What happens at the end of the beginning? What major decision does the protagonist make? This time there are really only two possible answers. The doctor, after witnessing the prejudice firsthand, decides to stay and fight it out; or the doctor decides to seek revenge. (Other answers are possible, but any answer that takes the protagonist and antagonist out of contact with each other is undramatic and won't work.) The answer to this question is important because it defines what the play is about. More than likely the first answer is the way to go. Just as with Romeo and Juliet, who knew falling in love was not going to be easy, and with Rambo, who understood the consequence of walking back into town, so too, our doctor decides to stay in a town where he is not wanted.

Now, let's go back to the beginning. What could the opening event be? The family arriving at their new home seems to be the most natural place to begin. The story is about the family and their relationship to the town, not about the doctor graduating from medical school, or the family protesting the move.

What have we so far? A black doctor moves his family to a small northern town that is desperate for a doctor. The doctor invites the neighbors over for dinner. Tensions rise during the meal. The neighbors and the black family have little in common with one another. After the main course, the neighbors politely ask the doctor's family to leave town. Insulted, the father tells them he has every right to live there and makes the major decision not to move. As it's a morally correct decision, we know the beginning will be short.

Now we work through the middle. *What conflicts/crises, obstacles, and complications result from the doctor's decision?* Hundreds of possibilities exist. Here are ten:

1. The wife condemns the doctor for not doing more research into the town before they moved.

2. The family quarrels over their future.

3. The son runs away from home.

4. The parents are disturbed to find that their daughter rejects her blackness.

5. A burning cross is found in the yard.

6. With no patients, the doctor is going bankrupt.

7. The community sues them on some trumped up charges concerning property lines, or ownership of the house.

8. The doctor finally gets his first patient. The next day he is visited by a lawyer and handed a malpractice suit.

9. The only white patient who comes in is ostracized by the other townspeople.

10. The family discovers that the father knew all along this was an all-white community and purposely brought his family here to break the color barrier.

Does the story contain enough conflict/crises, obstacles, and complications to sustain the middle? Undoubtedly. With only a few hours of work, the list could be pages long. The writer picks her favorite conflicts and then arranges them so they're governed by rising action. So far, the formula is doing its job. It's making it easy on the playwright.

What is the dark moment? Simple. The formula states the doctor must fail. He will give up the fight and decide to leave. Perhaps the malpractice suit goes to court. It looks as if he'll lose his license. Rather than sacrifice his family and future, the doctor makes a deal; he'll leave if they drop the court case. The family is disappointed. They begin packing.

Now for the ending. *What is the enlightenment?* What has the family learned by enduring the conflicts, obstacles, and complications of the middle? Is enlightenment possible? If they haven't learned a lesson, perhaps their skin is thicker now. Or could there be enlightenment with the white families, or both? What if Ms. Burns throws a derisive good-bye party for the black family? In the midst of the party, her mother has a heart attack. The doctor must save the white woman and, in doing so, reminds himself he is still a good doctor. Enlightenment! Does this sound like stories you've heard before? It should, it's formula! It follows the same pattern as a thousand other stories.

What is the climax? The formulaic answer is clear. The protagonist must succeed, and the antagonist be defeated. Ms. Burns realizes the truth: the doctor saved her mother's life, and she may be wrong. Or better yet, she doesn't change her mind, but her hardness makes the townspeople realize they are wrong and they turn against her.

What is the catharsis? The black family stays, and there is a bright future. Ms. Burns is still an old biddy, but the black family has learned that not everyone will like them and those people must be tolerated, just as Ms. Burns will have to tolerate them. The white families accept their new black doctor, and they live happily ever after.

What's happened here? With little work, we have come up with a basic outline of what might be a good story. But notice the characters are being created to support the action, the action is based on a formula, and therefore, the characters are formula. For example, the doctor was made a skiing and hunting enthusiast not because of the character's needs, but because it would help justify the story. The whole thing has a stereotypical familiarity about it. It's predictable.

THE KING OF FORMULA WRITERS

The master formula playwright was Eugene Scribe (1791–1861), who wrote more than five hundred dramas and short skits, and whose plays are now all but forgotten. He's remembered solely for his almost machinelike technique for structuring plays. Pure formula plays such as his are called *well-made plays,* a curious handle because his plays were ill made. They sacrificed plausible characterization, logic, and truth to make the story interesting. His formula included: a secret known to the audience but unknown to the characters, intense action and suspense, a series of ups and downs for the protagonist, an obligatory scene in which secrets are exposed, and a strong denouement or solution. What's so wrong with this? The problem is that none of his stories depended on or were motivated by the characters.

MELODRAMA

The most popular method of formula writing is *melodrama*. Melodrama has consumed the American entertainment industry. Nearly all films, television shows, made-for-television movies, and sitcoms are melodramas. Melodrama is also alive and well on the stage. Its roots go back to the Greeks and New Comedy about 400 B.C. The term "melodrama" dates to the nineteenth century when a play's dialogue was often accompanied by music, much the same as today's movies have a background score.

Melodrama is associated with the flimsy "good versus evil" plots of the turn of the century that all seemed to have a falsely accused hero who fights the good fight, struggling against shipwreck and earthquakes to proclaim his innocence. However, melodrama has evolved into an advanced method of storytelling with clear divisions between good and evil, and enough twists and turns in the plot to keep the majority of audiences interested. It keeps them absorbed because melodrama, like formula writing, concentrates on the story rather than the characters. The characters in melodrama *can* be well developed and powerful, but the emphasis leans toward what the characters *do* rather than *who they are*.

THE PROPER USE OF FORMULA

To use formula properly or avoid it altogether, a playwright must first study and understand it. A student once approached us after a playwriting seminar and told us about his brilliant solution to his story problems. He had invented a "framework" into which he could plug in an idea and quickly develop it into a full story. He had spent two years test-marketing his theories and was going to let us in on his little secret. As he began explaining the mechanics of his "framework," it occurred to us what he had invented (or reinvented) was the standard modern formula. If you do not study formula you will end up reinventing it.

A playwright should also understand the advantages and disadvantages of working with formula. The playwright who follows the rules of formula exactly will produce a predictable, uninteresting drama, just as the poet who follows a perfect iambic stress will probably write a rather bland poem. The chief disadvantage of formula is that it's comfortable. It's a trap in which playwrights can manage to write without using the full extent of their imaginations.

If formula can be a harmful contrivance, then why do playwrights use it? Most beginning playwrights are unaware they are using a predetermined formula; they think they're simply following their instincts. Only by studying the formula do they become aware of what they're doing. Other playwrights use it because it gives proven results. After all, in the history of mankind, melodrama and formula are the most successful methods for storytelling. The Irish writer William Butler Yeats wrote, "When the imagination begins to cool, the writer begins to be less alive and seeks external aids, tricks of the theatre that have proven themselves again and again. He feels himself fortunate when there is nothing in his play that has not succeeded a thousand times before. . . ." Formula is *safe*.

Using formula *successfully* requires creativity. Rather than reinventing dramatic structures extant for hundreds of years, a good formula writer uses formula to release her imagination. Formula is a crutch that allows a writer to quickly set the story so she can concentrate on character and dialogue development. Later, when the characters can stand on their own, the writer discards the crutch and finds new and interesting developments. The problem is, many writers forget to throw away the crutch.

Playwright #11 has at least three ways to save *Black as Snow*. First, the writer must find inspired answers to the structural questions. For example, what would be a more interesting, less predictable enlightenment? What less expected decision could the protagonist make at the end of the beginning? Second, where can the writer deviate from the formula? Formula doesn't have sacred laws that we must blindly obey. A successful formula writer always allows structure to take a second seat to the writer's impulses and creativity. This is not to say that the writer should break all the rules. Successful writers seldom break the rules. Dramatic rules, such as the rules that dictate the structure of a sentence, should not be broken, but improved upon. To improve a rule, you must first know it, understand why it exists, and then creatively deviate from it. Creative deviation will make the story seem new and less like one told before. Third, and most importantly, the characters must be given more weight. As long as the characters are subordinate to an action, which in turn is subordinate to a formula, the play will never explore the truth of the situation.

Many writers enjoy working within the precise framework that formula provides. For example, a sonnet has a strict formula, and yet we would never condemn Shakespeare as a formula writer. According to the English writer Gilbert Keith (G. K.) Chesterton (1874–1936) sonnets are easier to write than other verse because they are restricted. Formula writing, like a sonnet, can be a framework that sets some writers free to think and be creative.

The key is character. Before you can take the next step in story development, you must have a deep understanding of the techniques and principles of character development.

EXERCISES

Exercise #1
Work out your idea using formula. Remember, creative and logical deviations from the rules are the key to success.

Working Title: _____

Opening Event: _____

Basic Situation: _____

Protagonist: _____

Antagonist: _____

Disturbance: _____

Dramatic Question: _____

End of the Beginning: _____

The Middle: _____

Conflicts: _____

Crises: _____

Obstacles: _____

Complications: _____

Dark Moment: _____

Enlightenment: _____

Climax: _____

Catharsis: _____

Exercise #2
Write a short play that follows formula entirely. Allow yourself only one line of dialogue for each structural element. That is, allow one line for the event, one line to reveal the protagonist, one line to reveal the antagonist, one line for the disturbance, one line for the major decision, and so on.

Exercise #3
Romeo and Juliet begins with an event, the gang fight. What other events could Shakespeare have used to begin the play? Examine the reason each might or might not be a natural place to start the play. For example:

Possible Beginning	Evaluation of Suitability
1. It could have begun with the event that started the two families warring.	This might be a natural place to begin if the reason the families were warring was important to the story. Yet, in *Romeo and Juliet* the justification for the battle is not central to the love story that follows. Romeo and Juliet do not try to bring their families together, so this would not be a natural place to begin.
2. The play could begin with Rosaline (Romeo's previous love interest) and Romeo breaking up.	It could if this were a story about Romeo trying to repair the relationship with her, or if Romeo were torn between Juliet and Rosaline.
3. It could begin with Romeo proclaiming his need to fall in love.	It's an event and it's central to the story, but it lacks conflict.

Now try the same exercise with your play. List several possible opening events. Why would each be a natural place to begin your story? Does each idea contain the essence of the story that follows?

Exercise #4

List the conflict/crises, complications, and obstacles contained within your play idea. There is no set rule as to how many conflicts you need. You must decide: Do you have enough to sustain the middle of your play?

Chapter 3

CHARACTERS IN ACTION

The surest way to get a play produced is to write one with interesting, genuine characters that push the story forward. Character is the best plot there is. Playwright John Howard Lawson said, "A play may contain

> *No play can rise above the level of its characterization.*
>
> George Pierce Baker

a duel in every scene, a pitched battle in every act and the spectators be sound asleep, or be kept awake only by the noise." Action and story are often not enough. Plays are about people. Character development separates the playwriting pro from the beginner. It's one area in which most playwrights fail, yet there are many techniques to help a playwright achieve greater understanding of the elusive qualities of powerful, fully dimensional characterizations.

Years ago we met an old Parisian street artist who was delicately adding the final touches to his creation. When he finished, I asked what was the most common mistake made by beginning painters. He answered, "They look at the canvas too much." The same is true of beginning playwrights. They spend too much time looking at the page and not enough studying the people they're writing about. A playwright is a student; human life is the teacher. If you simply attempt to invent a character, you're spending too much time looking at the canvas and not enough studying real life. A playwright must take the time to study human beings, for they're the stuff on which strong, believable characters are based. A character is built from bits and pieces of human lives, so a playwright's ability to create characters is based on his ability to examine and understand the motivations and emotions of this creature called a human being. When a playwright develops a strong character, the result is an alloy made from a great deal of the playwright's emotions, experiences, observations, and only a touch of invention.

WRITE ABOUT *WHO* YOU KNOW

Playwrights write about people they know, whom they personally feel for and understand, and with whom they have experience. Playwrights don't *become* the character, but rather find the feelings and thoughts of the character that are inside themselves. You certainly can't feel anyone else's emotions but your own. No matter how hard you try, when you develop a character, you're simply highlighting a particular side of your own thoughts and feelings. Your own core emotions, sensations, and experiences are the principal building blocks in creating characters. This is not to say you must behave like the characters you write, but you have inside you the senses and memories that allow you to understand why strangers act as they do. Playwrights select and modify their own personalities to fit different characters. By empathizing and remembering similar events and emotions in your own life, you can find common ground with your characters. It's not uncommon for a playwright to say a particular character is this or that side of his own personality. Only then can the playwright understand the character's rhythm of life, thoughts, feelings, motivations, and actions.

EMPATHY

Sympathy is compassion, commiseration, even understanding, but *empathy* is more. It's as close to knowing someone else as is humanly possible. Empathy is substituting your emotions for the emotions of another. When you feel empathy, you're feeling yourself in the place of another. It's as close as human beings can come to a shared experience. If your friend's father dies and you have never experienced the death of a close relative, you have sympathy. If you have experienced the death of your own father, then you have empathy. Only when there is empathy can a playwright truly know and write a character. This doesn't mean that to write about the death of a father you must wait until your father dies, or you must face death to understand how a terminal patient feels, or murder in order to feel the inner thoughts of a killer. Empathy is also possible when a person imagines himself in the place of another, builds a vivid image of what the situation would be like, and reacts.

The great acting teacher Constantin Stanislavski used an exercise called the "magic if" to stimulate the imagination; the technique involved one question, "What would I do if I were this character under these circumstances?" A playwright uses the "magic if" to find the similarities between himself and the character, and explores the intimate emotions and thoughts that result. Yet raw emotions are not enough. The magic question is "What would I *do*?" Emotional similarities between the playwright and character are good as long as they result in outward movement. In other words, the common emotion must lead the playwright to understand the character's impulse toward action.

To illustrate this point, let's go back to playwright #6 (chapter 1). Her working title was *Fathers & Daughters,* the story about a daughter who comes home to confront her dying father. At first the playwright had little empathy with the father even though she based the story on her own difficult childhood. Her father was a desperate man who had struggled for ten years toward his doctoral degree. As she began to write, the role of the father was a one-dimensional, hateful man who yelled at his daughter and caused the family no end of trouble with his tirades. The first draft met with total failure. The script was nothing more than a melodrama in which the good daughter triumphed over the evil father; a personal fancy that failed to communicate with or entertain the audience. She gave up.

Years later she called to say she had rewritten the script and won her first contest. This time the play worked beautifully. The father was a well-rounded, three-dimensional character; he was still a hateful man, still yelled at his daughter, but this time the play was motivated and a success. What happened?

As it turned out, the playwright's most vivid image of her father came from her childhood. She was in the car with him when a woman cut them off in traffic. Her father always hated female drivers. Infuriated, he chased the guilty driver down and began telling her what a jackass she was. It was a small town, everybody knew everyone, and the daughter was terribly embarrassed. In the middle of the father's tirade the guilty driver cracked her window and said, "Why don't you go to college?"—the worst thing one could say to a man who had been struggling for ten years to get his Ph.D. Her father stood speechless for a moment and then spit on the woman's windshield. The event was forever burned into the daughter's mind. From her point of view, her father was unbalanced and possibly insane. This was the point of view from which she wrote the first draft—the miserable failure.

Fifteen years later, this same playwright was a struggling artist in Los Angeles. Things weren't going well for her career, she was nearly bankrupt and flunking out of grad school. Late one night she was driving home from her night job when a car suddenly cut her off, almost causing an accident. It was a male driver. She hated male drivers. Infuriated, the playwright chased the car down, stopped it at a light, and began telling the driver what type of idiot he was. (This is not recommended in Los Angeles.) The man totally ignored her. Suddenly the playwright's mission became clear. Standing on the cold, wet street, she felt the old glands working in her mouth. She knew what she had to do. She spit on the driver's windshield (again, not recommended in L.A.). That evening, she thought about her father, dug out the old play, and began to rewrite. Now she had, at least for a moment, seen life from her father's point of view and understood the strain and pressures. By chance, she had built a vivid emotional image and reacted to it. Now she had the ability to find the good in her bad characters and the bad in her good ones. She understood that all people think they have "good" reasons for what they do. She had empathy.

Author David Rintels put it another way: "Presenting one side of the story is not drama. One side is polemic or propaganda. The best drama comes when you let both sides make their best case—winner take all. It's not drama to have only one side of an issue." In order to present both sides of the story, the writer must understand that one of the highest forms of intelligence is the ability to see life from someone else's point of view.

Empathy can be a lasting, deeply personal understanding or only a flash waiting to be mined for greater perception. Empathy happens when a playwright allows a brief moment of insight to unlock the door to heightened understanding. Empathy makes it possible for a man to write an accurate woman and a woman to write a believable man. A black writer can understand a white character. An old man can create the role of a child. It's popular today to say, "only my kind can understand my feelings," but playwrights transcend barriers and find the common ground between the races, genders, and ages.

OBJECTIVITY

Objectivity, allowing the least possible distortion from personal feelings, prejudices, or interpretations, is difficult when you are writing a deeply personal story with characters you know all too well. Writing a play may be therapeutic, but a play that serves only the playwright's needs is nothing more than a diary entry. Playwrights communicate. Each word is not only written for the playwright's benefit, but as a gift to others. In order to communicate, a playwright must have a deeply personal relationship with the characters and yet remain objective. Playwrights split themselves into two writers: the emotional writer involved with the character's thoughts and feelings, and the analytical writer who judges everything from a distance.

Time is the best way to gain distance. One student playwright desperately wanted to write about the tragic death of his sister, but every time he tried, he came up short. He knew his sister, had plenty of empathy, he understood what happened, but without perspective, he couldn't separate himself from the characters. Most of his writing sessions ended with few pages and many tears. Several years from now, time may give him perspective on the events and he may write a good play. Eugene O'Neill didn't write his autobiographical plays until years after his family had passed away.

Sometimes a playwright doesn't have the option of time, or the characters and events are so personal that time has little effect. In these cases, a playwright can gain perspective by changing the original character's gender, age, or race. The playwright may also modify the time or location of the story.

Once, while working with a beginning playwright, I noticed he was getting more and more upset with my suggested changes. As I showed him how to make the characters more real and the situation believable, he suddenly shouted, "But that's not the way it happened!" Plays aren't about what happened; they are an *imitative interpretation* of the facts. Playwrights are not journalists. We are allowed to interpret and alter reality in order to find our truth. In science, truth is achieved by adhering to facts. In the arts, truth can be achieved by interpreting, manipulating, even distorting facts.

S U B S T I T U T I O N

Even with empathy, not every playwright has the personal experience and understanding to write every role. Occasionally, a story demands a character with which the playwright has no experience, no emotional bond, a character beyond the playwright's knowledge.

This problem can be solved with an old acting technique called *substitution*. When actors must play a role for which they have little or no emotional bond they sometimes replace the character's emotions with ones closer to their own. For example, if the character must kill someone, and the actress can't find the emotion within herself, she'll substitute a similar emotion. This concept can also apply to playwrights.

Recently a student finished a play about a young man who was torn between his love for a coed and his need to belong to a fraternity. The girl didn't want the protagonist to belong to the rowdy frat house, while the frats, jealous of the boy's relationship, demanded he break up with the girl. The play was read in class to a chorus of yawns. It was a deeply personal story for the nineteen-year-old playwright, yet no one cared. The class thought the story and characters weren't worth the time, yet the play was not a total loss. The playwright saved it by using his own emotions as a substitution and wrote a play about a priest who falls in love and is torn between his duty to the church and a woman. The parallels between the fraternity house and the Catholic Church were just similar enough to bring the playwright's emotions and experience into play. Through substitution, he could use his emotions to understand what a priest in love might feel, think, and do. He researched the Catholic Church, rewrote the play, and produced a rather interesting story about a priest who falls in love with a Baptist deacon's daughter. It never won an award, but during the public reading, the audience was absorbed. Afterward, one audience member, a nun, wondered how a nineteen-year-old could've written such a deeply emotional and uplifting piece. We never bothered to tell her the playwright was really writing about his frat house.

A substitution can go even further and cover unrelated emotions. An actor acquaintance of ours was playing the role of Solness in Ibsen's *The Master Builder.* The character of Solness is haunted by the tragic deaths of his children. After they died in a fire, Solness switched from building churches to homes and made a personal fortune in the process. Solness was troubled because he believed the deaths worked to his advantage. He couldn't bring himself to look on a church, let alone build one. The actor playing the role was childless, hadn't been to church in years, and couldn't bring himself to feel for Solness. He felt no empathy, so he used a substitution based on something that happened to him when he was fifteen. It was late at night and he was walking home from a friend's house, when he felt someone was watching him. He turned and looked up to find, silhouetted in the moonlight, a gargoyle sitting on the peak of a clapboard house across the street. He had lived in this neighborhood for years, walked down the street a thousand times, and had never seen the gargoyle. He stood there staring at this little figure perched in the darkness. Suddenly, the small figure turned its head and looked at him. Its yellow eyes sparkled in the moonlight. He didn't stop running until he got home. Even the next day, when he discovered an escaped pet monkey was his horrible gargoyle, he would not be comforted.

To this day, he is haunted by the sight. Although this had nothing to do with what haunts the character of Solness, he was able to substitute this emotion and play the part. The same is true for a playwright. If you have little in common with the character, you can still substitute and write a strong character as long as you communicate your own believable emotions. Producer and director Arthur Hopkins summed it up nicely by saying, "Heartaches are heartaches in the Avenue or the Bowery, and love and trouble and weakness and strength are pretty much common to all kinds of people."

CHARACTER ANALYSIS

When analyzing a character, there are hundreds of questions a writer might ask:

What is the character's self-image?

How highly does the character regard himself?

How does the character handle different situations?

Does the character admire herself?

Does the character hate himself?

What are the character's vulnerabilities?

Why is the character vulnerable?

What are the character's obsessions?

What are the character's unmet needs?

What are the character's habits?

What haunts the character?

What are the character's idiosyncrasies?

What drives the character's relationships?

What drives the character?

What was the happiest moment in the character's life?

What is the worst thing the character has ever done?

What does the character dream about?

What is the best thing the character has ever done?

What were the character's high school years like?

What does the character know about herself that others don't know?

This list could go on for pages. The sum total of a character's personality, emotions, thoughts, and motivations is often too much for a playwright, or anyone, to comprehend. (Psychiatrists spend years trying to understand the basic human mental processes and have only scratched the surface.) This is why a playwright doesn't have to totally understand a character before writing begins. The act of writing is a process of discovery. From outline, through drafts, rehearsals, and performance, a character is always growing. Pages of character analysis may help the playwright to understand part of a character, but true comprehension seldom comes before the playwright starts writing. Just as in life, you don't totally understand a person on the first, second, or even third meeting. The same is true of characters. To begin writing, a playwright must have only a *workable* understanding of the characters. This basic understanding is fine as long as a deeply personal, empathetic understanding of the character occurs during the process.

A workable understanding comes through character analysis. Character analysis depends upon the playwright's ability to dissect a character. Most playwrights do this by dividing a character into practical bits and pieces. In reality, it's impossible to break a person's character into such components because everything is interrelated, but a writer will do this in an attempt to clarify a character. One way to analyze a character is to divide it into four basic elements: the four dimensions of character.

DIMENSIONS OF A CHARACTER

Several years ago a student got tired of his characters being described as two-dimensional. "What's wrong with two-dimensional characters?" he asked, "I see so many of them in real life." He was right. There seem to be many shallow, two-dimensional people out there, but they don't belong on the stage. A strong, stageworthy character has at least three and possibly four dimensions.

THE FIRST AND SECOND DIMENSIONS OF CHARACTER

The first dimension of character is the *public side*. What a character seems like from the outside and what she is like from the inside can differ greatly. For example, from the outside, or public side, a character may be described as:

Irritating	Anxious
Exasperating	Work centered
Controlling	Domineering
Perfectionist	Fault finding
Hypercritical	

You may recognize this person. It's the classic definition of an obsessive-compulsive personality. But does this really tell you who the character is? Here is another:

Fears disapproval

Self-doubting

Anticipates catastrophe

Wants to be admired for ability

Wishes people valued his or her self-discipline

Feels wounded when others don't value his or her helpful hints

Feels there is a right way and a wrong way

Rarely feels support

This sounds completely different, but in fact it's also a description of an obsessive-compulsive person, viewed now from the inside, the personal side, the second dimension of character. To develop a strong, unique character, a playwright must always look at the public side filtered through the personal side. Here's another example, a classic description of a hysteric. The public side:

Overdramatic	Eager
Playacting	Superficial
Receptive	Can't really be trusted

Personal side:

Finds others so hard to please

Believes passive people aren't attacked

Looking for a prince or princess

When a playwright cannot justify and understand all of a character's actions, then he is writing from only a public view of the character, and will never achieve the characterization the stage requires. All attitudes, traits, fears, hopes, everything that distinguishes and individualizes character, no matter how strange or irrational, must be justified and understood. For example, a student playwright was writing about a woman whose husband beat her. She described the character of the husband as an evil man who beat his wife "for no reason." Not possible. All humans have reasons and rationales for everything they do. No character or person sets out to be evil. The wife beater might appear evil and irrational from the public side, but from the personal side (his point of view) he believes his actions are highly justified and even logical. This playwright, as callous as it sounds, needs to find the husband's personal positive reasons for his actions, and then must search for a similar side of herself. If she fails, she will write a one-dimensional, uninteresting stereotype unworthy of the stage.

POSITIVE VERSUS NEGATIVE CHOICES

Playwrights try to find the positive choices a character makes, rather than the negative ones. A classic example of positive choices comes from Tennessee Williams's *Cat On A Hot Tin Roof.* In the play, Mae, (also called "Sister Woman") is constantly fighting for a piece of her father-in-law's plantation. Many actresses choose to play her as motivated by *greed,* which invariably leads to a tiresome, shrieking caricature. To truly understand the character we must look at what positive motivations the playwright includes. In Mae's case, the author has given her a once wealthy background, many children to support, and a husband who feels slighted by his father. Mae believes she is motivated by *need* (for recognition and family) instead of greed (for money); the former is a positive choice, the latter is not. She may in fact be greedy, but she doesn't see herself that way, and so the playwright has given the character a positive choice.

People may be misguided, even totally wrong, but they seldom see their motivations or actions as negative or evil. For example, the mother who leaves her children because she is hateful is not as interesting as one who tries to justify her actions by thinking it's best for the children. A playwright looks at life from the character's point of view, and understands why each character views himself or herself as a good person with constructive motivations and actions (even though the end result may be destructive).

CHARACTER CONFLICT AND CHARACTER FLAW

Just as conflict and crisis are the core of a good play, they are also the core of a good character. Strong characters are often at odds with themselves. The public and personal sides are in crisis or conflict. Jean Vilar, the French actor and producer, said, "Few, if any, of our admirations and loves are free of illusion; that is, of errors of judgment, if not of outright lies. . . . There is no human work or creature which . . . is not finally seen in its true contradictions." Characters without inner conflicts, who never have errors of judgment are either boring or are wonderfully complete, emotionally healthy people. In either case, they don't belong on stage. Plays are about imperfect people with problems, crises, and inner conflicts. Drama is possible because of human errors.

When the character experiences conflict, an interesting and exact statement about the conflict can be drawn. For example:

He wants to fall in love but feels unworthy.

She wants to be trusted, yet she trusts no one.

She needs to have a child but believes she is too old.

He knows he has the talent but is afraid of failure.

If this inner conflict is powerful enough to affect the character's good judgment, then it's a character flaw (sometimes called a fatal flaw or tragic flaw). This is the personality imperfection that trips the character and prevents him from achieving a goal. Usually a character flaw comes about because a character doesn't have an accurate picture of his private, personal self. All plays are about characters with limited self-awareness. Why? Because the same is true in life!

Arthur Miller used *Oedipus* (the Greek tragedy about the king who rips his eyes out when he discovers he has married his mother and killed his father) to make the point. If Oedipus had a great deal of self-awareness, Miller states, he would have seen that ". . . he was not really to blame for having cohabitated with his mother, since neither he nor anyone else knew she was his mother. He would have decided to divorce her, provide for their children, firmly resolve to investigate the family background of his next wife, and thus deprived us of a very fine play." Oedipus doesn't have clear, perfect knowledge of himself, and so discovery, growth, and a great play are possible.

All characters are mired in a limited view of life. This limited view results in some sort of flaw, vice, error in judgment, or frailty. If your play has a weak middle, one problem could be that your protagonist is too proficient at dealing with the problems facing her. All characters have flaws. Find the flaws and you will achieve greater understanding of character.

THE THIRD DIMENSION — MOTIVATED ACTION

The third dimension of character is *action*. Action and character are inseparable. Character defines the action and the action is justified through character. Any attempt to develop one without the other will result either in simple characters designed only to serve the story or in limited stories that give the characters nothing to do. Writing long character analyses separate from any action is nothing more than an interesting exercise. It assumes that the characters are stagnant; they aren't. Characters change, characters do things, characters are action.

This aspect of character is unique to playwriting. It's possible to write a novel, poem, or short story and never have the characters do anything, but a play is driven by the characters' action. Without action there is no play.

Aristotle said plot is the first principle and soul of a play; the only way to bring character up to the level of plot is to imbue character with the same element that makes plot so important. That element is action. Only when the characters have strong, well-motivated action can they share focus with plot.

As an example, idea #2 (from chapter 1), *A Hard Act to Follow,* about the playwright's grandfather, is in character trouble—because there is no action. No doubt the character of the grandfather is real and multidimensional. The playwright is basing it on her own grandfather, for whom she has great empathy. But, as far as writing for the stage is concerned, the character has no conflict or crisis or action and is stagnant and incomplete. Maurice Maeterlinck, the Belgian poet, said, "An old man, seated in his armchair, waiting patiently, with his lamp beside him—submitting with bent head to the presence of his soul and his destiny—motionless as he is, does yet live in a reality—a deeper, more human, and more universal life—than the lover who strangles his mistress, the captain who conquers in battle, or the husband who avenges his honor." Yes, a person who is taking no action can be just as deep as a character who sets out against a sea of troubles, but without action, there is no play. And so the lover who strangles his mistress or the husband who avenges his honor are far better stage characters than the old man sitting near the lamp. Action can be a desire, a want, a goal, anything that pushes the character to *do,* say, or challenge.

Yet, a character's action doesn't have to be some lofty quest. Though some characters do set out to save the world, most action is small by comparison. For example, playwright #6, while writing *Fathers & Daughters,* thought she understood the character of the mother. The playwright could easily state the public and private side of the character, she thought she had empathy, but was lost when it came to the mother's action. "The mother is a sad lady who is dominated by her husband," the playwright stated. "She takes no action." When asked if life for the mother would be easier if she left her husband, the answer was, "Of course." Then there must be a reason she stays. That reason is expressed in an action (hopefully a positive action).

It took several days of soul-searching and analyzing before playwright #6 came up with the answer, "Mother stays because of her deep desire to take care of someone, anyone. Her children have grown and left. The grandchildren are far away. The only child left in her world is her domineering husband. If she left him, she would have no one but herself to take care of. If someone is not dependent on her, her life is meaningless. Her action, then, is mothering her husband." Perfect! This action, from the public side, makes her appear to be a mere servant, but from the personal side, it makes her life worth living. Her need to be a mother makes it a positive choice. Understanding a character comes when the playwright places the character in action and understands the true, positive motivations for that action.

Motivation is the reason a character starts a particular action. This motivation is embodied in the character's conscious or unconscious personality. It can come from some dark part of the character's history or be as simple as the desire to do the right thing. Wherever it comes from, people seldom have complicated motivations for what they do; the character may be complicated, the motivation may be hidden deep within the character's phobias or personality traits, but once found the motivation can usually be stated in a simple sentence:

I want to kill my uncle, because he killed my father.

I have to make a better life for myself to prove my parents wrong.

I must be with Romeo because I'm in love with him.

I need to prove myself a man.

One of the fastest ways to lose an audience's attention is to have a character with unclear or weak motivation. But the motivation shouldn't be too obvious. Characters can become shallow if they wear their motivations on their sleeves, constantly reminding the audience why they're acting as they do.

THE FOURTH DIMENSION—
THE SUBCONSCIOUS

The fourth dimension of a character is the *subconscious*. This is largely out of the control of the playwright, for the playwright's own subconscious is automatically embodied in the character's. The fourth dimension of character is affected by the playwright's own times, values, and desires. This is why some playwrights fail when they attempt to direct their own work; they're unaware of the subconscious side of their characters. Often, it takes another point of view, an outsider, to fully understand what a playwright has written.

BUILDING A CHARACTER

A basic understanding of character occurs when the playwright stacks all the opposing facets of character into a cohesive whole. The public side, private side, the character's action, and all the interconflicts, flaws, and motivations can lead to a total greater than the sum of the parts. A gestalt occurs. But to do this, a playwright must be able to analyze characters, tear them down to their individual elements, and then rebuild them as the playwright sees fit. In this way, a character in a play can be made up of several people whom the playwright intimately knows, including the playwright herself.

For clarity, let's follow a playwright as he builds a basic understanding of a character, one dimension at a time. First the public side:

> Bob Sticklmire is six feet tall and has brown hair. His nose looks one size too big, and he covers a bad case of acne with a beard. His fellow workers like him because he is on time, he always throws himself into his work, and he will readily admit when he is wrong.

What do you know about Bob Sticklmire? Not much. You could guess that Bob is sensitive about his acne and you might be able to draw the conclusion about him being closed or shy, but the public impression is not enough. Many possibilities exist, and few facts. Here are some details about Bob's private side:

> Bob doesn't understand why he hasn't been promoted to vice president. He believes he can never miss a day of work or they'll discover he's not really needed. He goes into the office an hour early every day in the hope that someday someone will realize how hard he works; he knows, in his soul, that he cannot move up in the company until he finishes his degree.

These personality traits give you a clearer picture of Bob. He's much like thousands of other people out there, but if we add in what Bob does—his actions—who Bob is becomes much clearer:

> At Christmas, Bob never gives his son gifts, but presents him with a clean, crisp, new one hundred dollar bill, which he steals from petty cash.

From this one little action, we can draw all sorts of conclusions about Bob's character. What type of father would only give a one hundred dollar bill and no presents year after year? Most likely Bob doesn't believe the theft is wrong, but justifies it as a positive action toward his son. Also, his exact feelings toward the company and work are clearer. You could now begin to fill in the blanks concerning Bob's life. He believes the company owes him something. Does he think the same about his son? His wife? One Christmas action opens up hundreds of possible questions and answers about the real Bob Sticklmire.

When a public side is in conflict with a private side and there is a clear action or reaction, you have the bare beginnings of a character. The playwright is launched on a path of discovery, but discovery cannot be separate from the playwright's own thoughts and emotions. The answers must come from within as the playwright tries to find a part of himself that would react as Bob Sticklmire reacts. Character analysis must lead to an empathetic understanding of character.

In this case, our playwright remembers the time he stole from his mother's purse. His mother wouldn't let him have a toy, so he took the money to get even. Then he had a change of heart, but thought if he put the money back he would get caught, so he gave the money to a girl he really liked. Notice how the character is beginning to grow from basic information to personal understanding. The process is repeated over and over as the playwright digs deeper to find an understanding for the core of Bob Sticklmire.

Next, the playwright must be able to hear the voice of Bob Sticklmire. After years of study and practice, a musician can develop the ability to hear music without any sound being present. A similar process happens to playwrights. After years of writing, they develop the ability to see and hear imaginary characters. Their acute ear for rhythm, tempo, speech patterns, and the ability to analyze and understand the essence of a character allows them to wrap themselves in characters as real as the people they meet on the street. To anyone else this might appear a form of schizophrenia, but to a playwright, it's the highest form of creativity. This is the extraordinary instant when the character of Bob Sticklmire seems to write himself, as if the playwright were no longer part of the equation. The character has now taken on a life of his own.

TECHNIQUES IN CHARACTER BUILDING

Just as there are techniques to help a playwright organize the structure of a play, there are techniques to help a playwright develop a character. Some of these techniques include individualization, basing characters on real people, stereotypes, adding a "piece of sugar," character arc, character catalyst, limiting and combining characters, and character details.

Individualization: This is an individual trademark in a character (a unique gesture, phrase, or quirk) that sets him or her apart from all others. For example, a student writer created the role of a policewoman, a strong, effective officer who could hold her own with any man, but had a fear of being intimate. She expressed the fear in a rather odd way. Every time she was intimate with a man, she would start talking about jelly-filled doughnuts. This nervous habit upset the men in her life, but endeared the character to the audience. The individual trademarks should never be just added to a character, but must be motivated from within.

Basing Characters on Real People: Some playwrights write with a particular actor or person in mind. By imitating the speech patterns and style of a real person, they can create believable dialogue and personalities. For example, a student playwright based a character on Henry Fonda by imitating the actor's style and speech. The result was a realistic sounding character who no one would've guessed was Henry Fonda.

There are three keys to imitation. First, choose the right person to imitate. The person should be close in type to the character you're creating and also someone you know well enough to consistently imitate. Second, simple imitation is sufficient only to start the process. If the imitation does not lead to greater understanding of the character, it's only a trick, and the final result will lack depth. Third, once you have used this technique, let the source of your character be your little secret. Never admit to anyone you've used her as a model. Knowing a character has been based on them will often embarrass or anger them.

Stereotypes: Just as there are formulas for building a story, there are also formulas for building characters. These formulas are called *stereotypes*. Stereotypes are oversimplified character types. They occur when we leap to conclusions about a character and assign labels rather than discover attributes. For example, playwright #11's story idea about the black family moving into a white neighborhood could easily contain white and black stereotypes. To avoid stereotypes, a playwright must find the traits unique to each character and no other. Never use typical reactions to justify an individual's actions. For example, a student playwright wrote about a child who blames himself for his parents' divorce. When questioned why this child blames himself the playwright answered, "that's what children do." True, many children do blame themselves for their parents' problems, but the child character will be stereotypical unless the playwright digs deeper and finds the unique, individual reasons this particular child blames himself.

Piece of Sugar: Occasionally a playwright creates a protagonist whose personal flaws or traits make the character disagreeable to the audience. One way to solve this problem is with a "piece of sugar." This device gives the protagonist dialogue or action that proves, somewhere deep in her soul, she is really a nice person. The phrase "piece of sugar" comes from a James Cagney movie in which he played a vicious outlaw. In one scene, he takes a lump of sugar and gives it to a horse, thus showing the audience he isn't all bad. If you have a protagonist who's about to lose sympathy with the audience, you might create a "piece of sugar."

Character Arc: Just as a story has a beginning, a middle, and an end, so do most characters. Character arc is the growth or change in a character caused by the events of the story. It can be considerable, but more often it's a slight change in direction that leads the character to greater understanding or awareness. Too often playwrights think of people and characters as fixed. In high school, we are taught to "be ourselves," yet we seldom consider that part of ourselves is growth and change. Who you are today is not the exact same person you'll be tomorrow. The same is true of the characters in a play. Through trials, tribulations, conflicts, and enlightenments, characters can adjust, grow, and change.

Not all characters in a play have to have character arc. Those that don't are set in their ways. Their personalities reflect self-fulfilling prophecy that they can never escape. But if characters do change, they should never change so dramatically that they're no longer the same character. When considering a character, plot the individual's arc and make sure the change is believable and motivated.

Character Catalyst: There is a difference between character motivation and character catalyst. A *motivation* is a deep reason behind a character's action. A *catalyst* is a temporary event that causes the character to react. For example, a beginning playwright had a character get drunk and tell his wife off. When asked the motivation, the playwright answered, "He's drunk." Drunkenness is *never* a motivation. The desires, needs, and motivations of a character exist whether he is drunk or sober. In this case, the husband's drunkenness is only a catalyst that causes the action to occur at this moment; it is not the real motivation behind the action.

Limiting and Combining Characters: Today most professional theatres are fiscally strapped. In order to keep the payroll down they are forced to look for plays with smaller casts. Once you have more than six characters in a play, you lower the chance of getting it produced. This is by no means a hard and fast rule, but a playwright should make sure all the characters in a play are needed. If you have smaller parts that serve only one function or appear for only a few minutes, try to combine them into a major character. Exceptions to this rule are college and community theatres, which are seldom limited by payroll (because they don't pay the actors), so cast size is not a hindrance. In fact, most college and community theatres look for plays with larger casts so they can keep their students and membership happy.

Character Details: Years ago I was acting in a play, and the director suddenly stopped the rehearsal and signaled me down from the stage. He put an arm on my shoulder and asked for specifics about my character.

"How old are you?"

"The script says I'm thirty."

"More specific?"

"Thirty-and-a-half," I answered tentatively.

Overjoyed with my exactness, he sent me back on stage. Exactness and details are important when it comes to building a character, but sometimes they can get out of hand. In this case, whether the character was thirty-and-a-half rather than thirty was not important to the story, the character's emotions, or motivations. The art of building a character, like all arts, is selecting and arranging the important elements of character into a unified whole. Details are important, but only the details that affect a character during the traffic of the play.

FINAL THOUGHTS ON CHARACTER

A good playwright develops a poet-like ability to see and hear life from all points of view. Only when playwrights are alive and aware of themselves and the people around them do they draw strong, realistic characters. This is why some playwrights take notepads or tape recorders with them and record snatches of dialogue and observations. This is the reason playwrights don't limit themselves to observing one particular social class, gender, or age. William Archer said, ". . . specific directions for character-drawing would be like rules for becoming six feet high. Either you have it in you, or you have it not."

EXERCISES

Exercise #1
Write a short scene in which you find positive motivation for what the antagonist in your story idea does. Don't merely justify emotions and actions, but try to find a part of yourself similar to the character.

Exercise #2
Write a brief scene in which your protagonist and antagonist are in conflict. Make sure the reader's sympathy is with your protagonist. Then rewrite the scene, adjusting so that the reader's sympathy falls with the antagonist because his or her positive motivations are now clear. (The key to this exercise is to rewrite the scene as little as possible.)

Exercise #3
Select the one character in your story idea with whom you have the least in common. Attempt to find events, an emotion, or motivation in your life that you could substitute for the character's own events, emotion, or motivation.

Exercise #4

Pick one of the characters you want to write about and attempt to find the character's flaw. Write an interesting and exact statement about the parts of his or her personality that are in conflict.

Example:

He needs to be free but can't leave his three children.
She wanted to be a teacher but hates the children.

Exercise #5

Write a brief description of each character in your play. Include the characters' public, personal, and motivated action sides.

Exercise #6

In order to develop your descriptive powers, play the game "Essence." This game begins with a student thinking of a famous person and stating, "I am a living American," or "I am a dead Frenchman," or whatever. Then the other students must ask questions such as, "What kind of cloud would you be?" or "What kind of car are you?" None of the questions can be direct; they must all attempt to show the essence of the character. This forces players to think in specific metaphors and abstractions. In the end, the students write down who they think the main student has in mind.

THE WRITER'S TEN COMMANDMENTS

Author Tom Shadyac was up one night after a UCLA writers' party and said that his savior, Lajos Ergi, spoke to him from a burning box of erasable bond paper so that he might know his laws.

I. Thou shalt love the Lord thy God, CONFLICT, as thyself.

II. Thou shalt not have false gods, PLOT, DIALOGUE, STORYLINE, before character.

III. Thou shalt not steal—but thou mayst borrow and make it thine own.

IV. Thou shalt not kill character with stereotypes, shallowness, or two dimensionality.

V. Thou shalt not commit a*dull*tery—for, as the great prophet, Richard Walterious, has said after me, "The greatest sin of art is dullness."

VI. Thou shalt not lie—that's what agents are for.

VII. Thou shalt keep thy premise holy.

VIII. Thou shalt honor thy father and mother—for it is from them that one learns about oneself and from oneself that all art emanates.

IX. Thou shalt love thy neighbor as thyself—for this will cause Conflict (the source of all drama) with thy neighbor's husband.

X. Thou shalt keep the Sabbath—unless thou hast a deadline.

Reprinted with permission of the author.

Chapter 4

FORM WRITING

When playwrights develop the ability to analyze, understand, build, and
write multidimensional characters,
they're ready to take the first steps
away from formula writing. Without
formula, the playwright lets the story
grow naturally from the characters
rather than following preset guide-

*The Dramatist who hangs his characters
to his plot, instead of hanging his plot
to his characters, is guilty of cardinal
sin. . . . Character is the best plot there is.*

John Galworthy

lines. The label "form play" has nothing to do with genre, it's simply the process
by which the playwright conceives and writes the play. William Archer said,
"The difference between a live play and a dead one is that in the former the
characters control the plot, while in the latter the plot controls the characters.
Which is not to say, of course, that there may not be clever and entertaining plays which are 'dead' in this sense, and dull and unattractive plays which
are 'alive'."

A good how-to book gives its reader recipes. Formula is a recipe, but a
form play has no recipe, so form writing is difficult to teach. All we can do
is give the playwright the ingredients; the exact recipe is left open to the individual writer. The most important ingredient in a form play is character, but
other elements come under three major categories: dramatic principles, plot-
structure, and technique.

DRAMATIC PRINCIPLES

There's a difference between dramatic rules and principles. *Rules* are the special
techniques, even regulations, applied to playwriting during a particular period
of history. A *principle* is a dramatic axiom that has changed little through history
and applies to all plays in all ages. The years have produced many dramatic

rules, but only a few basic dramatic principles. For example, the sixteenth-century French tragic playwrights followed formulaic rules. Their rules (called the Unities) stated that the action of a play must take place within a twenty-four-hour period, with no subplots and no mixing of tragedy and comedy. Sixteenth-century French playwrights would have insisted that these were more than just dramatic rules. They are, however, only rules and now outdated. Most modern playwrights would never consider them. On the other hand, the same basic dramatic principles that bound these French Neoclassic playwrights also apply to the ancient Greeks, to Shakespeare, to Eastern plays, and are still valid today. Dramatic principles are essentials that all good plays share. They define the nature of drama.

The most famous list of dramatic principles was written by Aristotle in *Poetics*. This twenty-three-century-old document defines six elements: plot, character, diction, thought, spectacle, and song. A strong argument can be made for each, except of course, song. Portions of ancient tragedies were sung, but it's certainly been proven since that singing isn't necessary in a fine tragedy. Even Aristotle mixed his dramatic rules and principles.

The debate over what elements make up a play and their order of importance has raged for thousands of years. From Aristotle to Horace to John Dryden, all have attempted to define the conventions of what makes a play. One interesting note is that when playwrights turn to criticism and attempt to define the exact elements of the art, their playwriting abilities often take a downward turn (George Bernard Shaw is a notable exception). Plato pointed out in *Apology* that playwrights (poets) are unable to give a coherent account of their process. The same is true today. Playwrights seldom have a highly objective understanding of what they do or how they do it. What a playwright needs is a practical understanding of dramatic principles. The order of their importance or exact meaning we leave to those on the outside of playwriting, to those who can examine, analyze, and debate, but never have to write a play.

A playwright's working list of dramatic principles would include: character, action, conflict/crisis, truth, spectacle, unity, and plot-structure. A play that lacks these qualities is not a play. We'll briefly review these principles and then cover them in detail in other chapters.

Character: Not all characters are good material for the stage. John Howard Lawson says, "Drama cannot deal with people whose wills are atrophied, who are unable to make decisions which have even temporary meaning, who adopt no conscious attitude toward events, who make no effort to control their environment." Stage characters are unique from those written for novels, poems, or short stories. Stage characters are full of action and able to express themselves.

Action: Aristotle said, "Action implies distinctive qualities both of character and thought; for it is by these that we qualify actions themselves, and these—thought and character—are the two natural causes from which action springs." Action is movement. A play, like life, changes and grows. The fundamental law of life is change. Everything changes, we grow old, we learn, seasons come and go, so the fundamental law of plays must also be changed. Plays are about what happens when change causes change. Another word for change causing change is action.

Conflict/Crisis: Plays are about human struggles. Whether it's good against evil, good against good, the individual against social forces, human nature against environment, thesis against antithesis, or mankind against itself, a play is about a clash of wills. As John Howard Lawson points out, "It is difficult to imagine a play in which forces of nature are pitted against other forces of nature." It's difficult because it's not a play. A play is about human conflicts and the answers that result. Crisis is the core of a play. George Pierce Baker, Eugene O'Neill's playwriting professor, said, "A play is the shortest distance from emotions to emotions." In other words, plays are about conflict occurring in crisis.

Truth: Playwrights are philosophers. They attempt to understand human beings and the world on which they're trapped. They may do this by selecting a realistic view of people or by emphasizing the fantastic side of human existence. The playwright's search for order and truth may result in a statement about the absurdity of life, a simple theme, or complex thesis.

Spectacle: We borrow Aristotle's term "spectacle" to say that theater is a performing art. A play is written for live performance. It's the only form of writing that must work on the page and live on stage. The ultimate test of a play occurs when it goes in front of an audience.

Unity: Tchaikovsky said, "What has been written with passion must now be looked upon critically, corrected, extended and most of all, condensed to fit the requirements of the form." A play's form requires a coherence in action and continuity from beginning to middle to end. Unity is the absolute and essential relation of all the parts to the whole.

These principles are necessary in playwriting, but they don't help the playwright build a story from character. This is where plot-structure becomes important.

PLOT-STRUCTURE

A play is a reflection of life (through one particular playwright's eyes), only sharpened, edited, and intensified. Therefore a playwright must learn to select, compress, and organize actions and characters into a compact whole. Plot-structure is the way a dramatist forms reality into a play. *Structure* is necessary because it creates a logical sequence from chaos, it turns the random action of life into the structured action of a play.

Some contemporary critics view structure as superficial; they say art should never be mechanical. These critics fail to understand that all plays, all art, have some sort of mechanical structure. Strindberg's expressionistic *A Dream Play* may appear to follow flow of consciousness, but it has a logically unified plot-structure. Japanese Kabuki plays, in which a performer's style is often more important than story, have structure. Even absurdist plays have a plot-structure. All good plays have a structure, just as language has syntax.

A play without plot-structure will wander and appear cluttered, erratic, and pointless; it will fail to communicate. Some playwrights purposely write erratic, pointless plays with the intent to show how erratic and pointless life is. This always fails. All they do is confuse the audience. It's a paradox that the only way a playwright can communicate that life is erratic and pointless is by constructing a stable, consistent, meaningful plot-structure.

Formula allows the playwright to structure a play by following a predetermined plot-structure. With form writing, playwrights are cut loose to create a unique plot-structure. Playwrights may free themselves from formula, but they must never lose structure. Whether you use formula, form, or both, the one thing you don't want your play to be is formless.

PLOT AND STORY

Plot and *story* are not interchangeable. Story is the basic outline of the play. If you briefly pitch your play idea to friends, you'll most likely tell them the story. For example:

> Dr. Stockmann is a little naive when it comes to people. When he discovers that the local mineral baths are contaminated, he thinks he'll be a hero for exposing the facts. He writes letters to the local papers only to be attacked by the mayor and townspeople, who don't want to lose their livelihood. In the end, the doctor learns an important lesson about the nature of people. He maintains his lonely battle and loses everything except his right to think.

This is the fundamental story of Ibsen's *An Enemy of the People*. Story provides only the basics. Plot, on the other hand, takes the basics of conflict, character, action, and so on, and proportions them into an exact order that achieves the playwright's purpose.

Some playwrights say that story is no longer important. They believe television and movies are now the best medium to tell stories, so they proclaim their plays free from story. This is fine as long as their plays have a strong plot.

PLOT POINTS

If you use form to write a play, the best way to build a plot is by using structural reference points called *plot points*. Plot points can take many forms: a character's realization or decision, a twist or turn in events, or a simple dramatic moment.

Formula plays are full of plot points that follow a predetermined order. In form, however, each plot point is simply the next logical, motivated step in the characters' lives. In other words, when a formula writer asks the question "What happens next?" she's really asking, "What could be the opening event? What is the opening balance? What major decision can the protagonist make that will cause conflict? What is the dark moment?" The form writer, on the other hand, asks only one question, "What would these particular characters in this situation do next?" The logical answers to this question are then strung together to form a series of plot points that make a unique framework. This natural framework is governed only by strong characters and dramatic principles.

DEVELOPING AN IDEA WITH PLOT POINTS

The only way to learn form writing is to enter into the deeply personal world of the playwright. It's a process that's too private to share, and yet, without sharing it, the methods of the form writer cannot be taught. Playwright #6 (chapter 1) agreed to let us examine her deeply personal process. Her story was *Fathers & Daughters,* about the woman who comes home to confront her dying father.

To work with form and plot points, a writer starts with characters. Who are they? At first, playwright #6 said she wasn't really sure. Because playwrights write about characters they know, she began by looking at her own father, an amateur philosopher who had an opinion on everything. The playwright spent weeks, even months, mulling over the characters. She spent little time at the keyboard, but still she was writing, for writing is the process of understanding. F. Scott Fitzgerald said that he could never convince his wife that the time he spent staring out his window was time spent writing. In one of these staring out the window sessions, playwright #6 remembered something that had happened years before. It was evening, her father had come to visit and they somehow got into a heated argument about how the human race was destroying itself through overpopulation. Her father built himself into a frenzy telling her that a responsible parent would only have one child. The playwright broke down in tears, because she was holding her second baby, his grandson.

"What are you trying to say, I shouldn't have had this baby?" she said as she ran into the bedroom crying. Her father muttered to himself, "It's nothing personal," and left.

An interesting image. What does it tell us about their relationship? The father seems to need an audience for his ideas, but he doesn't consider their effects. The playwright went on to remember that her father was "French vanilla; all the time I was growing up, it was the only flavor of ice cream allowed in the house." She was in college before she discovered chocolate and strawberry. The next day she made the following note about the characters:

> The night of the "one baby per woman fight," my father could not deal with my "illogical tears." Two hours later, near midnight, he returned with a small white paper bag. Inside was a half pint of *peach* ice cream. He never said he was sorry. He never brought up population control. He just served up two small plates of ice

cream and we sat there eating in the dark. I hate peach ice cream, but it didn't seem to matter. I knew that he was trying to say he was sorry. That's the type of man he was, he never took the time to ask what kind of ice cream his daughter liked, but the fact that it wasn't French vanilla was enough. Reaching out was so hard for him—except for that night, just sitting in the dark eating peach ice cream.

This is a good plot point. Could it be the end of the play? If so, what leads us to this final moment? The form writer begins to toy with the idea, asking more questions about this father and daughter relationship. Who are they? What do they want? What makes them tick? Three days later the playwright's notes read:

I had this older friend who was a wonderful character actor but never really made it big. One day I was visiting when he told me he was going into the hospital for cancer surgery and he might not be coming back. He was serious. He then asked if I'd go into the attic and retrieve an old dusty box, which I did. When I got back, he took the box, went outside, and threw it away. What could it have been? What dark secret was he trying to hide? What about his life did he want to hide after his life was over? I had to find out. After we said good-bye, I snuck around back and opened the trash. The box was filled with old *Playboy* magazines. How can I use this in the story? A mystery box could make an interesting dramatic question. Maybe the daughter thinks that it's something very personal, something which, when revealed, will bring forgiveness and understanding, but then she discovers it's only *Playboys*. Here was a man facing death and all he could think about was his old box of *Playboys* he hadn't touched in years. Could this send the daughter in the play over the top? Would this allow her to attack his selfishness?

Add this to the peach ice cream plot point and she's getting a much clearer idea of this father. What have we got so far? A daughter comes home to confront her father only to discover that he's more interested in throwing out the old *Playboys* than helping her. The playwright continues building characters and discovering plot points by combining images and ideas. What if this philosopher father was going into the hospital and the daughter was set to drive him? She doesn't know how serious it is until she discovers the *Playboys*. The ice cream would have to be set up. No problem, the father is having surgery, he's not allowed to eat solids so the daughter brings over his favorite, French vanilla.

The analyzing and developing of character continues. The daughter is dominated by her father, not physically, but mentally. The playwright next remembered how her father seldom listened to her and never valued her opinion.

We were driving along one day and I was giving him directions on how to get where we were going. I told him to turn here, but rather than trusting me, he flagged down another car and asked a total stranger for directions.

Another good character moment for the father, but what does it say about this daughter? The playwright wasn't sure. As is often the case, when a playwright is writing a highly personal story, the character representing the playwright is the weakest, for it requires much self-analysis and understanding. The next note read:

> The daughter wants to grow up, but few women can, due to treatment by fathers. Why do fathers continue to treat them like children? What if the woman has just gone through her second divorce? Often women seem to pick husbands like their fathers. She's desperate to find a dominating man who'll value her. It's a paradox. Dominating men never value their wives. She's searching for a man who doesn't criticize. After a failed second marriage, she comes home to confront her father.

This diary entry contains some good observations as the playwright continues to search for and analyze her memories and experiences, but she's beginning to feel dry.

"I've been thinking too much," was her comment one day, "I feel I've come up with everything I can." So, she headed to the library and began reading about other people's experiences with their fathers. This recharged her. A few days later she was back working.

"Why does she have to be divorced? Why is that important to the story?" I asked.

The playwright thought about it, then, "Two reasons. First, I've never been divorced and I think it will separate myself from the character, at least a little bit. And second, it'll give my two characters something to talk about. Perhaps the father really liked this ex-husband, because he was a lot like him, and the father and daughter can have conflict over the divorce, while in reality, they're talking about their own relationship. In the beginning, she doesn't realize the men she marries are just like her father. In fact, her problems with men revert back to childhood. During the course of the play, she'll discover the truth about her relationship with men."

That discovery will be another plot point. Notice also that her plot points are all character motivated. There isn't really an order to them yet, but the story is growing naturally from character.

Where are we so far? This is the story of a woman who is dominated by men and her realization that she must take control. She knows she must stop seeking her father's approval. The process will take weeks, if not months, as the playwright explores the possibilities. This is why many writers rely on formula, because it takes a much shorter time to come up with the story. It's safer.

Several days later, the playwright had made new discoveries. She questioned why so many fathers draw away from their daughters as they grow older.

"Something about reaching puberty caused the end of the 'daddy's little girl' relationship. Perhaps fathers don't trust themselves, so they would rather break the emotional bond than take the chance of being tempted. This doesn't mean that all fathers want to go to bed with their daughters," she continued. "It's just that they hate themselves for even being tempted or thinking about it."

"Interesting," I said. "Where did you get this?"

"I interviewed fathers about their relationships with their daughters."

Good. It's based on real emotions. But it's not yet specific to these characters and this play. Why does this particular father pull away?

Several days later she created a scene between the daughter and father in which the daughter reveals that she is pregnant. A new plot point. The daughter wants to grow up, and having a child is the only way she knows how. The twist, however, is that the daughter's revenge is to have a child through artificial insemination. She is going to cut all the men out of her life. At this point the playwright was beginning to write bits of dialogue and brief scenes rather than notes:

DAUGHTER
Look, I paid fifteen hundred. Everything I had.

FATHER
And you don't even know who the father is!

DAUGHTER
Well, not entirely. I read his sperm report. Most of the donors there are Texas A&M students. This one was, I think. He was six foot two, curly hair, and brown eyes. From the Midwest and a football player with 3.01 grade point average.

FATHER
A sperm report?

DAUGHTER
They give you an information card about the donors and you choose what you're looking for. You can find anything.

FATHER
How do you know it's true?

DAUGHTER
The donors only get twenty-five dollars per donation, the difference is quality control.

FATHER
QUALITY CONTROL! This could be bull sperm they've implanted in you and how would you know?!

DAUGHTER
I guess I don't know. But I have confidence in them. They were awfully nice.

FATHER
Of course they were nice, they charged fifteen hundred

(CONTINUED)

```
                        FATHER (CONT'D)
bucks per ounce! God, that's great! My daughter's been
home three weeks. Where was she? She spent the time
downtown, layin' there with her skirt up, legs all
akimbo, bein' shot full of bull sperm! I'm such a happy
parent!


                        DAUGHTER
It's a very respected cryo bank! Highly recommended.


                        FATHER
Christ almighty, what do you want me to say?


                        DAUGHTER
I don't want your approval! I just want you to know.
You're going to be a grandfather.
```

Later, the playwright was exploring possible plot climaxes.

"There has to be a climax, right?"

"Not necessarily in a form play," I answered, "It's possible but optional."

She continued, "So what if the climax was the moment of recognition where the father learns a lesson about women and his daughter?"

"That's exactly what would happen in a formula melodrama," I answered. "So you can use that as a safety factor, a crutch. But a form play doesn't have to have a formal climax. What are other possible plot points? What would be consistent with these characters? Could the daughter come to realize that the father is set in his ways and that it's essential she work out her problems on her own? Could the father die and leave the daughter alone? There are hundreds of other possible climaxes. Throw out the formula and explore. What does the daughter do next? What does her character allow? Don't worry about the formula answers, they will always be there."

The playwright goes back to her plot points; the climax will be discovered when she gets there. She decides to make a list. Here's what she has in the way of plot points:

Plot point #1	The daughter comes home. She has just been divorced and needs comfort, but doesn't want to admit it to her father.
Plot point #2	She tells her father that she is getting another divorce. He really liked the guy and can't believe she's left him. They argue.
Plot point #3	He wants her to go get a box from the attic. The daughter wonders what it could be.
Plot point #4	She tells him she is pregnant and is going to raise the child alone. Set in his ways, he attacks her for trying to live without a man.
Plot point #5	She sneaks a peek into the box and discovers that it's only *Playboys*. She explodes.

| Plot point #6 | She discovers that all of her husbands and lovers have been just like her father. |
| Plot point #7 | Peach ice cream scene. |

There are holes, but the writer is beginning to have an idea of what the plot-structure will be. Through logical thought and character development, the plot points are becoming clearer. Notice that the process includes little talk of who is the protagonist, who is the antagonist, what is the end of the beginning, what is the dark moment, and so on. In place of the formula, the writer is coming up with a string of character-motivated plot points that will soon logically link together to form a compelling story.

Form writing can be frustrating because, in the beginning, the few strokes of story and character don't look like much. Unlike formula writers, who can work out the story in a matter of days, form writers, in the beginning, often have trouble pinpointing their story. The form writer is led by images and bits of characters. It's only after long analysis that the play becomes an organized plot built around real characters.

A few days later, the playwright decided she was spending too much emotional time with the daughter and should spend more with the character of the father. She needed to understand why he was so standoffish. She had to find a *positive reason* for his coldness. Why does the father think his actions are positive? Her long hours led to thoughts of her dog.

The poor thing lived the last three years of his life with cancer, and the time had finally come to put him to sleep. The playwright remembered that on that last trip to the vet's office she had wanted to cry and hug her pet but couldn't. First, she was worried that it would upset her little friend, and second, she wanted to ease the transition. She wanted to prove to herself that she could go through with this. She also felt as if once she started crying, she would never recover. Could the father be the same? Could he think that he must be strong for his daughter's sake, that if he wasn't strong he could never leave her? It works. The playwright has found a positive reason (and a substitution) for the father's strength, which the daughter views as coldness.

The development continued until she had a basic outline of the story and workable understanding of the characters. One day she discovered that at some point she had made an almost seamless transition from making notes to writing a play. I noticed that she hadn't called in several weeks, so I called her. She didn't have time to talk. The play was alive. The number of plot points had grown from five to twenty well-motivated, logical steps in a story. She had to get back to it. She was with the people in her play and had no time for any reality but theirs.

The strange part was that when the script *Fathers & Daughters* was finished, it followed the exact order of a formula play. That's fine, because form writing is about the process. *If the plot points are created as a result of character, then the process is form. If the characters are changed to follow the plot, the process is formula.*

COMPARING FORM TO FORMULA

As we mentioned before, we're so familiar with the conventions of formula, we tend to measure other methods and plot-structures as deviations. Measuring that deviation can be of some use, for it highlights the differences between formula and form. Because no two form plays have the same structure we must compare one at a time. For comparison, let's look at Marsha Norman's Pulitzer Prize–winning play, *'Night Mother.* Column one is the standard formula, column two is how Ms. Norman's play follows or doesn't follow the formula.

FORMULA	'NIGHT MOTHER
BEGINNING	
Event	Jessie tells her mother that she is going to kill herself.
Protagonist and Antagonist	It's not clear which character is the protagonist and antagonist. This is not a play about good against evil.
Disturbance	The disturbance happens long before the play begins.
Decision	Again, Jessie's decision to kill herself happens before the play begins.
MIDDLE	
Conflict Crises Obstacles Complications	There is a great deal of crisis and conflict as Mother tries to talk Jessie out of killing herself, but few complications. Nothing happens that makes Jessie reconsider or blocks her attempted suicide.
Dark Moment	No one moment can be called the dark moment.
END	
Enlightenment	Jessie kills herself. But the enlightenment that brings her to this point happens before the play begins. Also, there doesn't appear to be any major enlightenment between Jessie and her mother.
Climax	Jessie kills herself.
Catharsis	Her mother calls for help, but is there catharsis? We don't know.

Formula is only one method of story telling. It is reliable, safe, and it works, but there are many other plot-structures, as many as there are playwrights.

INDIVIDUAL STYLE

When a playwright frees herself from pure formula she becomes free to develop her own style. *Style* is the sum of a particular person's ability, imagination, and taste. All playwrights want to be distinctive, but if you pursue stylistic uniqueness, you may end up being different without uncovering your own personal style.

For centuries, imitation was the method used to train young painters and writers; once they mastered someone else's technique and style, they were set free to discover their own. Today, many young playwrights believe that if they learn someone else's technique they'll inherit that writer's style. This is not necessarily true. Style and technique are related, but they are not inseparable.

Strict imitation will produce static clones, but you can sample and survey other writers' techniques without inheriting their style. The key is to write about what you find interesting, from your own point of view and unique imagination. You'll find your voice if you live life, listen, learn, and write. Don't worry if it takes several plays and years before you understand your own style. Someday you'll see common themes, a unique interpretation of the facts, and the repetition of techniques. Only then will you know you have a style all your own. In other words, style should take care of itself.

TECHNIQUES IN STORY BUILDING

An old adage of writing is, "Before writers learn technique they are fools; while learning it they are weak; only after they master technique can writers become creative." For example, a cabinetmaker, before learning the techniques of working with wood and tools, struggles to make a simple box. While learning, he can build a pretty average cabinet, but he's not yet free to make the wood do exactly what he wants. Only when he has mastered the techniques, knows how to choose which wood to use, how to plane it, how to join and carve, is the cabinetmaker set free to be truly creative.

The playwright who uses form must be an expert at technique. Dramatic techniques, like the carpenter's knowledge, are those processes that have repeatedly been shown to work. Call them a bag of tricks if you wish, but techniques are procedures by which a complex task, such as writing a play, is accomplished. They're methods and devices playwrights have discovered and used through the ages to help build strong characters and good plot-structure. Every chapter of this book covers technique. Here, however, is a good place to add a few techniques that don't seem to fit any one particular chapter.

Time Lock: Time limits everything in drama. You have only a short amount of time to tell your story, reveal your characters, and come to some conclusion. When a plot seems to lack drive it may need a time lock, a device that heightens tension and crisis by placing a deadline on the shoulders of the protagonist. A classic example comes from *Romeo and Juliet,* where the lovers are forced to take action because Juliet's parents have arranged for her to marry Count Paris, a man she does not love. If that impending marriage were not limiting their time, the lovers might consider their options, plan a strategy, and decide the best action to take. Instead, the marriage is a time lock that forces them to act without delay. Juliet takes the potion, and their love comes to its tragic conclusion.

For example, in playwright #6's *Fathers & Daughters,* the time lock is the father's cancer. This forces the daughter to confront the father now rather than putting it off till tomorrow. If a problem can wait until tomorrow, most people will let it go. A time lock is the reason the characters must confront each other *now.*

Trap: Some playwrights attempt to trap the characters in a location they can't leave and therefore stay and work out their problems. The trap prevents the characters from telling each other off and leaving. William Inge uses this device in *Bus Stop,* in which the characters are trapped at a bus stop during a snow-storm. Another example is Shakespeare's *The Tempest,* in which the characters are shipwrecked on an island. Bad sitcoms use cliche traps all the time—the writers will "trap" the characters in an elevator, where they are forced to look back and remember past episodes. Yet, if it's justified and an integral part of the plot, a trap can act as a pressure cooker and multiply the heat of any conflict.

Coincidence: A play is a compression of life. This compression is sometimes called the telescoping of time. *Long Day's Journey Into Night,* for example, compresses all the family's problems—a history of addiction, blame, and self-hate—into one day. To make this compression believable, a playwright must limit the number of coincidences. A coincidence is a sequence of events or turns in the story that, although accidental, seems to have been planned or arranged. The audience will allow one major coincidence before they begin to question the plausibility of the plot. For example, if two old friends bump into each other on a street corner in Times Square, the audience will accept it as possible (even if one is now living in Iowa and the other in Spain, it's an allowable coinci-dence). If you start adding more coincidences, such as the two old friends have both traveled to New York to find the same mail-order bride, you will begin to lose the audience and the story will appear forced. The old argument that "truth is stranger than fiction" doesn't work in a play. Limit the number of coincidences and your play will appear more truthful. Aristotle said, "the probable impossible is to be preferred to the improbable possible." (By the way, this technique does not apply to farce.)

Sarcey's Principle of Offstage Action: Francisque Sarcey (1827–1899) was a French dramatic critic who theorized that an audience was less likely to scru-tinize the plausibility of an event if it occurs offstage or before the play begins. In other words, if the story demands a questionable coincidence, the audience will be more forgiving if a character tells them, through exposition, about a coincidence rather than staging it before their eyes. For example, in *Oedipus Rex* it seems rather strange, knowing the oracle's prophecy (that Oedipus will kill his father and marry his mother), that Oedipus isn't careful about marrying a woman who is obviously older than himself and, while he's at it, inquiring into the circumstances of Laius's death. Yet, most audience members never question this because the killing of Laius and marriage occur outside the frame of the play. Sarcey was known for his unreliable theories, but this one might have some validity.

Answering a Dramatic Question with a Dramatic Question: A play can have one major dramatic question and/or several smaller dramatic questions. Either way, a good playwright enjoys teasing the audience by holding off the answers. One technique is to answer a dramatic question with another dramatic question. For example, at the beginning of a play a son comes home and tells his mother he's been discharged from the army. The dramatic question is "Why?" Later, the answer comes out: the son was forced out because of psychological problems. But the answer only leads to new dramatic questions: what type of psychological problems and what caused them?

First Question Asked is the Last Question Answered: This is one of the oldest techniques of playwriting. It means that the playwright asks a major dramatic question in the first few minutes of the play and holds off answering it until the very end. The moment the major dramatic question is answered, the suspense ends, and so does the play. For example, in *Romeo and Juliet,* the major dramatic question "Will love triumph over jealousies and hate?" is answered, but only at the very end of the play when the warring families end their feud.

Interruption: Interruption is a technique whereby a playwright temporarily suspends or interrupts the main action of the story to create greater crisis. An interruption of action that has been taken to the very brink of crisis whets the audience's appetite. For example, Hamlet's advice to the players momentarily diverts the main action of the play. The brief beat relaxes the story's progress, which in turn causes greater suspense, tension, and crisis. One student's play interrupted a suicide attempt so that the character could remember his father's first new car after World War II. A Packard. A beautiful machine. This is an excellent example of interruption. The primary action is suspended to recall a minor moment in the character's life, thereby adding to the crisis of the primary action.

The Victorian novelist Wilkie Collins said, "Make 'em laugh, make 'em cry, make 'em wait." Interruptions in story must be carefully planned and exactly executed. William Archer said, "When once a play has begun to move, its movement ought to be continuous, and with gathering momentum; or, if it stands still for a space, the stoppage should be deliberate and purposeful. It is fatal when the author thinks it is moving, while in fact it is only revolving on its own axis."

Avoid Sentimentality: There is a difference between sympathy and sentimentality. Sympathy occurs when the audience knows the character, understands the situation, and has an emotional response to the character's misfortunes. Sentimentality occurs when a writer forces the audience to feel for a character by making the characters endure, helplessly, circumstances that they have not initiated. For example, a recent student play started with the main character's wedding being called off, a good event, but within three pages the poor woman had run from the wedding, been mugged and beaten, and was lying in the hospital where none of her friends had time to visit. The audience should feel sympathy, right?

Most audience members are callous. Every day they hear about lives that are full of misfortune. You can't force an audience to feel for a character by telling them that this particular person is innocent or oppressed. To care, the audience must first know the person. A good playwright establishes the character before asking for sympathy. You earn the audience's sentiment through strong characterization and a logical story.

Open Story, Closed Story: An open story is one in which the audience is in on the truth. A closed story is one in which the author chooses to withhold crucial information in order to maintain the audience's interest. For example, the play *Dial M for Murder* is an open story. The audience knows all along who the bad guy is. The same is true of *Othello* and *Tartuffe*. The audience is in on the fact that Iago and Tartuffe are corrupt. On the other hand, the old *Perry Mason* television series and most Agatha Christie mysteries used closed stories. The audience doesn't know who the bad guy is and enjoys trying to solve the case with the characters.

Antagonist/Protagonist, the Same Character: Sometimes the protagonist and antagonist are the same character. An example would be a protagonist who is fighting a battle with alcoholism. This can be difficult to write, unless you pair your protagonist with another character who represents the protagonist's problem, in this case another alcoholic. This gives your protagonist someone to reject—someone to have the climactic scene with. It gives your character someone to talk to.

FINAL THOUGHTS

Often playwrights will use both form and formula. They use form until the story becomes bogged down and then switch to formula to solve a few problems. The line between these two processes is fuzzy. Both types of writing use dramatic principles, technique, and plot-structure. The only real difference is process. The formula writer applies the same rules to every play. The form writer seldom applies the same rule twice. To label yourself a form writer might be good for the ego, but unless it turns out a quality play, the label is meaningless. Both form and formula can turn out a quality product.

A few years ago, a college director told me about a play he directed that, according to the audience, was a total failure. They walked out in droves, but he still considered the play a success because they had had such a fine process. They drew together as a cast and had a lot of fun. This type of logic doesn't work for a playwright. For us, the process is a failure unless it turns out a quality play or, at the very least, teaches us how to turn out a quality play the next time. If the play is a failure, if you haven't learned anything, change the process.

EXERCISES

Exercise #1
Look at your play idea. Does it contain a time lock? Would a time lock help the plot?

Exercise #2
Draw up a list of plot points for your play idea. Do the plot points come from the characters or from formula?

Exercise #3
How many coincidences does your play contain? If more than one, can they be justified?

Exercise #4
Chart your play's plot-structure as compared with the standard formula. Where do you follow formula, where do you differ? Use the following chart to plot the differences.

FORMULA	FORM
BEGINNING	
Event	
Protagonist and Antagonist	
Disturbance	
Decision	
MIDDLE	
Conflict Crises Obstacles Complications	
Dark Moment	

END _____

Enlightenment   _____

_____

Climax   _____

Catharsis   _____

Chapter 5

DIALOGUE

Plays are about people on particularly talkative days.[1] The act of writing a play is the process of assembling it from its smaller units, the characters' individual words. When it comes right down to it, a playwright merely selects and arranges words from the dictionary. When properly strung together, these words become dialogue. But dialogue does not begin with words, it begins with the need to talk.

> *Vigorous writing is concise. A sentence should contain no unnecessary words, a paragraph no unnecessary sentences, for the same reason that a drawing should have no unnecessary lines and a machine no unnecessary parts.*
>
> William Strunk, Jr.

Dialogue is a combination of what a character needs to say, compounded by what the character is compelled to say. It's simple communication colored by a character's environment, history, emotions, and situation. It's the utterance of a human being who has a unique way of communicating. Dialogue is not everyday speech. It's speech that has been heightened, shaped, and edited, yet it must *appear* as normal speech to the audience.

A playwright's characters cannot employ the novelist's resource of description and explanation but must reveal themselves through talk. Good dialogue is a result of a strong characterization and a well-structured story that places the characters in a situation and time where communication is not only necessary, but notable.

Dialogue is also a controlled medium a playwright uses to convey a point of view, cover exposition, and push a story forward. **Every line of dialogue must advance the character or advance the story.** In order to advance the

---

[1] Except of course mime plays.

story, a playwright becomes adept at writing exposition. In order to advance the character, a playwright works with speech, subtext, sound, imagery, rhythm, tempo, pace, beats, and of course words.

SPEECH

I was a freshman in college when I wrote my first play, and guess what? My playwriting professor didn't care for it. He told me that my main character, a professor, didn't sound like any professor he'd known. So, I hauled out the old thesaurus and gave the character a lot of big words. It was my first attempt at making a character speak like someone other than me, and it failed miserably. The character ended up sounding more like an egomaniacal robot than a professor. At nineteen years old, it never occurred to me that it might be helpful to go out and listen to how real professors actually talk. I depended on my imagination, even though I was surrounded every day by real professors. Playwrights don't create characters from thin air. They first listen, then imitate, analyze, and finally create.

Years later, in Hollywood, I ran into a similar problem. I was paired off with a screenwriter to rewrite a movie in which several scenes took place in a logging camp. Having spent four years in the Upper Peninsula of Michigan, I had at least a vague idea of how real lumberjacks spoke and believed I could write something close to their speech. My partner was born and reared in Los Angeles and had never met a lumberjack or spent any time in the woods, but he plowed forward anyway. As we worked on the rewrite, his suggestions seemed cliche and his dialogue sounded familiar. Finally, when I questioned him, he admitted that his only experience of lumberjacks was from watching the late sixties television series *Here Come the Brides*. What made this Hollywood experience even more absurd was that the writers of *Here Come the Brides* more than likely had never met a real lumberjack either! You can't base dialogue on someone else's idea of how people talk. Playwrights have to get out, experience life firsthand, and study real people (including themselves). The only way to know whether the words fit the character is to listen to real people.

SUBTEXT

When a character says exactly what's on her mind, it's called *on-the-nose dialogue*. It's on-the-nose because the characters are only speaking the *subtext*. Subtext is the second meaning of a line of dialogue, the hidden meaning behind the words, the real reason a character chooses to speak. It's a character's underlying emotions, thoughts, and ideas. In other words, dialogue is like an iceberg; only part of the meaning can be seen above the waterline, yet all the meaning is present. The line "I hate you" is simple, with few interpretations. But when a playwright adds a character's subtext, it can take on hundreds of possible meanings. "I hate you" could mean "I love you," or "I miss you," or "I wish I were you." A line of dialogue must have two levels, what the character says and what the character means, or subtext.

Dialogue and its subtext can be compared to a word's connotation and denotation. A particular word can be chosen for its denotation, which is its dictionary definition, or its connotation, the feeling it invokes when used. For example, the *denotation* of Hiroshima is a city in Japan. Its *connotation* is nuclear war. Subtext is the dialogue's connotation.

Think of subtext as coming in the back door of a house. If you walk in the front door, your purpose is clear, and the result is on-the-nose. But people, or characters, seldom approach a subject through the front door. Either they don't know exactly what they feel or how to express themselves, or they hold back and test the waters. Good playwriting often comes in the back door by creating dialogue that avoids the direct approach.

One way to avoid on-the-nose dialogue and create subtext is to make the characters speak about a completely different subject. For example, a woman who's worried that her husband is involved in an affair might bring up the subject of having another baby. This way she tests her husband to see if he's still interested in a long-term relationship without revealing her true purpose. The dialogue concerns having another baby, but the subtext is "Do you want a divorce?" You need to find what the characters are *not* talking about in order to discover the core of what they *are* talking about. This is sometimes known as "writing between the lines," because what is not said is often more important than what is.

WORDS

Words are the playwright's paint. When mixed properly they can glance or glaze, collide or clip, to reveal the heart, thoughts, truths, and lies of a character. A playwright must understand the effect achieved by mixing words so that each work will reveal the deepest thoughts of the character as well as what needs to be said to move the story forward. In order to understand words and how they relate to each other in dialogue, playwrights must have a strong grasp of diction and usage, but they must also know imagery, rhythm, tempo, pace, and sound.

IMAGERY

Both playwrights and poets deal with detailed observations that create mental mirages for the audience. These observations, or images, are the fastest method of communication, for they cut the idea, concept, or emotion down to its essence.

Imagery is not a part of everyday speech. Only when one is at his highest emotions, only when one is at or near some great understanding, does verbal imagery occur. The classic example comes from Eugene O'Neill's *Long Day's*

Journey Into Night. The character of Edmund, as he recounts his days at sea, reveals what verbal imagery is all about:

> EDMUND
> I was on the *Squarehead* square rigger, bound for Buenos
> Aires. Full moon in the trades. The old hooker driving
> fourteen knots. I lay on the bowsprit, facing astern,
> with the water foaming into spume under me, the masts
> with every sail white in the moonlight, towering high
> above me. I became drunk with the beauty and singing
> rhythm of it, and for a moment I lost myself--actually
> lost my life. I was set free! I dissolved in the sea,
> became white sails and flying spray, became beauty and
> rhythm, became moonlight and the ship and the high dim-
> starred sky! I belonged, without past or future, within
> peace and unity and a wild joy, within something greater
> than my own life, or the life of Man, to Life itself! To
> God, if you want to put it that way. Then another time,
> on the American Line, when I was lookout on the crow's
> nest in the dawn watch. A calm sea, that time. Only a
> lazy ground swell and a slow drowsy roll of the ship.
> The passengers asleep and none of the crew in sight.
> No sound of man. Black smoke pouring from the funnels
> behind and beneath me. Dreaming, not keeping lookout,
> feeling alone, and above, and apart, watching the dawn
> creep like a painted dream over the sky and sea which
> slept together. Then the moment of ecstatic freedom
> came. The peace, the end of the quest, the last harbor,
> the joy of belonging to a fulfillment beyond men's
> lousy, pitiful, greedy fears and hopes and dreams!

People tend to talk in conclusionary terms. Statements such as "He was mean to me," "The house is red and white, you can't miss it," are the results of thought processes that reached a conclusion. Edmund's speech ends with a conclusionary statement that joy is being fulfilled beyond man's lousy, pitiful, greedy fears and hopes and dreams. An interesting statement, but the verbal imagery before the conclusion breaks the conclusion into the supporting details. It helps the audience enter into Edmund's world and see why he drew that particular conclusion.

In order to achieve verbal imagery, therefore, a playwright breaks conclusionary statements into the exciting facts, observations, and thoughts that lead the character to the conclusion.

Consider the following when writing dialogue that contains verbal imagery. First, imagery for imagery's sake is unacceptable. A poet might be able to get away with this, but a playwright must tie all images into character and story. The images must mean something to the audience or they don't belong in a play. Recently, we attended a reading packed with provocative verbal images.

References to Indians holding toasters, blood pouring from an elephant's eyes, and sweet lakes in the sun certainly piqued some audience members' interest, but none of these images tied into character or the story. They were just provocative. In the theatre, all imagery (and symbols for that matter) must relate directly to the story, theme, and characters, or they are unimportant details and must be cut.

Second, detailed imagery can save what might be a mundane speech or scene. We'll use an example from a student play, this time a play about a prostitute. In a long speech toward the middle of Act Two, the call girl recounted the story of how she became a woman of the street. She recalled that she had been raped at seventeen in the back seat of a Pierce Arrow.[2] It should have been an engaging speech, but instead grew predictable and boring. After the reading, the student realized her mistake: she had simply told the story, event to event, and never found the imagery needed to convey it.

On the rewrite, she looked deeper into the character and found the imagery she was looking for. As the prostitute told the story, she stopped to say that this was the first time she had ever been in such an expensive car. While she was being brutalized, she tried to concentrate on the car's ivory door handles. The monologue described them in detail. She had never seen ivory door handles before, and she thought of the elephants that died to make them. It seemed to her to be such a waste. The powerful speech made the audience feel for this poor woman; the moment had been transformed from a simple recounting of events, full of conclusionary terms, to a detailed, emotional speech expressing meaningful verbal images that led to the conclusion of how she fell into prostitution.

RHYTHM, TEMPO, AND SOUND

Some of the most difficult concepts for a beginning playwright to understand are rhythm, tempo, and sound. An advanced playwright is able to adjust rhythm, tempo, and sound to match the characters, emotions, and mood of the scene. The use of consonance and assonance in a character's dialogue goes a long way toward describing that character's motivations. As an example, in the play *Cat on a Hot Tin Roof,* Maggie the Cat describes her sister-in-law, her rival for Big Daddy's money, as a former "Cotton Carnival Queen." The hard sound of each of the first letters gives the character a chance to show jealousy, derision, and coarseness through the action of simply saying those three seemingly complimentary words. The playwright is giving the actress a chance to comment without being on-the-nose.

Shakespeare also uses this technique exquisitely in all his plays. Let's look at an example in *Much Ado About Nothing.* When Claudio disgraces Hero at the

---

[2] A expensive automobile of the 1930s.

marriage altar over a supposed infidelity she's committed, Shakespeare has given him the words:

> Sweet Prince, you learn me noble thankfulness.
> There, Leonato, take her back again.
> Give not this rotten orange to your friend.
> She's but the sign and semblance of her honor.
> Behold how like a maid she blushes here!
> O, what authority and show of truth
> Can cunning sin cover itself withal!
> Comes not that blood as modest evidence
> To witness simple virtue? Would you not swear,
> All you that see her, that she were a maid,
> By these exterior shows? But she is none;
> She knows the heat of a luxurious bed;
> Her blush is guiltiness, not modesty.

You can see the hissing sounds of the sibilant "s" recur; in this way, Shakespeare is enabling Claudio to call his highborn bride a "slut" and "snake" without having to speak the words in front of her family. Such underlying action through sound ties into the character.

Rhythm: More than just timing, rhythm is a verbal variation that creates a pattern. Each individual character has his or her own rhythm, which manifests itself in the dialogue. Unlike the rhythm of poetry, the rhythm of dialogue is much more subtle. It's the gentle adjusting of a line's sounds, stress, and tempo to help reveal the character and the emotion at the moment. Given the needs of the moment, dialogue should pulsate or flow, swing or jingle, oscillate or tranquilize. To understand rhythm, look at the following line:

> The right word in the right place.

Notice the particular rhythm imparted by the "r" sound repeated three times, juxtaposed to the soft ending word, "place." Now explore the following lines, which are similar but carry different rhythms:

> The perfect word, perfectly placed.

> An accurate word, in its correct location.

> A proper expression placed with perfection.

Notice that each has different rhythms and sounds. A rhythm conveys a particular *tone,* but most of all, it engenders a particular character who might say the line. The first line, "The perfect word, perfectly placed," is dominated by *P*s and

Os and *Ths* and gives the line what some might call a comfortable feminine sound, and we might see a young woman resting in her lover's arms. The second, "An accurate word, in its correct location," is more precise and "harder" sounding and brings to mind a businessman praising a subordinate. The third, "A proper expression placed with perfection," is dominated by *Ps*; we might envision a matronly woman impressing friends. No two people talk the same way or use the same rhythms. A playwright adjusts each line so that the words reveal that particular character's inner rhythm.

Tempo: Dialogue is designed to be spoken at a particular speed (fast, slow, and so on.) All characters (and people) have an inner clock that forces them to speak at a certain speed. This designed-in speed is called tempo. Perhaps it's the heart beating inside of us that makes us so aware of tempo. Tempo can convey emotions as strongly as any words. It gives a feeling of motion to a speech or scene.

   Composers place a notation in music that tells the musician at what rate and with what feeling it should be played. A playwright can't be so obvious. A good line of dialogue has an internal clock that makes the tempo unmistakable to the reader or actor. Indeed, Shakespeare was also a master at using Leontes's tempo-rhythm to expose ambitions, true nature, and purpose in *The Winter's Tale.*

> Is whispering nothing?
> Is leaning cheek to cheek? Is meeting noses?
> Kissing with inside lip? Stopping the career
> of laughter with a sigh? (a note infallible
> of breaking honesty) horsing foot on foot?
> Skulking in corners? wishing clocks more swift?
> Hours, minutes? Noon, midnight? and all eyes
> Blind with the pin and web, but theirs; theirs only;
> That would unseen be wicked? Is this nothing?

Here Shakespeare has given the usually level-headed and happy King Leontes a fervent, crazy rhythm in suspecting his wife of adultery. The first verse is short and those after it are long, and the many stops after the questions reveal thoughts tumbling at breakneck speed.

   There are no hard and fast rules concerning tempo. The playwright must have an inner sense of what works and what doesn't. More often than not, a playwright doesn't look to tempo unless there's something wrong with a scene or character. Usually, tempo is written intuitively. Frustrated because something isn't working, the playwright goes back to examine specifically a character's tempo to see if it's inconsistent with the mood or moment. Here is an example of a speech in which the tempo is out of sync with the action and character:

> (The DARK MAN approaches
> BETH. She backs toward the
> bed.)
>
> BETH
>
> Stay away from me! You aren't getting near me again or
> I'll have to tell your father and mother and anyone else
> who will listen to my story. Get your hands off me now
> because I will not put up with you or any other man again
> as long as I live.

It's obviously a frantic moment, yet Beth speaks in long, complete sentences, which makes for a slow tempo. To solve this problem a playwright will often use line length to control tempo. A scene in which two characters exchange many short lines will tend to have a fast tempo, whereas longer lines will slow the tempo. This is by no means a rule. Longer lines may sometimes speed a speech, and many short lines will break the speech up and make it read slower. Read the following similar speeches and notice how the first speech seems to read slower than the second.

> SPEECH ONE
>
> What's your problem? Don't tell me. You don't have any.
> Yeah right. Know you do. So does everyone on the block.
> You're not Mr. Sociable. Give up the pride. Call her.
> You won't regret it.
>
> SPEECH TWO
>
> What's your problem and don't tell me that you don't
> have any problems because I know you do and so does
> everyone on the block. You're not exactly Mr. Sociable,
> so give up the pride and call her or you'll regret it.

If a playwright has a strong understanding of the characters before she writes, the rhythm and tempo of a character will come naturally. A true understanding of rhythm, tempo, and sounds cannot be taught; it comes from years of writing dialogue. In the meantime, when writing realistic dialogue, try to base your characters on real people, people you know. If you're a good listener, the natural sounds, tempo, and rhythm of that person will invade the characters you're trying to write. When you finish a draft, the best way to know if the rhythms and tempos are working is to read the play aloud.

Pace: Dialogue can also affect the play's pace. *Pace* is the rate of speed at which a scene or act runs. If a scene fails because of a ponderous or sagging pace, the problem can usually be traced to lack of content. Look at the amount of information being conveyed. If a section seems to drag, more than likely it lacks action, dramatic questions, and conflict or crisis.

DIALOGUE AND BEATS

Dialogue can be broken down into small structural units called *beats*. A beat is a single unit of thought. It's a small section of the dialogue that's accented by a particular emotion, subject, or idea. A change in emotion, subject, or idea means the beginning of a new beat. The following dialogue is divided into beats.

                          BURMA JEAN
Do you know an Ed Overball?

                          SHIRLEY
From PTA, why?

                          BURMA JEAN
Man, he's got some ugly kids.

                          SHIRLEY
Burma Jean!

                          (BURMA JEAN turns the page
                          in the newspaper.)
                          * New beat

                          BURMA JEAN
Oh my God.

                          SHIRLEY
What?

                          BURMA JEAN
Donald Wayne Hill got married. Here's a picture of him
and his bride.
                          * New beat
Looks kinda pregnant, doesn't she? God, that bouquet
must be two and a half feet across. You can't hide that
kind of thing behind gladiolas and baby's breath.

                          SHIRLEY
                          (Suspicious)
When I was going out with him, he told me his sperms had
two tails. Said they couldn't go nowhere, just swam
around in circles.
                          * New beat

                          BURMA JEAN
Oh, look! Estelle Prudence! She knows I can't stand her.
God. Her card's got some little dog holding mistletoe in
its teeth. You know her little dog died of cancer last
year?

                          SHIRLEY
No. Well, bless her heart.
                    * *New beat*

                        BURMA JEAN
Probably to get away from her. Says here she keeps busy
by cooking meals for the elderly. Oh, I'm just sure she
jumps in her car and runs all over town on her lunch
break from the Charmin Factory. Delivering hot meals
here, delivering hot meals there. . . . with her husband
not working, I'm sure she just has all the time in the
world.
                    * *New beat*

                          (ROXANN, lissome and
                          pregnant, wafts in carrying
                          a papier-mâché bust of
                          Elvis. She efficiently hangs
                          it from the dryer head.)

                          ROXANN
Do you mind if we exhibit this? It was Cameron's idea
for his class piñata. We are *so* proud.

                        BURMA JEAN
Piñata?

                          ROXANN
Well, everybody does a pig or a donkey head. I thought
this showed a little flair. Hey, I thought it'd go nice
as the centerpiece at the church banquet, what do you
think? We *were* going to fill it with candy and stuff but
the thought of cutting a hole in Elvis' head and letting
little children beat it with sticks . . . I just
couldn't.

                          (A beat of silence. The
                          women grow wistful.)
                          * *New beat*

                        BURMA JEAN
It just made me feel funny the way Priscilla and Elvis
looked so much alike. Like they were brother and sister.

                          ROXANN
I read where Egyptians used to marry their own brothers
and sisters. Had children with heads like hatboxes.
                    * *New beat*

                          SHIRLEY
How's Cameron's asthma?

ROXANN

Cleared up.

BURMA JEAN

And the wandering eye?

The fiction writer has paragraphs; the playwright has beats. Each beat must have action. The action of a beat can be stated in a verb. This verb is the task that the characters try to complete during that small section of the dialogue. When each beat is properly written, the conflict and motivation can be charted. For example:

Beat/Bit	Conflict	Motivation
#1 The play begins. Sally is upset because she lost her job.	Ralph thinks she should have worked harder. She thinks she was over-worked.	She thinks she works harder than he does. He doesn't want to lose her income.
#2 Sally states that she was a victim of sexual harassment.	Ralph is shocked. He wants her to call a lawyer. Sally wants to let it go.	Sally must stop Ralph from blaming her.
#3 Sally brings up the subject of his mother and how she is always pushing Sally to earn more money.	Ralph accuses her of being illogical.	Sally must cover her lie.

Why do we use the word "beat," which seems to suggest a rhythmical unit of time, common cadence, or a brief pause, rather than "unit" or "section"? The theory as to how this musical term has come to its nonmusical dramatic meaning comes from when the disciples of Constantin Stanislavski (the head of the Moscow Art Theatre and often called the father of modern acting) came to the United States to teach. Some people believe Americans were confused by the Russians' thick accents and mistook the word "bit" for "beat." If you say the line, "First you must split the play into little bits," with a Russian accent, you'll find some truth to this theory.

Whether it's true or not, looking at "beats" as "bits" makes a lot of sense.[3] A playwright, like an actor, divides dialogue into bits or beats to understand the character's actions and motivations, moment by moment. In order for a beat to work, each new beat must be motivated by something in one of the preceding beats, must also have conflict or crisis, and must logically interlock with the beats before and after it.

---

[3] Here the word "bit" denotes a small piece or portion of a play, not to be confused with "comic bit" which is a humorous routine.

A playwright can also use beats to diagnose the problem of a scene already written. By checking beats for proper motivation and conflict, a playwright may be able to single out the exact moment a particular bit of dialogue fails. Any beat that doesn't advance the story or characters is excess weight and should be cut from the script.

DIALOGUE TECHNIQUES

A playwright must have intimate knowledge of syntax and grammar and a strong vocabulary. But even so armed, a writer may find it difficult to write dialogue. The following are tools, writing devices, and techniques that a playwright may use to improve the chances of writing strong dialogue.

Line Construction: Often, a playwright will move the most important element to the end of a line. For example, "I love you more than the moon, the stars, or the heavens above," places the most important element, "I love you," at the beginning, where it creates little suspense. Placing the modifiers first will delay the point of the sentence and cause a dramatic question that keeps the audience's interest. "More than the moon, the stars, or the heavens above, I *hate* you." The most interesting point (the climax), is generally toward the end. But don't take this to the extreme, for if you place the modifier first in *every* line you'll write robot-like dialogue. Occasionally, when a line of dialogue doesn't seem to work, check to see where the climax falls.

Show Emotions, Don't Tell: Show the characters' emotions rather than have them talk about their emotions. For example, instead of having a character talk about how depressed she is, show how her depression is affecting her. The following is bad dialogue:

```
                    MRS. WALLACE
Oh, I'm so unhappy. I don't think I've ever been so
upset. It just eats at me. Every day I think it's going
to get better and I just get more depressed.
```

If the writer was showing the emotion, Mrs. Wallace might be talking about her child, her job, her day, or any of a thousand other subjects, but her depression would be *implicit* in the lines. People seldom analyze their own emotions. When was the last time you heard someone, in the heat of a crisis, stop to neatly scrutinize how and why she feels the way she does? Most people and characters don't have deep self-awareness. A character in a play, just as a real person, should *live in the moment* and say what occurs to her at that moment. A character who stands outside herself and describes what she feels is really the author in disguise.

Avoid Generalities: People are seldom general in their speech. They refer to exact situations and specific details rather than broad concepts. Stanislavski said that "in general" is the death of all dramatic conflict. Audiences come to see specific people at a particular point in time. A wife may tell her husband that his mother is nosy, but this is usually followed by *exactly* what the mother did to earn the title. The following line is too general:

> BETH
> Your mother was over today. She's so nosy. We have to do something. She's driving me nuts.

By making the line more specific, it might read:

> BETH
> Your mother was over today. In the first twenty minutes she tried to potty train Ben, lectured me on which bleach I should use, and asked me what type of birth control we practice. We have to do something!

Inherent in the second line is the fact that the mother is "nosy." Replace generalities with specifics. A good playwright knows that specific examples lead to better dialogue and eliminate the obvious.

However, don't let your specifics get the upper hand. Referring to obscure details may confuse your audience. Years ago we attended a reading of a new script of the Circle Rep in New York and were quite lost during most of the reading. When it was over, the audience thought the play was wonderful, but we couldn't grasp the story. Several audience members were quite put out, but took the time to explain to me that the two main characters were gay. We were amazed. There was no indication of this in the script. They never talked about it, nor did they do anything that might lead to that conclusion. I questioned how they knew, and one audience member said, "It's so obvious, they talked about how much they want to go to Franco's Bar." This was, apparently, a famous gay bar in New York. The whole play hung on this one reference, and, because I didn't know this, I was left in the dark. Being too specific might be fine for a small local audience (like the one at the now defunct Circle Rep in New York), but most dramatists maintain that plays in New York should make sense in Wyoming.

Monologues: A monologue is a long speech made by one character to another character or characters. In real life, people generally don't monopolize a conversation with long discourse, so monologues are a bit unnatural. This is true in drama as well. Long unbroken monologues often slow the pace of a play, because the other characters become static. Experienced playwrights can handle monologues, but the novice should try to break monologues into shorter, more realistic dialogue.

The key to a good monologue can be found in Eudora Welty's book *One Writer's Beginnings*. She tells a story about her mother talking on the phone. Sometimes her mother would just sit and listen for long periods, punctuated by an occasional "Well, I declare," and "You don't say." After one of these single-sided conversations, Eudora asked what it was all about, and her mother answered that it was the woman from down the road, "She was just ready to talk."

The same is true in a monologue. Good monologue requires a reason why this character chooses this moment to link thoughts together into a long speech. The character must be emotionally ready to talk.

Often a monologue is the place where a character works out his problems or adds up what has happened so far and tries to understand what it means. Avoid stagnant monologues in which a character simply recalls past events. The character should be *compelled* to recall the events. Also, avoid didactic monologues in which the playwright's opinion reveals itself. A monologue is a special moment in a play where a character has so much to say, so many feelings to communicate, that he or she cannot be interrupted. Thus, monologues must be full of action. In the following monologue, the character of Ira recalls his relationship with his father; he is active because it leads him to a conclusion about himself.

```
                         IRA
On his death bed he told me that makin' money was evil.
That I was not a "good" black man because I was fat cat.
Hell, I drove a black Volvo. That was rich by his
standards. He called out for the great white Ruler of
Heaven, the Hebrew God to bring down the stones of
hell-fire on the white Sodom and Gomorrah that I was
participatin' in. He called out to the children of
Israel. But I couldn't. All I saw was a beaten man. On
his last mornin', I told him like it is. Told him that
Christianity was simply to serve the needs of the white
masters. That's the type of son I am, I told an old man,
on his last breath, that his deep religious beliefs were
intolerable. I calls him a psalms-singin' hypocrite! And
then I buried him, not in the plain pine box he picked
out, but in the best gold-leafed mahogany coffin money
could buy! That's the type of son I am.
```

Listening: Let's look at a simple exchange of dialogue between two characters looking for coffee:

```
                         JOHN
Honey, where's the coffee?

                         SALLY
In the fridge.

                         JOHN
And sugar?

                         SALLY
Right beside it, on the left.
```

This is bad dialogue. Why? The characters are simply asking and answering questions. The dialogue is not affected by the characters' ability to listen. Seldom do characters hear exactly what another is saying. More often than not, characters (just like people) filter what they hear through their own needs. We interpret, misinterpret, and read special meanings into everything. When writing dialogue you must ask yourself what is being said and how it is being heard. They can be two very different matters. When we take this into account the dialogue may come out differently:

                         JOHN
Honey, where's the coffee?

                         SALLY
Are you testing me?

                         JOHN
And sugar?

                         SALLY
You don't think I know, do you.

Or perhaps:

                         JOHN
Honey, where's the coffee?

                         SALLY
The doctor said no more caffeine.

                         JOHN
And sugar?

                         SALLY
Did you take your medication?

When writing dialogue, always take into account what the character is saying as well as what the character is hearing.

DIALOGUE AND EXPOSITION

Exposition lets the audience in on the given circumstances of the play, important offstage action, and what has happened to the characters between scenes and before the play began. It's also how a playwright reveals the back story of the characters and plot that doesn't fall within the frame of the play. By the "back story" we mean the history of the characters and plot, and by "frame of the play" we mean everything that happens on stage and in the present. Exposition covers what happens offstage and in the past, outside the frame of the play. Some plays have no need for exposition because all of the important action occurs on stage and in the present. Plays such as *Othello* and *King Lear* were written with little exposition. Other plays such as *Hamlet* rely on exposition to set up information that the audience needs to know in order to make sense of events that occurred within the frame of the play. Today, it is difficult to write a play in which the whole crisis plays out on stage, and so playwrights must have a detailed knowledge of how to use exposition.

The ancient Greek playwrights had it easy when it came to exposition, for the audience usually knew the story before the play began; other information was related through a chorus that spoke directly to the audience. Shakespeare also got around exposition with few problems, for he could write a prologue in which an actor would state details about the back story or write a soliloquy in which such information could be easily conveyed. A hundred years ago, playwrights still used asides and soliloquies to recite the necessary facts. To-day, however, choruses, prologues, soliloquies, and asides are considered old-fashioned and are seldom used. In a modern, realistic play, the playwright must hide the exposition in the dialogue and yet keep the exposition obvious enough that the audience can immediately absorb it. A play doesn't allow for going back and rereading. Good exposition is the art of conspicuous concealment. The trick is to expose the needed information as efficiently as possible without the audience realizing it.

Good playwriting avoids *obvious exposition*. Obvious exposition is dialogue full of on-the-nose back story. The characters aren't communicating with each other, they're simply filling in the audience. The lights rise, the play begins, the phone rings, a maid answers, and the audience laughs. Why? Because a character answering a phone at the beginning of the play is one of the more obvious devices for conveying mere exposition:

MAID
(on the phone)

Hello . . . Bob! Good to hear from you . . . No, my lady is still at school. I can't believe she's going to get her high school diploma at fifty . . . Master Wellington is taking it pretty hard. Still thinks it's an embarrassment . . . No, he hasn't taken a drink since Friday . . . Yes, that's a new record.

Years ago a friend of mine at the Second City improvisation company did a skit called the *Obvious Exposition Players*. It went something like this:

SON #1

How's Mom?

SON #2

Considering the fact that she's nearly seventy, she's doing just fine.

SON #1

If only she hadn't had that heart attack last year.

                              SON #2
That was a bad one. Left her in the hospital for three
months.

                              SON #1
I took care of her, remember? I was here every night
'til the nurse kicked me out.

                              SON #2
What about me? I was there every morning.

                              SON #1
You were. She's been a good mother. Remember the time
she lied about your age so that you could join Little
League?

                              SON #2
How could I forget. I'd never be a big league pitcher if
it wasn't for her.

                              SON #1
And I'd never be a barber if she didn't let me
experiment on her head.

If the purpose of a scene or dialogue is to "fill the audience in" then it will fail, because the action has nothing to do with the story or characters. Yet, a story can't move forward unless the audience is aware of some background information.

This appears to some playwrights as a catch-22, but can be solved using certain techniques that allow the exposition to be integrated into a play. These methods include hiding the exposition by use of conflict, humor, question and answer, confidant, and the less often used flashback and narrator.

Exposition Through Conflict: The simplest and most often used method to hide exposition is through conflict. If the characters are arguing or having a disagreement, their dispute, debate, or squabbling will allow the audience to hook into the emotional conflict without consciously hearing the exposition. For example, if two sons are arguing about whether their mother should be put in a nursing home, a great deal of information can be given to the audience concerning the mother's condition and the sons' feelings toward her. The fight, of course, must be a natural part of the story and characters. This shouldn't be a problem, because a play is never about people who agree with one another.

If you engage an audience's emotions through conflict, you can slip them the exposition. In the following dialogue, a lawyer and an expert witness clash about how to present a case. While the audience is engaged in the conflict, they are given a great deal of back story concerning the victim:

                              ACEY
The method of death?

                              PHILIP
Strangulation.

                              ACEY
You're sure?

                              PHILIP
Yes.

                              ACEY
Work with me! Are you sure?

                              PHILIP
It's hard to tell.

                              ACEY
Isn't it possible the skeletonized cartilage around the
larynx was fractured after the body was placed in the
ground? Isn't it possible that the weight of the earth
over thirty years could have crushed the larynx?

                              PHILIP
I guess anything is possible.

                              ACEY
"Anything is possible?" What the hell jury is going to
believe an expert witness who says that? Fight fact with
fiction, not with generalizations. Is it possible that
the cartilage could be fractured after the body was in
the ground? "Yes!" The hundreds of pounds of earth piled
on top of the body could've fractured it. "Yes!" See
what I'm askin'?

                              PHILIP
You make me nervous.

                              ACEY
Then how the hell are you going to react when you're
cross-examined! Now answer the question! Could the
cartilage be fractured after death?!

                              PHILIP
Yes!

                              ACEY
How?

                              PHILIP
I don't know, but if you'll let me be an expert rather
than telling me what to say then maybe I could come up
with a possible answer!

Exposition Through Humor: If the audience is laughing, they're seldom aware that the scene (or line) contains expositional information. In the following brief bit of dialogue, we're given the back story concerning the father's relationship with the mother and we find out that he's been in the hospital. Yet neither is the subject of the scene:

>   HENRY
> Seen your Mama lately?
>
>   DARLA
> It's been a while.
>
>   HENRY
> Think she's startin' to look like Bozo?
>
>   DARLA
> Daddy!
>
>   HENRY
> It's true. While she was losin' her sight she just kept
> pilin' on that Max Factor lipshit and with that red
> Church of God hairdo, twice the size of a human head,
> she started lookin' like Bozo. I had to ask her to stop
> comin' to the hospital cause she was scarin' the hell
> out of the nurses.
>
>   DARLA
> She does not look like Bozo!
>
>   HENRY
> Your mother, a tenth of a ton of thrills and fun.
>
>
>   (He notices Darla glaring at
>   him.)
>
>   HENRY *(cont'd)*
> What's wrong? You need money?

Exposition Through Question and Answer: This is a simple method in which one character asks questions about a situation and another answers, thereby filling in the character and the audience at the same time. This will only work if one character legitimately needs to know the information. Question and answer can be effective for only a short bit of dialogue before it becomes repetitive. In the following scene a son comes home after a long absence and confronts his older sister.

>   CASEY
> God, you must be hungry. I saved a couple of Whoppers.

>   (She pulls from the Captain
>   Kangaroo pockets of her
>   Burger King uniform a
>   handful of greasy
>   hamburgers.)
>
>   NORMAN JR.
> No thanks.
>
>   CASEY
> They're still good. They just look like hell.
>
>   NORMAN JR.
> You got a job?
>
>   CASEY
> Yeah, Dad started charging me rent.
>
>   NORMAN JR.
> How is he?
>
>   CASEY
> Father? His motor functions are good. This week he spit
> on the windshield of a van full of nuns who pulled out in
> front of him, and he got into an argument with the goof
> at the auto parts store.
>
>   NORMAN JR.
> So you're trying to tell me that everything is normal?
>
>   CASEY
> You got it.

Exposition Through a Confidant: As realism took over the modern theatre, asides and soliloquies became outdated. It just wasn't realistic to have characters talking about their problems to thin air. Yet, the authors still needed a way to let characters express back story. They solved the problem by introducing a confidant, a character (usually an outsider, stranger, servant, or visitor) there to give the main character someone to talk to. As the confidant is filled in, so is the audience. The trick is to make sure the confidant's reason for being in the story is more than just being a confidant.

All characters must advance the play and not just serve the playwright's need to hide exposition. A good example would be Edward Albee's *Who's Afraid of Virginia Woolf* or Henrik Ibsen's *A Doll House,* which both have uninformed characters who must be filled in on the peripheral information.

Here is an example of a playwright using a confidante, in this brief scene from a student written play, a fiancee (the confidante) must be told of her new family's little idiosyncrasies.

> KAROLINE

Casey, would you tell your brother that it's perfectly natural to think your own parents are strange or different.

> CASEY

Norman, our parents are perfectly natural. Karoline, there's something I have to warn you about, you have to ask permission to go to the bathroom at night. You see, our father has been in charge of an assembly line his entire life.

> KAROLINE

Buick, right?

> CASEY

Right. What you got to understand is that in order to go to the bathroom on the assembly line, you have to ask permission. Our father is the one who grants permission.

> NORMAN JR.

He does more than that. He's an executive.

> CASEY

To understand our father, you must see the logic in installing this quaint little custom at home. In order to go to the bathroom at night, you'll have to first yell, "I Have To Go To The Bathroom."

> KAROLINE

You're kidding.

> NORMAN JR.

Casey's not telling it right.

> CASEY

When we were young, he was afraid we'd fall in. It's twenty years later, his hearing is shot, so in order to get permission, you have to stand out in the hall and yell, at the top of your lungs, "I HAVE TO GO TO THE BATHROOM!"

> KAROLINE(trying to remain positive)

All families have their ways.

Exposition Through Flashback: It's not a good idea for a beginning playwright to use flashbacks. This is not to say that it can't be done. Some of the finest plays ever written have flashbacks. But if your first impulse is to write a flashback in order to cover the needed exposition, you're most likely hiding your inability to write good expositional dialogue. If you must have a flashback, consider the following. First, the mood and tone of the play should allow flashbacks. The play should be the kind in which time is adjustable. This means that you'll have more than just one flashback. Second, the story must provide a reason for the flashback. Something in the present essentially causes the character to relive the past. The present emotions or events must draw a parallel to the past and cause the flashback. Third, make sure the flashback doesn't repeat information. We recall a student's work in which one character said, "Remember those high school days, that touchdown? No doubt about it, I was good," and the scene dissolved to the character, twenty years earlier, running for the touchdown (also an example of cinematic thinking). If in the flashback the character had fumbled the ball and failed to get the touchdown, perhaps the scene would have advanced the story and been worthwhile (although it is still cinematic and difficult to stage).

One possibility is to avoid flashbacks by making the past and present concurrent. A perfect example of this is Arthur Miller's *Death of a Salesman,* in which the boundaries between then and now are lifted, allowing Willy Loman to see both worlds. *Death of a Salesman* has no flashbacks, only two realities running at once.

Exposition Through a Narrator: Using a narrator is another form of covering exposition for young playwrights to avoid. Too often a narrator is a simple commentator who is in the story because the writer doesn't know how to deal with exposition. It can be done, however. Some great plays, such as Thorton Wilder's *Our Town* and Tennessee Williams's *The Glass Menagerie,* use narrators. If you're going to try it, be *sure* your narrator is an integral part of the story, a full character, and rich in personal conflict. Also, decide who the narrator is talking to; who is the audience in the narrator's mind?

SPRINKLE EXPOSITION

Exposition doesn't only occur at the beginning of a play. A playwright will hold back bits of exposition and release information as needed to keep the story moving and the audience interested. It's possible to have exposition revealed from page one to the final line of the play and anywhere in between. If you give all the exposition at the beginning, you'll leave little for the audience to wonder about. For example, a student wrote a play about a young woman who was kicked out of the military. The exposition concerning her dismissal was not revealed until page forty! By delaying this important information, the writer asked a dramatic question and kept the audience wondering.

THREE EXPOSITION METHODS PLAYWRIGHTS SHOULD AVOID

First, characters should never speak their thoughts into a tape recorder or make diary entries that turn into monologues. These are just modern versions of a soliloquy and seldom work. They are no better than having the phone ringing as the lights rise. Characters need to play off other characters. Talking into a tape recorder or making diary entries is seldom dramatic.

Second, characters should never be the type of people who talk to themselves. Again, this is usually just a ploy. Characters who talk to themselves are boring. Interaction makes a play exciting.

Third, characters should avoid reminiscing about the past. There is nothing more monotonous than two characters sitting on the sofa and enjoying a glass of wine while remembering the old college days. If characters are going to reminisce, then some immediate conflict must happen within the scene that forces them to remember the past. They must be compelled to speak about the past, not placidly recall events. At the very least, have them disagree about the past.

UNNECESSARY EXPOSITION

The most common mistake new playwrights make is to put too much exposition in a play. Information that fails to move the story forward is unnecessary exposition. Playwrights can learn a lot from attorneys who present a case to a jury by giving them what they need to know and no more. Kenney F. Hegland, professor of law, in his book *Trial and Practice Skills* writes, ". . . the discipline is to force yourself to say—and prove—what is relevant. Not to say—and prove—everything; if you do, you have said nothing." The same is true with playwrights. If everything is important, then nothing is important.

Good exposition is lean. Here's an example: how many children does Lady Macbeth have? Shakespeare does not say. This information doesn't advance the overall plot, so it's left out. All we need to know is that Lady Macbeth has children. The exact number of children or their names would only cloud and slow the story. Another example: In *Romeo and Juliet,* what are the Capulet and Montague families fighting about? What started the feud? It's never mentioned in the play because it's not important to the action of the love story. You don't have to tell all the back story, only the bits and pieces important to the two-hour traffic of the stage. Art emphasizes the important bits.

Only occasionally does a play give the facts. Most of the time a playwright need only hint at the probabilities or possibilities of what happened in the past.

The other mistake new playwrights make is repeated exposition. It's an old-fashioned idea that everything in a play should be stated at least three times in order to make sure the entire audience gets it. The Spanish dramatist Jacinto Benavente (1866–1954) said, "The first time, one half of the audience will understand it, the second time the other half, only on the third occasion may we be sure that everybody understands." Another saying comes from Tom Taylor, the Victorian playwright, who ventured, "When you have something to say to an audience, tell them you're going to say it. Tell them you're saying it. Then, tell 'em what you've said. Perhaps then, they'll understand it." Both Jacinto Benavente and Tom Taylor's statements no longer apply. If the play is well written and the exposition clearly stated, it's seldom necessary for a playwright to repeat it. Tell your audience clearly and tell your audience once. The second time you repeat information you'll bore them. The third time you'll lose them.

FINAL THOUGHTS ON EXPOSITION

All exposition must be invisible to the audience. To make it so, the back story is revealed in a natural way. The best way to do this is to invent dialogue that advances the story and characters first and conveys exposition second. Never develop a character whose only purpose is to provide exposition. Also, avoid blocks of dialogue or scenes that are nothing but exposition. Scatter the exposition throughout the play. Let the audience in on the exposition only on a need-to-know basis. Good exposition is swiftly absorbed by the audience; it's shown through dramatic events and dialogue, not laboriously explained.

DIALOGUE AND SIGN POSTS

The opposite of exposition is the *sign post* (sometimes called a setup or fore-shadowing). This is dialogue (or action) that justifies future events within the play. In *Romeo and Juliet,* the friar's speech about his garden and his knowledge of herbs is a sign post that sets up the fact that he (later in the play) knows which chemical will make the potion. Without the sign post the later action would not seem credible. Sign posts prepare the audience for future events. The key is to make the sign post memorable yet subtle enough that it only hints at future possible events. Alexandre Dumas, the French Romantic playwright, said, "The art of the theatre is the art of preparations." William Archer added to Dumas's often quoted remark, "On the other hand, it is also the art of avoiding laborious, artificial, and obvious preparations which lead to little or nothing." Just as exposition tells only what is needed to clarify the story, sign posts should set up only essentials.

Dialects: Playwrights no longer spell out phonetically the dialect of a character. The following speech in a southern accent is written as a playwright might have written it fifty years ago:

> DARLA
> That's cawse meyun don't train boys to be meyun, mamas do. And whether you lahke it owuh not, a fathuh trains a gull to be a woman, but they nevuh finish. They leave us incomplete. Wah? I don't know, mebbe theyur scayud of us. Mebbe the minute we staht growin' boobs they back awf. Owur mebbe they need us and if they finished the jahb we'd be too indepindint. Straynge how they nevuh set us free and yet fawlt us for owuh depindince.

Today, the same speech would be written with only the rhythm, tempo, and words of the dialect, leaving the exact sounds for the actor to find through dialect (phonetic) work. The script would indicate that this character speaks with a southern twang, or would perhaps reveal exactly which region of the South the character comes from, but it definitely wouldn't go into such phonetic detail. This makes the script difficult to read. Today, the same speech would read:

```
                    DARLA
That's because men don't train boys to be men, mamas do.
And whether you like it or not, a father trains a girl
to be a woman, but they seldom finish. They leave us
incomplete. Why? I don't know, maybe they're scared of
us. Maybe the minute we start growin' boobs they back
off. Or maybe they need us and if they finished the job
we'd be too independent. Strange how they never set us
free and yet fault us for our dependence.
```

It's crucial that the playwright who thinks in the dialect of a character she's writing first understands the sensibilities of the character—the background and opinions that shape an area and its people. A playwright certainly wouldn't imbue the farmer from Providence, Rhode Island, with the same tempo-rhythm as the farmer from Cuthbert, Georgia. There are simply too many known divergent socioeconomic, religious, and historical forces working on each of those specific characters.

If we take as an example from what is arguably the best-known American dialect—New York-Brooklynese—we can identify what outside forces have shaped the tempo-rhythms. In doing research, you'll find that the New York-Brooklynese tempo we know today is a direct descendant from the flood of Irish immigrants. These immigrants quickly assimilated into every aspect of the city's culture, bringing with them their hallmark lilting speech pattern and penchant for changing the initial *th* in words such as "these," "them," "those" to *d* to make the familiar "dese," "dem," "dose." You also know then, that the Irish sensibilities of forced deprivation, independence, and the deep desire for roots might come to play into your modern New Yorker's character. You may also factor in that the New Yorker's reputation for being loud—another tempo result—is affected by his environment, for he competes with the constant din of city noises and the effects of pollution on his respiratory system. All these things as a whole may account for the large number of husky, insistent, and seemingly assertive New York voices.

Do not assume that you know how one part of the country speaks. Research is necessary. Above all, don't rely on what you hear on television. Hollywood seldom goes to the trouble of hiring a dialect coach. I attended a recent Hollywood audition for a play that was set in Iowa. The actors all assumed they knew how people in Iowa spoke, so they put on a horrible drawl. Iowa is standard Midwestern American, but none of the actors knew this and made fools of themselves.

DIALOGUE TO AVOID

Certain lines of dialogue just don't work. No rule states that you can't use them, but normally they're a warning that something is wrong. For example, avoid lines such as "What do you mean by that?" or "What're you trying to tell me?" A new writer will use such lines to fill space between real thoughts. Lines such as "I can't believe you're moving to Alaska," or "So what do you think?" are often there simply to start a conversation. If the situation is alive and full of energy, conversations will start spontaneously without false prompting. Other phrases that don't work are "As you know, . . ." or "As I told you, . . ." or ". . . remember?" and "Like I told you yesterday. . . ." If the other character already knows or was told yesterday, then why is the information being stated again? These lines almost always mean that obvious exposition lurks nearby. Lines such as "Sit down and let me tell you about it," tells the audience that a long, boring speech is coming and is a cue for them to nap for a while. First drafts are often filled with lines that begin with "so" or "well." By the second draft, you'll discover that most of the "so's" and "well's" can be eliminated, as this example illustrates:

> JOE
>
> So, are you going to the funeral?

> ALLEN
>
> Well, I don't know. I need time.

> JOE
>
> Well, I think you should. You need to end this part of your life.

> ALLEN
>
> So, are you telling me or asking me?

Another type of dialogue to avoid is *name calling*. This happens when characters consistently call each other by their given names:

> JOE
>
> Allen, how are you?

> ALLEN
>
> Joe, boy, it's good to see you.

> JOE
>
> I was just thinking that, Allen.

```
                    ALLEN
How long has it been? Gosh, Joe, what? Three years?
```

CLICHE

A cliche is a worn out or commonplace phrase that has become trite. Phrases such as "beyond the shadow of a doubt," "beat swords into plow shares," "it'll all come out in the wash," "water under the bridge," or "as alike as peas in a pod," are cliches and should be avoided. People *do* talk in cliches, but a play deals with heightened language, so a playwright should try to come up with new ways for characters to state old cliches.

EDITING

Each line of dialogue should advance the characters or the story. Too often, dialogue contains excess words that are unnecessary and weigh it down. Use only the words necessary for the line to communicate the thought, clarify the subtext, fit the tone, reveal the pace, tempo, and rhythm, and reflect character.

PUNCTUATION MARKS

Punctuation marks clarify the dialogue's meaning. All the standard practices concerning punctuation apply to dialogue, but a few are unique in playwriting.

Double Dash: The double dash (--) is used to indicate when a speech or line has been interrupted. Example:

```
                    FRED
If you ever talk to Kathy again, I'll teach you a few
things! Just look at her and I'll--

                    SAM
Shut up and get out!
```

Ellipsis: An ellipsis (. . .)shows the omission of a word, phrase, or the beginning or end of a sentence or where the character loses the train of thought, drifts off, or fade off to another subject. For example:

```
                    BUDDY
I'm not sure if you realize what just happened. With one
line, I started a conversation. Paid you a compliment.
Showed interest and . . . but you're really not
interested.
```

During a phone conversation an ellipsis mark the moments when the other, offstage party is speaking. Example:

GRACE
(on the phone)

No, you're lying. He really asked you to marry him?
When? . . . You're joking! . . . But you can't, you have
to tell Fred. . . . You don't mean that.

Italics and Capitalization: Occasionally, a playwright will use italics to emphasize a particular line or word in a speech. This is acceptable as long as it's used sparingly. Capitalization is sometimes used to indicate when a speech or line is shouted. Again, this should be used sparingly. Example:

BETH

You mean me? You are talking about me. ME! In front of *my*
face. Fine! YOU CAN ALL GO TO HELL!

Abbreviations: Abbreviations are used in dialogue only if the character also used the abbreviation. For example, if you want the character to say "TV" instead of "television," then the abbreviation is acceptable. Other abbreviations should be eliminated. For example, don't write "Dr. Jones." Instead use "Doctor Jones." Numbers should be written out. Instead of writing "15," write "fifteen." The only exception is if the number requires more than a few words, like "1,433," in which case use the number and not the word(s).

Comma: In dialogue the *comma* (,) is used to show a slight hesitation. Hesitations occur naturally in speech, so it's important to indicate them. But if you don't intend a hesitation you needn't use a comma in the traditional way. The following lines differ greatly in meaning with and without commas.

BETTY

My baby, my baby, my baby.

And

BETTY

My baby my baby my baby.

The first indicates that each "my baby" is said with the slightest of hesitations. This might mean that each word is given a different weight or perhaps the line is said slowly. The second line shows the playwright intended not even the slightest gap between words and so they run together and are given similar stress. By carefully adjusting commas, a playwright can help actors understand the tempo of a given line of dialogue.

FINAL THOUGHTS ON DIALOGUE

Dialogue is a reflection of the characters who speak. Most people, and therefore most characters, don't speak in complete, well-thought-out sentences with proper grammatical awareness. They stumble, feel their way, and only during brief moments of understanding or when torn by deep emotional conflict, do they become poetic.

Your dialogue must properly reflect the character's thoughts and feelings, yet it must move the story forward, reveal the back story, plant sign posts, and express the mood of the piece. The only way to become proficient at writing dialogue is to first listen to people talk, learn how different types communicate, and then imitate. Years of imitation and study will lead to the heightened reflection of everyday speech called dialogue.

EXERCISES

Exercise #1

The English author George Orwell, in his essay "Politics and the English Language," pointed out that too many vague words will cloud a work and "fall upon the facts like soft snow, blurring the outlines and covering up all the details." Study the following dialogue. How many words can you cut and still make it convey the characters and story?

                         ACE
You're still talking to him?

                       SANDRA
He comes over on Sunday afternoons, and we act happy
together for a few hours so that his daughter will
think he's a great guy. Ace, he's been talking about
this case. He told me a cash offer was made to you
and you turned it down. Ace, that wasn't smart. The
landlord probably used that same money to bribe my
boss . . .

                         ACE
Ah ha! Then you admit it?

                       SANDRA
No, I just wouldn't doubt it.

                         ACE
So what are you telling me? We're up against New York
City? This I know. Five thousand dollars doesn't keep
you out of the rain in New York for very long. Nope, for
New York City is a hard, hard place. Listen, the only
reason I got this place to live was because a Mrs.
Greenwall was kind enough to have a heart attack in the
lobby. While everyone ran over to watch her die, I made
a beeline for the front desk to check on her room.

> SANDRA
>
> Five thousand dollars. You said five thousand dollars.
>
> ACE
>
> Would you move out of a place as perfect as this for so little?
>
> SANDRA
>
> Oh my God. I really think you should drop my husband as your attorney. You know, he wasn't even a "B" student. The only reason he got the job at Leibowitz, Wasserstein, and Ryan was because his great uncle was once a partner.
>
> ACE
>
> So what are you saying?
>
> SANDRA
>
> Ace, my husband mentioned a dollar amount, but it wasn't five thousand dollars. It was . . . it was fifty thousand dollars!

Now look at one of your own scenes. How many words can you cut and still make it convey the characters and story?

Exercise #2

Write a two-character scene in which you reveal the exposition using the following methods:

> Conflict
>
> Humor
>
> Question and answer
>
> Confidant

Exercise #3

The following dialogue is neutral. Rewrite the dialogue, keeping the same situation but adding character. Remember the tempo, rhythm, sounds, and speech of a particular character. Or rewrite it with characters from your own plays, or use people from class or family as templates:

> PERSON #1
>
> Did you tell him?
>
> PERSON #2
>
> I'm not going to tell him, you tell him.

                         PERSON #1
I would, but now is not the right time.

                         PERSON #2
Then maybe we should wait.

                         PERSON #1
Or you could tell him.

                         PERSON #2
I don't see why I should tell him when it's your job to
tell him.

                         PERSON #1
My job? Since when is it my job?

                         PERSON #2
It's not my job.

                         PERSON #1
Well, it's not my job either.

                         PERSON #2
Then let's not tell him.

                         PERSON #1
Agreed?

                         PERSON #2
Agreed.

Exercise #4

The following speech is full of conclusionary terms. Can you rewrite the speech, adding the verbal imagery that breaks the conclusion into the supporting details?

                         FATHER
Norman, in your desperate attempt to live your own life,
don't you see you're repeating the same mistakes I made?
I was twenty years old once and I thought I knew what I
wanted from my life. Funny how your dreams change. Funny
how ridiculous they become.

Exercise #5

Take one of your own scenes and divide it into bits/beats and check for proper motivation and conflict. Chart the scene using the following:

Bit/Beat	Conflict	Motivation
#1		
#2		
#3		
#4		
#5		
#6		
#7		
#8		
#9		
#10		
#11		

Chapter 6

SCENARIO, WRITING, AND REWRITING

A play can come from many places. Ibsen and Shaw each started with a theme, a basic point they wanted to make; Shakespeare began with stories he usually borrowed from history or Italian romances; Eugene O'Neill's plays originate with character. Whatever process you use, it's a good idea to have a basic scenario before writing.

> *You should not begin your work until you have your concluding scene, movement and speech clear in your mind. . . . You cannot very well know where you should come out, when you don't know where you are going.*
>
> Alexandre Dumas

SCENARIO

A *scenario* is a playwright's prep work, and is made up of notes on character, action, location, thematic ideas, and a story outline. This groundwork can take longer to construct than writing the play. Some playwrights think about the scenario for years before they write the first line of dialogue. Others are hit with inspiration and need only a few scratchy notes. If you're writing your first play, it's best to have a detailed scenario.

A scenario is both the mechanical task of constructing and the creative joy of drawing interesting characters and story. It's exploring the question, "What if? . . ." The formula writer will use the scenario to answer the basic structural questions (What is the end of the beginning? What is the dark moment? What is the enlightenment?), whereas the form writer will pencil in the plot points. A finished scenario is a blueprint full of reference points that, in turn, are beacons within the dark void of an unwritten play. A scenario may also point out a play's faults and inconsistencies before it's written (for example, a weak middle, or a lack of conflict). A scenario doesn't necessarily make writing easy, but it can free up the writer's creativity so that he may deal with the problems within an individual scene or moment and not constantly ask himself where the play is going.

A good scenario shouldn't be fixed in stone, but be designed to give the writer room to maneuver. The English dramatist Sir Arthur Pinero said, "Before beginning to write a play, I always make sure, by means of a definite scheme, that there is a way of doing it, but whether I ultimately follow that way is a totally different matter."

As you write, interesting possibilities will reveal themselves and new discoveries will change the story and characters, sometimes subtly, sometimes drastically. Often a writer will finish the play and look back at the scenario only to be amazed at how little of it was actually used. A playwright should never have an ironclad scenario, yet if the scenario has too many holes and leaps of faith, the playwright is not ready to write.

The basic elements of a scenario are working title, character names, outline of the plot-structure, place, setting, acts, scenes, French scenes, and perhaps a theme.

Working Title: The title brings a play into focus. It should represent the whole work, its mood, style, and subject matter. Often the playwright must write the entire play in order to discover the perfect title. To begin with you only need a *working title*. A working title gives a play some identity. It christens a few snatches of dialogue and notes on character and story with the hope that it will someday become a full play. Tennessee Williams understood the importance of an evocative working title. *The Glass Menagerie*'s working title was *The Gentleman Caller; A Streetcar Named Desire* was first called *The Poker Party*. Titles can come from many sources:

A quotation	*The Little Foxes*
An image	*Summer and Smoke*
A poem	*A Raisin in the Sun*
The Bible	*The Runner Stumbles*
A character's name	*Marty*
An action	*The Homecoming*
A place	*Tobacco Road*
Humor	*Oh Dad, Poor Dad, Mamma's Hung You in the Closet and I'm Feelin' So Sad*

For now, the working title need only appeal to you, but the final title must stimulate others. The first thing anyone knows about your play is its title. First impressions are so important that some playwrights test-market their titles. They're looking for that combination of words which piques curiosity. You want the title to represent the work, but you also want it to interest potential directors and audiences.

Character Names: Name your characters as early in the process as possible. This helps you think of them as people rather than just types. For example, "the father" or "the boyfriend" are archetypes, not flesh and blood. You can also enhance a character by finding names that reflect the character's rhythm, personality, geographical region, education, and ethnic background. Among the many good sources for names are baby name books and your phone book. If those don't help, graveyards are gold mines of interesting names.

Sometimes a playwright gives two characters similar names. Although there may be valid artistic reasons for using such combinations as Harry and Hazel, Sam and Sid, or Jerry and Berry, they can cause confusion. Most readers and directors don't take the time to go back and reread; once lost, they stay lost, and the script is tossed in the rejection pile. Give each of your characters unique names and you will avoid this problem.

Outline of Story: Whether the playwright uses formula or form, the structure of the story becomes clear when it's divided into smaller segments. These segments start with acts, scenes, French scenes, and, finally, individual beats.

Acts: The largest segment in a play is an *act*. Acts are divisions within the story marked by an *act break* or intermission. Each act is one major unit or section of the story in which the events are related. William Archer said, "It is a grave error to suppose that the act is a mere division of convenience, imposed by the limited power of attention of the human mind, or by the need of the human body for occasional refreshment. A play with a well-marked, well-balanced act-structure is a higher artistic organism than a play with no act structure, just as a vertebrate animal is higher than a mollusk." In today's theatre playwrights use acts in several ways, the most common being full-length one-acts, two-act plays, three-act plays, and short one-acts.

Full-Length One-Act Play: There is no intermission in this type of full-length play, so the beginning, middle, and end flow without interruption. In the modern theatre the idea was first tried by August Strindberg in 1888 when he abolished the acts from his play *Miss Julie*. In the introduction to that play he explains,

I have done so because I have come to fear that our decreasing capacity for illusion might be unfavorably affected by intermission, during which the spectator would have time to reflect and to get away from the suggestive influence of the author-hypnotist. My play will probably last an hour-and-a-half and, as it's possible to listen that length of time, or longer, to a lecture, a sermon, or a debate, I have imagined that the theatrical performance could not become fatiguing in the same time.

Few of these long one-acts are in use today, but they're becoming popular. If you're planning such a play, be concerned, as Strindberg was, about how long the audience can sit without the expected intermission. Our attention span is certainly shorter than it was in 1888. The general theatre-going public expects at least one intermission, and as a result full-length one-act plays are generally shorter than two- or three-act full-length plays (usually between eighty minutes and a *maximum* of ninety-five minutes). When your play is produced, you may want to make sure that a note is placed in the program explaining to your audience that this is a full-length one-act play so that they won't think the play is three hours long. It's also not uncommon to list the play's running time to make your audience less restless.

Two-Act Plays: This is the most common way to divide a full-length play. The act break is generally taken just after the middle of the story. Your audience will expect the first act to be slightly longer than the second.

One common way to end an act is with a *plot twist*. This is a revelation or turn in the story that will lead to greater conflict and crisis. It can also be a simple dramatic moment that will make the audience want to come back after the intermission. To quote Emmett Jacobs of the American College Theater Festival, "You have to get a pretty good inferno going in the first act to jump that fire-break of intermission."

Three-Act Plays: The three-act format is rarely used now. The double intermission makes the play longer and more formal. Two-act full-lengths are the norm.

Short One-Acts: Most beginning playwrights start with a one-act play. A short one-act play can be anywhere from several seconds to about an hour long. A one-act may be shorter than a full-length, but it requires the same detailed work on structure and character.

When writing a one-act, you are working under time constraints, so the story shouldn't be complex. The scope must be severely limited. One-act plays generally revolve around one narrow incident or occurrence in a character's life. Some formula writers condense the span of a short one-act by beginning the story near the middle of the conventional structure (before the dark moment) and tell only the second half. Through exposition, the playwright quickly fills in the elements contained within the missing beginning and most of the middle and then lets the play continue from there. When a form writer writes a one-act she uses a limited number of plot points.

Theatres seldom perform a single short one-act. More often than not, they'll produce an evening of one-acts. This means it's essential that you keep your one-act simple. The set must be modest so it can be quickly changed during the intermission between plays. It would also be a good idea to limit the size of your cast. With the theatre doing several one-acts in an evening, many actors will be involved. This could place financial strains on the theatre. Keep your one-act simple, keep it small, and it'll stand a better chance of being produced.

Sometimes a playwright will write several one-act plays as *companion pieces,* which are designed to be performed on the same night. By doing this, the playwright doesn't have to share the evening with other one-acts. Companion pieces can have related or unrelated themes and stories. Examples of related one-acts are *Lone Star* and *Laundry & Bourbon* by James McLure. Examples of unrelated one-acts are Christopher Durang's *Sister Mary Ignatius Explains It All For You* and *The Actor's Nightmare.*

Ten-Minute Plays: For years playwriting professors have assigned ten-minute plays. These are short, (usually no more than ten pages) plays written as exercises to help the student understand dramatic techniques. Today, these exercises have become a popular form of playwriting. More and more contests and theatres are interested in ten-minute plays (sometimes called quickies).

In order to write one of these short one-acts, you must understand that such plays are extremely limited in scope. Sets are simple so that they can be changed in seconds (you're often allowed only a generic chair, sofa, and table), and the cast is usually limited to fewer than four. The structure of a ten-minute play includes an early point of attack, which commonly occurs at the bottom of the first page or top of the second. The play usually has one conflict only, which seldom allows time for more than one plot point. Also, the tight structure allows for little exposition; the entire story should fit with the frame of the play. The end of a ten-minute play falls close to the climax, giving only a line or two that hints at catharsis.

Theatres that produce ten-minute plays will stage as many as ten in one evening. Keep it simple, concentrate on one brief moment in the characters' lives, and your chances of being produced will increase.

Scenes: The next smallest unit in a play is a scene. A scene is a formal subdivision within an act. One scene ends and a new one begins when there is a change of time or place. If you have a play with many scenes, consider two things. First, make sure all the scenes are necessary. *Blackouts,* in which the lights are totally dimmed between scenes, can pull an audience out of a play, because the action continually starts and stops. This problem can be solved by eliminating some or all of the blackouts, so the actors walk from one scene directly into another.

If you're writing short scenes because you can't maintain the action for more than a few pages at a time, then you are writing from a television or movie point of view in which short scenes are the norm. In playwriting, however, a change of scene is desirable only when absolutely necessary. Try to group scenes together, and work at finding realistic transitions that can turn several short scenes into one powerful longer scene. This doesn't mean that all plays that have an abundance of scenes are poorly written. Many short scenes are fine, as long as the playwright is making the decision based on what's good for the plot-structure.

The second concern when writing many scenes is more mechanical. When you change scenes, make sure any change in costume or set can be achieved quickly. One young playwright wrote an end of a scene that called for the main character to be wearing a three-piece suit. Following a blackout, the next scene began with this character wearing a funny horse outfit. The logistics of a scene transition aren't the director's or costumer's responsibility. The onus is on the playwright to write a stageable play. In the case of the funny horse outfit, the playwright was forced to write what used to be called a *cover scene*. This is a scene or bit of dialogue designed to cover a set or costume change. It is seldom used anymore, because few modern plays have many sets or costume changes (it's just too expensive), but the principle still works. The playwright writes into the story a scene that continues the action on stage while the actor is offstage changing into the all-important horse outfit. A cover will only work if the scene and dialogue move the characters and action forward.

FRENCH SCENES

The next smallest segments of a play are *French scenes*. A French scene begins whenever a character enters or exits and continues until the next entrance or exit. For example, if a scene has John and Bob fighting and Mom comes in, Mom's entrance marks the beginning of a new French scene. Bob then storms off, and we have another new French scene. The length of each French scene varies, as does the number of French scenes within a play, act, or scene. A farce may have tens of dozens of French scenes, while a play with no entrances or exits has only one.

The French scene originated in, of course, France where hundreds of years ago the printing press was still a novelty and quite expensive. To cut costs, a theatre would give an actor only those pages of the script that concerned his or her character rather than the full script. The most cost-efficient way of dividing a play was from one entrance or exit to the next entrance or exit. Although this did little to help the actors with character analysis and continuity, it did save a few precious pages.

This antiquated method of dividing a play would have been long forgotten had it not been such a help in playwriting. Because a French scene deals with only certain characters at a particular point in the play, it divides a play into small, workable units.[1] A playwright treats each French scene as a miniplay that can have the structural elements (beginning, middle, end) of a full play. As each

---

[1] There is no formal curtain or dimming of the lights between French scenes. The audience or reader is unaware that one French scene has ended and another begun. In addition, French scenes are not marked in a script. This is just a device to help the playwright structure the action of the plot. It is an armature, and the audience should not be aware of it.

entrance or exit occurs, the play changes, characters' attitudes adjust, and the story moves forward. If John and Bob are fighting about Mom's upcoming operation, and Mom enters (new French scene), John and Bob will react and, as a consequence, their argument will change. Perhaps they can't fight in front of Mom, or perhaps Bob now feels he can state the truth. When Bob storms off (new French scene), John and Mom are left alone, and again attitudes and intentions change.

When building a scenario, the playwright might make a list labeling the action in each French scene, thereby pinpointing what that particular moment in the play is about. Such a list might look like this:

French Scene	Characters Involved	Action
#1	Beth and Father	They accuse each other of ruining the mother's funeral.
#2	Beth, Father, and Marc	Beth introduces her boyfriend Marc to her father. The father hates him.
#3	Father and Marc	The Father announces that he's going to sell the house.
#4	Beth and Marc	Marc tells Beth of Father's decision. She decides she can't go home with Marc, but must work out the problems with her father.

A hundred years ago, writers of Victorian melodramas used to give each act an alluring title. Although this is now outdated, a beginning playwright might consider titling (in personal notes) each scene or French scene. This title is a label that pinpoints the conflicts and purposes the characters have at that particular moment. A playwright's list of French scene titles might look like this:

French Scene	Characters Involved	Minititle
#1	Beth and Father	The Temptation
#2	Beth, Father, and Marc	Assumption
#3	Father and Marc	The Crime
#4	Beth and Marc	Retribution

In most French scenes, the important bit of information (that is, the revelation, the confrontation, the twist in the plot, the best line, the miniclimax) comes near the end (just before the next entrance or exit). One trick is to interrupt a scene just before it hits its miniclimax. The entrance or exit of a character causes the conflict between hostile characters to remain unresolved and heightens the tension of the play. If the miniclimax occurs too early in a French scene, as in the dialogue that follows, the scene may appear to drag:

                              (The Guard exits.)

                         PHILIP
Sounds like there's insufficient evidence and our police
lieutenant is safe.

                         ACEY
I'd tend to agree, but the trial has taken some rather
serious turns of late. A responsible witness to the
affair has come forward with some sort of repressed
memories shit. And this mornin' we had the revelation
that my client, who claims to be an understanding
liberal, is really a racist SOB.

                         PHILIP
How did they prove that?

                         ACEY
McLuren's divorce decree, which was missin' since the
beginnin' of the trial, has somehow magically turned up
in the hands of the prosecution. It states that thirty
years ago our lieutenant divorced Mrs. McLuren for fear
of "black baby syndrome."

                         PHILIP
Which is?

                         ACEY
Some of you Caucasian-Americans seem to think that if a
white woman goes to bed with a black man, even once, she
may produce a black baby any time after that. Even years
or decades later.

                         PHILIP
That was thirty years ago. Things change. What's the
truth today?

                         ACEY
They simply questioned the truth. They hinted. It was
enough.

                         PHILIP
You should have said something.

                         ACEY
Thank you for tellin' me how to do my job.

                         PHILIP
What's wrong with demanding proof?!

                         ACEY
We adjourned before I could do so.

                         PHILIP
You should've objected!

                         ACEY
I couldn't! I feared the prosecution had exactly what I
have. Proof!

                         (ACEY pulls out a legal
                         document.)

                         ACEY (CONT'D)
Stole it from the county records when the trial began.

                         (PHILIP examines the divorce
                         decree.)

                         PHILIP
He can't be much of a racist if he hired you.

                         ACEY
When he secured the services of Koningsberg and Weiss
he insisted that I head the team defendin' him. Just
standard operating procedure. If you kill someone and
race is involved then be sure to hire a lawyer of the
same kind. It counts the same with gender. If you kill
or rape a woman, hire a woman to defend you. If you kill
a black man, hire a black lawyer!

                         PHILIP
                         (holding the divorce decree)
How did the prosecution get ahold of this?

                         ACEY
There are forces at work here. Most feel that the police
department needs a sacrificial lamb. Someone to take the
fall for thirty years of racial bigotry. Someone to hang
up in the town square so they can show how things have
changed.

                         PHILIP
You're good.

                         ACEY
I know.

                              PHILIP
So, where do we go from here?

                              ACEY
Good question.

                              (There is a hard knock at
                              the door. The DA enters with
                              a pizza.)

                              ACEY (CONT'D)
Lunch has arrived. You like pizza?

Notice that the French scene seems to hit its miniclimax somewhere toward the middle. If the playwright was interested in holding that tension into the next French scene he could move up the DA's entrance, thus not allowing the scene to relax. Things would be left unsaid, increasing the tension, as each entrance or exit cuts off the action before it's allowed to explode or resolve itself.

PLACE

Place refers to the geographical location, environment, country, state, city, or area. These elements can greatly affect the characters and story. Can you imagine *A Streetcar Named Desire* set in Minnesota? Various places have different social orders, accepted behavior, rules of etiquette, accents, and even different types of people. You should always select an interesting place, yet choose a location of which you have personal knowledge or have researched extensively.

One beginning student wrote a play that took place at a television studio in Hollywood. The fact that she had never seen a television studio and knew nothing of how a television show was produced didn't seem to bother her. She relied on her imagination and wasted her time writing a script that was full of errors, misconceptions, and stereotypes. Imagination is wonderful, but when it comes to place, it must be based in truth.

Place can be the single most important element in creating your play's environment. Just as playwrights are experts at observing and studying people, they should also have a keen eye for finding the individual traits of place and location, and the effects they have on character.

SETTING

Setting is what the audience sees on stage. The place is New Orleans and the setting Stanley Kowalski's living room and kitchen. Setting reflects the characters, environment, location, and time. Try to see the set in your mind's eye. Identify what makes it unique. What mood does it instill? How are story and character affected and reflected by this setting?

Also, a playwright must ask if the set can be built economically. Frequent shifting of scenery and many settings are no longer financially possible in most theatres. If you need more than one setting, try to use a neutral set. With these sets, a new location can be represented by the movement of a single object or the addition of one piece of scenery. Shakespeare's theatre did this all the time. A potted tree would be placed on a bare stage, two characters would walk out and say, "Here we are lost in the forest of Arden," and suddenly they were in the forest of Arden. This is known as "verbal scene painting." Another way to solve this problem is by using a multisetting, where several locations are included on one stage.

Recently a student playwright wrote a one-act play that required a two-story set. Few theatres are rich enough to produce such a play. Whether it's a one-act or a full-length, a play with a single, simple set has a better chance of being produced than one with many sets and effects. Almost all theatres are poor. You're shooting yourself in the figurative foot if you write a play that cannot be economically staged.

THEME

Theme is the primary statement of the play, the overall message, the truth behind the story. Sometimes the theme can be stated in a simple sentence: "A house divided against itself cannot stand," or "You can't keep a good woman down," or "Love conquers all." But more often it's a complex maxim or a discovery the author has made about human nature. For example, try to state the theme of *A Streetcar Named Desire* in a simple sentence: "If you're an emotionally disturbed Southerner, don't visit your lowbrow brother-in-law"? Nope, doesn't work. A play can have a single overall message or it can have several interwoven themes. For example, *Lysistrata* has at least three major themes: 1) war is ridiculous; 2) men and women become silly and illogical when sex is involved; 3) it's infantile for men and women to act as if they don't need each other.

Seldom does a writer sit down to write with a clear idea of theme. Theme reveals itself during the writing of the play. Arthur Miller said that he often didn't know what his plays were about until the second or third draft. What he meant was that he didn't yet have a clear theme. Labeling a theme too early in the process can inhibit the true, natural theme of the story from coming forward. This is not to say that it's impossible to start with a clear, well-defined theme, because Ibsen and many other writers certainly did, but be careful that you don't set your theme in stone. The writing process is full of delightful discovery, so allow your characters and story to reveal, improve, or change the theme as the plot grows. During the writing process theme should be treated as clay to be modeled and remodeled, and not marble to be unalterably carved.

A writer who's locked into a particular theme will likely sacrifice character and story to prove the theme correct. This could result in a didactic or propaganda play in which the characters are only mouthpieces for the author's message and editorials. Whether it's a complex motif or a simple idea, the theme is usually deeply embedded in the action. Theme should be *suggested* and not openly stated. The best way to avoid didactic plays is to shun themes that sound like political slogans, personal mottoes, or life lectures.

Interestingly, however, didactic plays are an acceptable form of theatre. *Mother Courage,* by Bertolt Brecht, is definitely and purposefully didactic. If you have consciously decided to write a didactic play, you should follow certain principles. First, attempt to *persuade* your audience, not *indoctrinate* them. Allow your audience a chance to think and consider. Second, don't let your characters in the play know the message. Let them be characters with real feelings and motivations, and not puppets who represent only one cause or philosophical idea.

If you finish a first draft and still don't know your theme, look at the reasons behind your need to write the play. Something is compelling you. What did you want to prove? If it's still not clear, move on, concentrate on story and character. With hard work and long hours of writing, the theme will usually reveal itself. In the end, the theme must be implicit. It must grow organically as the story and characters develop.

BUILDING A SCENARIO

A good play seldom jumps full blown into a playwright's head. It must be added to as the playwright fleshes out the story and characters. Each day the scenario should grow. Each question divulges new answers. Eventually, the play will reveal itself, and the writer will be ready to scratch down those first lines of dialogue. The finished scenario will have holes in the story, missing details, and areas left to be explored, but it still gives the writer an idea of what the finished play *might* be. The following is a rough scenario, a basic outline of character, French scenes, place, setting, time, and story for a two-act play.

Working Title: Ace in a Hole

Place: New York City

Setting: The William Henry Harrison, a transient hotel on the upper west side. The setting is Ace Campbell's old room. It's obvious from the faded clippings on the walls and the frayed upholstery that Ace has lived here many years.

Time: The present

Cast of Characters:

> MR. LAGATUTTA—a senile Italian Roman Catholic
>
> MRS. KONIGSBERG—an ancient Russian Jew
>
> WINK—a crazy man who doesn't understand English
>
> SHAPIRO—a lawyer
>
> SANDRA—a city employee
>
> ACE—an old stand-up comedian
>
> MRS. ROLAND DEFOE—a wealthy woman

Possible French Scenes

ACT ONE

French Scene	Characters	Action
1	Ace Mr. Lagatutta Mrs. Konigsberg Wink	It's another day of arguments at the transient hotel. Lagatutta hates Konigsberg. Ace tries out a new stand-up routine.
2	Ace Mr. Lagatutta Wink	Mrs. Konigsberg leaves to cook. Ace admits that his time here is up. He knows he will be evicted today.
3	Ace Wink	Mr. Lagatutta exits. Ace is left with Wink. We learn about their special relationship—good friends who will miss each other. Conflict?
4	Ace Wink Shapiro	Ace's lawyer, Shapiro, enters. He has a plan to save Ace from eviction.
5	Ace Mr. Lagatutta Mrs. Konigsberg Shapiro	Lagatutta and Konigsberg pledge their support, but it's obvious that they'll be of no help.
6	Ace Wink Shapiro	Shapiro has a private word with Ace; he tells Ace he must not leave the room. Eviction officers have been known to change the locks while tenants are out.
7	Ace Wink	Wink tries to cheer Ace with the only English words he knows, "Looks very bad."
8	Ace Wink Sandra	Sandra, a new eviction office trainee, comes to evict Ace.
9	Ace Sandra Mr. Lagatutta Mrs. Konigsberg	Trick or Treat—Comic bit with Lagatutta and Konigsberg.
10	Ace Wink Sandra	Sandra starts packing Ace's stuff.
11	Ace Sandra Mr. Lagatutta Mrs. Konigsberg	Lagatutta and Konigsberg forget their promise to help; they play childish games in the hall.
12	Ace Sandra	Ace is pushed too far and takes Sandra hostage.

13	Ace	They find out Shapiro is Sandra's ex-husband.
	Sandra	
	Mr. Lagatutta	
	Mrs. Konigsberg	

ACT TWO

French Scene	Characters	Action
14	Ace Wink Sandra Mr. Lagatutta Mrs. Konigsberg	Ace tells of his big break and how he became a failure. Sandra tries to make a compromise. They discover that Shapiro is really working for the landlord. Sandra is released and now wants to try to help them.
15	Ace Wink Sandra Mr. Lagatutta Mrs. Konigsberg Shapiro	Shapiro arrives and is forced to do a stand-up comedy act. Shapiro escapes.
16	Ace Wink Sandra Mr. Lagatutta Mrs. Konigsberg	Ace realizes that the gig is up. He jumps out the window.
17	Mrs. Defoe Wink Sandra Mr. Lagatutta Mrs. Konigsberg	Everyone is totally depressed. Mrs. Defoe enters. She is the new owner of the building and is looking for her designer.
18	Ace Mrs. Defoe Wink Sandra Mr. Lagatutta Mrs. Konigsberg	Ace returns. He has fallen on a window washer's platform and is still alive. He convinces the pretentious Mrs. Defoe that his crazy friend Wink is a famous designer. Sandra and Ace leave to start new lives.
19	Mrs. Defoe Wink	In the end, Mrs. Defoe goes over the design with the uncomprehending Wink.

Theme: Not sure yet, something about failure and being an artist. Perhaps how to deal with failure.

Notes: Must do more research into the world of the stand-up comic.

WRITING

Years ago, when a script was in trouble, a producer or director would turn to a script doctor. This was a writer who attempted to save another playwright's problem script by applying creativity, technique, dramatic principles, and even formula to identify and solve a script's problems. Today, playwrights must be their own script doctors. As the outline grows, the playwright should constantly ask, does it work? Does this communicate? Is it clear? Does the play tell the story in an organized, structured manner that allows the audience to follow and understand? Here are a few important tests the scenario should pass before you begin writing.

Will your play communicate to a diverse audience? A play should appeal to different races, genders, and regions. If you say you're writing to a select group of people, then you're defeating the purpose of writing a play. You don't want to preach the sermon to the choir. A play is never so personal only a select group can understand it. One student from Beverly Hills finished his scenario in which the antagonist was a leaf blower. Needless to say, it was an avant-garde piece. The play meant a lot to the playwright, for, at that time, there was a great deal of controversy in the city of Beverly Hills; they were thinking of banning the use of leaf blowers due to noise. To anyone who didn't live in or near Beverly Hills, however, the leaf blower analogy was meaningless. Playwriting is the art of communication. Does your play communicate?

Is your idea more like a movie than a play? Cinematic thinking is a major problem for some new playwrights. It can negatively affect a play in two ways. First, it can chop up a play with an abundance of scenes, giving the story an intermittent feeling. This style of writing is common to playwrights who grew up with a steady diet of television, in which sustained scenes are uncommon.

Look over your scenario. Are you telling a story that can live within the confines of a play? Playwriting is more limited than screenwriting. Limit the number of characters, limit the size of your story, and try to write sustained scenes that allow the audience time to get truly involved.

Second, cinematic thinking will hurt a script by including details that cannot be staged. We recently read a play in which the student included a montage and an auto accident—definitely cinematic. Try to imagine your play taking place on stage rather than in real life.

Where does your play deviate from the formula? If you're writing a formula play, where are you making the story interesting by deviating from the standard outline? The successful formula writer tests old conventions and satisfies the audience's expectations in unexpected ways.

Does your play contain too many or too few complications? Does your play deal with many complications rather than fully exploring all the possibilities of a few? Unless it's a farce, give yourself time to explore the characters' emotions and thoughts before you move on to the next complication.

Does it have unity? Do all the parts of the play—character, story, conflict/crisis, action, truth, French scenes, scenes, acts—combine into a united whole?

Does it contain any extraneous scenes or characters? Does the play have a purpose of action?

Do you still want to write it? Playwriting is hard enough even with the want, the *need* to write. If you have lost interest in the idea, this is a good time to abandon the project. Toss it in the scenario file, and maybe in the future it will again arouse your interest.

WRITING METHOD

If you feel satisfied with your scenario, if you have the passion, if you have a burning desire to write, then it's time to stop making plans and write. First, you need a place to write. This should be a permanent, private area, not something set up and torn down each writing session. The playwright who has to clear off the dining room table and set up the computer before writing won't accomplish as much as the writer who has a personal office. If you don't have room for an office, try to find a desk in the corner of the bedroom, a closet, a basement, someplace where you can close the door and get away from the noise of life.

A writer must also develop writing habits. Many writers set a schedule. Life is full of interruptions and problems that can limit the playwright's creative time. If you have a second job, as 99.9 percent of all playwrights do, then you need to set aside a part of each day for writing only. Start a tradition and do everything in your power to stick to it. Family members, lovers, and friends must understand that this is your time.

New writers are often told that they should write every day and it's true, but writing every day doesn't necessarily mean that you're sitting behind the computer; sometimes it means that you're thinking about your story or characters. If you don't feel like writing today, then write a letter, read a play, study a book on playwriting, but make sure that every day you spend some time as a playwright. You don't "give playwriting a try." That's like saying, "I think I'll try to be a doctor." It takes too much energy. Without commitment, you'll fail. Writing a play takes a commitment of time every day for months, even years.

Next, a writer must develop a method of writing. This is how the writer writes. Do you work best at night? Do you need music playing? Do you write fast, leaving problems to be solved later, and make many drafts, or are you more meticulous, making sure one scene is right before moving on to the next? If you're just starting, explore some ways to write that have been proven effective. Some writers find it helpful to write the first draft of a play quickly. Using their detailed outline, they charge right in, forging the first rough draft in only a few days or weeks. If they cannot write a section, they simply put "dialogue to come" or even "scene to come" and continue to rough out a first draft. This binge method of writing has some advantages, for it quickly gives a writer a rough first draft. It allows the playwright to explore the whole play and make broad discoveries as the writing flows from the heat of the moment. The finished first draft is always lacking, but then more meticulous rewriting can begin.

Other writers insist on making each page perfect before going to the next. This means that they go back and rewrite from page one each time a discovery is made. A change on page thirty means going back and rewriting pages one to twenty-nine. This is a tedious way to write, but can lead to a finished product in only a single draft. It worked for Sir Arthur Pinero, who said, "I can never go on to page two until I am sure that page one is as right as I can make it." This does not work for most writers, but it works for some, and that's all that matters. In addition, some writers write long first drafts, the reasoning being that it's easier to cut than to add, while others produce a rather short first draft, which is only a skeleton of the finished product.

While writing, writers seldom talk about their plays. If you tell friends and relatives the story over and over, there's a good chance the desire to write the story will wane. A playwright is a storyteller. If you have already told the story a dozen times, why spend the time writing it? Yet other writers find that by telling the story to a friend, they work out problems they never would have solved while sitting alone in front of the computer. Experiment. Find the time and method that works for you and then stick to it. Above all, remember, a writer writes.

R E W R I T I N G

When the first draft is finished, the playwright looks back objectively at what has been passionately written. Rewriting is repair work. Before beginning a new draft, a playwright should be clear on what needs to be repaired. Only when the playwright is armed with the script's problems and possible solutions should the next draft begin. In this way, rewriting is much like writing, it requires a plan of attack. The problem is, after weeks, months, or years of work on the same story and characters, a playwright's vision can become narrowed and the creative answers few.

There is a story about three Hollywood screenwriters who were doing a rewrite of a children's movie. They had been working on it for weeks, the deadline was near, but they just couldn't make the story work. The problem was that the original draft contained a horse that no longer seemed to work. They were pulling another all-nighter. It was getting near dawn when one of the writers said, "What horse?" It suddenly occurred to them that they were trying to adhere to a scenario now outdated. The story had grown; the horse was no longer needed. They cut the horse and finished the rewrite before the deadline. The lesson is, when rewriting, be open, willing to change, and ready to explore new possibilities.

F I N A L   T H O U G H T S   O N   R E W R I T I N G

Sometimes a playwright knows her script is not ready, yet can't figure out what's wrong. When this happens, the author needs *new eyes*. This is the ability to look at a script fresh, as if it were the first time. The best way to achieve this effect is to take some time away from the play. Some writers work on another project for a while, others simply take a vacation. (Everyone deserves vacations, even writers.) It seldom takes more than a week or two, but the writer should totally divorce himself or herself from the work. Lock it up, don't think about it. When you return, faults will reveal themselves and hidden problems will become obvious. Another method of achieving new eyes is to have a reading of the script. Plays are written to be heard, not silently read. A good reading is the fastest way to open a writer's eyes and launch into rewrite mode.[2]

The Irish-born American actor and playwright Dionysius Boucicault said, "Plays are not written; they're rewritten." A playwright should never place the words "Final Draft" on a script. There's no such thing as a final draft. Many playwrights have gone back, even to their most famous plays, and rewritten. Tennessee Williams was rewriting twenty-year-old plays two months before he died. Playwrights are always growing, learning, and changing, and so must their plays. A play is not finished when the playwright stops writing, or even when it's produced. A play isn't even finished when the playwright dies; the final draft of a play occurs when the last production closes, and the script moulders on a library shelf, forgotten by time.

EXERCISES

Exercise #1
Write a scenario of your play. Include all the elements needed. Include a working title, character names, outline of the plot-structure, place, setting, acts, scenes, French scenes, and perhaps a theme.

Exercise #2
Look at the place (geographical location, environment, country, state, city, or area) of your play. How will the place affect the characters and story?

Exercise #3
Look at the setting (what the audience sees on stage) of your play. How will the place affect the characters and story?

TOP TEN LIST FOR BECOMING A PLAYWRIGHT

Pat Gabridge, an award-winning playwright living in Colorado, came up with this insightful top ten list of reasons for becoming a playwright:

---

[2] Chapter 9 discusses how to stage a reading.

10. Be world famous when you're dead.

 9. Don't have to shave very often.

 8. Recession-proof. They don't make a living in good times or bad.

 7. Impress opposite sex at parties.

 6. No license required.

 5. Saves real jobs for other people.

 4. So your brother-in-law can ask: "Oh, what movie have you written?"

 3. Rejection letters are good for your health.

 2. Gives the radical right someone to pick on.

 1. Gives the IRS agents a good laugh.

Reprinted with permission of the author

Chapter 7

CREATIVITY

It's time to write. You go to your special place, start your computer, and concentrate on the blank screen. Minutes pass. Nothing happens. You concentrate harder, but you don't feel creative. You've drawn a blank. Eventually you give up. "I'm just not in the mood to write," you say as you snap off the hard drive and head for the door, another writing session lost. The next day, you're riding in an elevator, not thinking about much of anything, when suddenly you're hit with inspiration. Your subconscious has been working on a problem and now, between floors, it gives you the answer. You're inspired. You want to write, but it's impossible because you're at work and another writing session is lost.

It takes at least five years of rigorous training to be spontaneous . . .

Martha Graham

Writers are seldom in the mood to write. Flashes of creativity are few and far between. Rarely are we just hit, out of the blue, with inspiration, so it behooves us to rid ourselves of the idea that complete plays are written during inspirational flashes. We've all heard the story about Edward Albee writing *Who's Afraid of Virginia Woolf* in one weekend. Whether it's true or not is unimportant, because the vast majority of plays aren't finished in a rush. It takes many drafts, many weeks, even years to write a good play. If a writer must depend on or wait for random moments of creativity to hit, then she stands little chance of completing a play. Is it possible, then, to create a creative moment or inspire inspiration?

To answer this question we must ask, what is creativity? We know that creative people are those who find options and increase the range of choices. They're the ones whose mental mobility allows them to draw analogies and metaphors and find order in chaos. Above all, creative people are willing to experiment and take risks.

Creativity is a brief moment of insight. It can be a major flash or realization into characters, story, theme, or a small moment in which a minor problem is solved.

Creativity is seldom spontaneous. It usually has a source. Whether conscious or unconscious, something happens to cause a creative moment, so we need to explore ways to increase the chances of having creative thoughts.

Scientist Louis Pasteur said, "Chance favors the prepared mind." For a writer, this means writing. Writers write whether they feel like it or not. We write whether we're inspired or not. We write whether we're in the mood or not. Creativity may hit at any time, but it's more likely to occur if the writer is actively thinking. Yet how does a writer write without inspiration? Without being creative, can a playwright craft anything worth the paper it's written on? Yes, because a writer relies on *technique* until creativity hits.

Some writers blame their lack of creativity on *writer's block*. This is a rare psychological condition that prevents the writer from writing. Many claim to have it, but few actually suffer from it. Playwrights must eliminate the phrase "writer's block" from their thought processes. The term seems to express some mystical reason for not writing, when in most cases, it's only a writer not asking the right questions, not setting out to solve one small problem at a time, not using technique.

TECHNIQUE AND CREATIVITY

If creativity is a brief moment of insight, then technique is the principle or process that results from that insight. This means that a technique can be learned without having to repeat the original creative impulse. The first time you develop a discovery into a story or character, creativity is involved. The next time you use the lesson learned from that discovery, it's technique. You can't have the same brief moment of insight twice. When you lose your watch and discover it under the table, you don't leave it there, walk away, and come back minutes later to rediscover it.

Once you've had the moment, it becomes a part of your thinking that you can apply the next time you face a similar problem. Two weeks from now, when you again lose your watch, your watch-finding technique begins with a quick look under the table. Technique, then, may be defined as learned insight.

The same is true with an artist. It's possible for a great violinist to play an incredible, awe-inspiring concert and not once be creative. No brief moments of insight into the music or how to play the violin were made during the concert, so there was no creativity, only pure technique. Great emotion, yes, but no creativity.

Actors take the stage night after night, perform the same play numerous times, and can give a brilliant performance each night, but are they creative *every* night? Do they have a new moment of insight into the character or acting at every performance? Occasionally yes, but most of the creativity occurred during the rehearsal process; during the performance they're actively imitating the creativity that happened weeks before. Actors rely on technique, so an actor has no excuse not to take the stage and give a decent performance, even on an off night.

The same is true with playwrights. They can sit at the keyboard, not feel creative, not be in the mood, and still write pretty good dialogue. With technique, there are no excuses. For a playwright, technique is knowing the basic theorems of good dialogue, plot-structure, and character. Technique is knowing which question to ask and when to ask it. Even if the mood isn't right, the playwright can answer technical questions such as, what happens next? What does this particular character feel at this moment?

A playwright thinks by asking questions. The searching for answers can cause creativity. The best way to become creative is by being active. **Writing is being active, and creativity favors the active mind.**

Other methods that can also help a writer be more creative include an active point of view, direct experience, emotional recall, indirect experience, eliminating obstacles, problem solving, and separation of the critical and creative sides of the brain.

ACTIVE POINT OF VIEW

The scene: a grocery store checkout. A couple argues. Their hushed accusations grow louder. The clerk and customers gently stretch their necks to listen. The argument abruptly ends with the woman storming off. The customers go back to their *National Enquirer*s and coupon books, but each had distinctly different feelings about what had just occurred. One customer bitterly compares the argument to his failing marriage. A young professional woman is proud of the wife for not putting up with it. The checkout clerk can't understand why everything has to be so personal. Each person, depending on his or her point of view, interpreted the situation differently.

If the same scene were on stage, a playwright would structure the action and characters to allow limited interpretation. Armed with a point of view, a playwright can interpret what happened between that young couple in the checkout line, why they fought, who was right, and exactly what the argument meant.

A point of view is the writer's own logical, unique interpretation of the facts. It's a particular truth and conclusion a writer draws from living life.[1]

An *active* point of view simply means the playwright is always considering and judging. Playwrights evaluate, discriminate, and interpret. They witness life and create plays based on what they've seen and felt. Playwrights are no better

---

[1] Hollywood requires that writers be able to change their points of view and conform to what is popular. A true playwright will not sacrifice his point of view for a paycheck. Playwrights seldom consider the consequences of telling their own particular truths.

than their ability to select and arrange the parts of life they have witnessed, experienced, and examined. Without an active point of view, a playwright has less material to create with and will be less creative. An active point of view comes from long hours of observation and logical thought; logical thought is a result of an active mind, and an active mind is ripe for creativity.

DIRECT EXPERIENCE

A point of view is not fixed, but is always growing and changing. Life can be experienced two ways, directly or indirectly. Indirectly means through reading, seeing, and hearing others' reactions to their experiences. Direct experience is tasting life firsthand. It's an awareness, a heightened sense of life that leads to probing, listening, eavesdropping, participating, watching, and daydreaming.

A playwright must live life to write about life. Most people try to avoid emotions. We're told that the higher the joy, the greater the pain, and that only when we have seen the lowest valley can we experience the greatest mountain, so we do everything in our power to live in the gray area, sacrificing the bright highs so we can avoid the depressing lows.

Playwrights are different. They never shrink from emotions or experiences. This doesn't mean a playwright should get drunk and end up in jail. Deep awareness can make even the most mundane of moments interesting. It's said that most people are truly aware of their lives for only a few moments each day. Indeed, humans are known to be creatures of routine who will find any reason to go on automatic pilot. Playwrights have to avoid automatic pilot. They must constantly wake themselves up and experience life. This means playwrights must go out of their way to meet people, see new places, feel emotions, and above all, listen to the world.

EMOTIONAL RECALL

As the playwright experiences life, the events, conclusions, and emotions must stay with him. They should be on standby, ready when the playwright needs them, which requires an ardent memory. Even years after an experience, a playwright must be able to recall emotions and invest them in character. Stanislavski taught actors to "save" their sensory impressions and experiences so they could be recalled and experienced again. The same can apply to a playwright. The sense memories should be permanently stored and, when needed, revived and relived. The honest emotions that result can be mixed with the play's characters and, thus, lead to heightened awareness, a deep sense of character, an emotional stew where creativity is born. In short, a playwright must face life, experience life, listen to life, and remember.

INDIRECT EXPERIENCE

Indirect experience is viewing life through someone else's eyes. The most common way to do this is by reading and listening. A playwright is a reader of history books, novels, autobiographies, plays, true confessions, newspapers, anything available. From formal interviews to everyday conversations, a playwright listens, because good indirect experience can be just as powerful as direct. A playwright is not a sequestered person who seldom comes out of the dark study to face the day. No one is creative enough to write well about that which they have never experienced, either directly or indirectly.

ELIMINATING OBSTACLES

Another method of increasing the chances of becoming creative is to eliminate internal and external obstacles. To get rid of external obstacles, find a place to write, schedule time, and get adequate equipment. Accept no excuses; whatever it takes, find the time, a quiet place, and *write*. Internal, physiological obstacles can be more difficult to identify. Stanislavski suggested two things that might help eliminate internal obstacles. First, he said that a creative moment is more apt to occur if your body is free of *unnecessary* muscular and mental tension. Unnecessary tension absorbs inner energy, diverting it from higher centers.

Playwrights can learn from experienced actors. The moment they hit the rehearsal hall door, experienced actors center themselves and become receptive to the acting process. It becomes so habitual that, during these few hours, at this particular place they set aside whatever is happening in the world and concentrate on their art. For a playwright, this translates into a definite process to writing. Establish a strong routine or tradition that allows you to withdraw from unnecessary tension and enter your own little writing cocoon. This is not to say a playwright must be relaxed to be creative. If the tension is related to the emotions of the story and characters, then it's a good and useful tension.

Stanislavski also observed that creativity is significantly stifled by an actor's thoughts of the auditorium and public. If the actors are thinking of the audience, they're not concentrating on the artistic task. He said that an actor must be able to develop a "circle of his own attention," while concentrating on the task at hand. If you can't eliminate the outside world's interference, then find your own circle of attention or state of public solitude.

PROBLEM SOLVING

Another roadblock in the path of creativity can be the writer's inability to solve problems. This usually signals that the playwright is trying to solve too many problems at once. A play is made up of hundreds of small problems. As a result, script problems must be broken down into manageable components, each so small that there is a good chance you can solve them one at a time. Here are the steps to follow when trying to solve a problem:

1. Specify the problem. Don't be vague. Statements such as "the second act is boring" or "the character doesn't work" will not do. Which parts are boring? What French scenes? What aspect of the character?

2. Break the problem into manageable components. The smaller the better. Which beats? Exactly when is the character not working? What part of the character is inconsistent or underdeveloped?

3. Brainstorm possible solutions to each component. What techniques will solve the problem? Go back to the basics. If you can't find a solution, you're being too vague. Go back to steps one and two.

SEPARATION OF THE CREATIVE AND CRITICAL SIDES OF THE BRAIN

One roadblock to creativity is allowing yourself to be too critical of your new ideas. Creative and critical thinking come from opposite sides of the brain, and seldom operate at the same time. People are more creative when they come up with many imaginative possible solutions and hold off critical judgment until later.

One study placed a group of scientists in a think tank with a problem to solve. They were told that each time they came up with a possible solution they should all immediately analytically judge the idea before moving on to another. After a day of thinking and judging, they failed to solve the problem.

The next day they were given an equally difficult problem to solve, but this time they spent the morning pitching out possible solutions without critically judging them or even considering plausibility. That afternoon, the scientists returned and were asked to critically judge each solution they had come up with that morning. It worked. One of their morning pitches solved the problem. By turning off the critical side of the brain, they succeeded in increasing creativity.

The same is true for playwrights. By constantly judging your ideas you can stifle the creative side. The next time you have a problem to solve, write down one possible solution after another, without being critical. Don't judge whether they will work or not! Soon you'll have a list of possible solutions. Later, try to logically make each solution work or, in other words, use the critical side of your brain and you'll have a better chance of solving the problem.

Nothing is worse than the writer who judges everything the moment it's written. It's an open invitation to creative gridlock. Your creative side and critical side are of equal importance, but like children, they must be separated to get any work done.

EXERCISES

When excessive tension occurs, use your common sense and try to alleviate the root cause rather than the symptoms. If tension still persists, try the following relaxation exercises:

Exercise #1

Sit up comfortably, with your back in alignment; take three deep breaths, and let your shoulders relax.

Exercise #2

Close your eyes and bring your shoulders all the way up (aim to make them even with your ears). Hold for three seconds (your shoulders, not your breath) and release. Repeat, if necessary.

Exercise #3

With your eyes closed, breathe in deeply and slowly through your nose, allowing the exhale to come through your mouth. Repeat five times. (Note: never hold your breath during the above, and do it slowly, otherwise you could become dizzy.)

Chapter 8

FORMAT

Years ago, I sold a screenplay to Ron Howard's company, Imagine Films. After the contract was signed, the producer had me in for a "meet and greet." The first words out of her mouth were, "I took one look at your script and knew it was going to be an easy read."

You shall see them on a beautiful quarto page, where a neat rivulet of text shall meander through a meadow of margin.

Richard Sheridan

A new play should always look as if it's going to be an easy read. Place yourself in the reader's shoes. You've got to pore over five scripts tonight. The last ten you read were hard to follow, loaded with unclear characters and typos. You try to avoid these until the last moment. Now, late at night, you face the unenviable. The first script is 141 pages—too long. The next is titled *Death Walks Alone*—too dark. Two of the last three have a strange format you've never seen, so you look to the last script. It looks professional, it follows a proper format, and it begins with an attention-grabbing event. You're hooked, and the writer has won the first of many battles. Here are the basics of how to make your script appear professional.

TITLE PAGE

Your title page is the first thing anyone sees. Make the title interesting, something that'll attract the reader's attention. Years ago, I was at the home of Lew Hunter, the head of screenwriting at UCLA. He had several plays and screenplays to read that night. He opened his briefcase, dumped a load of scripts on his coffee table and sorted through. They had titles like *Bob & June, Memories, Impressions,* and *Frank's Story.* Without thinking, the first script he grabbed was

Love Stinks. Bob & June might have been a better script, but *Love Stinks* was read first simply because of its title.

Photocopy your title page on a heavier piece of paper (thirty-pound paper works just fine) and use that as the cover to make the title visible. Don't waste your money on vinyl or clear plastic covers. A sheet of heavier, colored paper will do just fine. Some writers decorate the cover with art in the hopes of attracting the reader's attention, but more often than not this detracts from the script and makes it look less professional. You can use a distinctive font, but that's about as fancy as you should get. Your title page should include the title, author's name, phone number(s), fax number, e-mail address, street address, agent, and a notice of copyright.

Author's Name: Your name should be centered under the title. A simple "by" is all that's necessary, though some writers prefer, "A new play by" or "A new comedy by," which are also acceptable. Some playwrights like to point out the obvious by stating, "An Original Play by." (We certainly hope it's original.) Whichever method you use, your billing should look something like this:

SHY KIDNEYS
a play by
Valerie MacKenzie

Phone and Address: This information should appear on the lower right side of the title page. It can take some theatres more than a year to read your script, so if you move a lot, you may want to list a permanent address. You may also want to list your fax number and e-mail address.

Agent: If you have an agent, you should also include his or her name, agency, address, phone, fax number, and e-mail address on the left side, across from your name and address. If you don't have an agent, leave this area blank (don't worry, most playwrights do not have an agent).

Copyright: A simple, small, unassuming notice of copyright is placed in the lower right corner under your phone and address. It should read, "copyright 199_" or "© 200_."

Some writers will place their names near the copyright notice: "©1999 Valerie MacKenzie." This isn't necessary. Your name is under the title, so we can assume you're the author and holder of the copyright. Also, you *shouldn't* include statements such as "All rights reserved" or "Property of Valerie MacKenzie." These facts are assumed by your simple copyright notice. If your title page is repetitious, what does that say about your script?

We once saw a title page with two copyright dates and three warnings that the script was the exclusive property of the author. In the process of making all these cautions, the author had forgotten to place his name on the script. Keep the copyright notice small and out of the way. The chances of someone stealing your script are minute.

COPYRIGHTING YOUR PLAY

When you copyright your play, you are guaranteeing yourself exclusive rights to your creation. Others will be breaking the law if they should copy, reproduce, perform, adapt, or in any way exploit your play without your permission. You can copyright plays, books, articles, screenplays, and even treatments. You cannot copyright titles, character names, short phrases, bits of dialogue, and general ideas or concepts. If you have an idea for a play, your best protection is to write the play and then copyright it.

All plays are automatically copyrighted from the moment of their creation, but this doesn't mean you shouldn't prove ownership through the Copyright Office of the Library of Congress. Copyrighting is easy. You need only send away for a form "PA." Write to:

Register of Copyrights

Copyright Office

Library of Congress

Washington D.C. 20540

You can also get information on copyrights through the World Wide Web. The Library of Congress' copyright general information web site is located at: http://lcweb.loc.gov/copyright/. The web site containing information on registering dramatic works is located at: http://home.earthlink.net/omniverse/elac-theatre/library/misc/copyrite.htm.

Or you can call the Library of Congress Forms Hotline at (202)707-9100 (24 hours a day). The form will take several weeks to arrive. Send the completed form and script, along with a check or money order to cover the specified nonrefundable filing fee, to the Register of Copyrights. If the play is unpublished you'll include one copy; if published, two copies of the best edition will be needed. Be sure to mail the form, your check, and the script(s) in the same envelope. You may wait up to sixteen weeks, but eventually you'll receive a certificate of registration, which is your official record of the copyright. File it and forget it until you need it, which most likely will be never. You need not recopyright a script every time you make changes. Only when the script has been significantly altered should you bother with recopyrighting. For more copyright information call (202) 707-3000.

COPYRIGHT TRICK

When submitting a script, some playwrights change the copyright date to match the year of submission. For example, if they're submitting a script they wrote and actually copyrighted six years ago, they'll change the copyright date to the present year. This isn't done for legal reasons but for effect. Directors, producers, and readers want new plays. An old copyright date might lead some to wonder why the play has been around for years and not produced. You want to submit an unpublished, unproduced script as if it just came out of your printer.

DEDICATIONS

Generally, unpublished plays do not have a dedication page. You may want to thank a spouse, teacher, or friend, but it's best to wait and thank them when the play is produced or published. The only exception is if you think thanking someone will help get the play produced. For example, you might say, "This play was developed through a grant from the Chicago Foundation for Abused Women," or "With grateful appreciation to the Southern Appalachian Playwrights Workshop."

TITLE PAGE DON'TS

Some playwrights list the name of a production company that supposedly owns the script. Usually this is done by playwrights who want to make the script appear more legit. Don't do it! Nothing is more amateur than seeing a script written by Tom K. Smithy and owned by Smithy & Associates.

Your title page should not mention which draft this manuscript represents. That information is for your own personal use or is used when you've been commissioned to write a play, and shouldn't appear on scripts you're submitting to a contest or theatre. Directors, producers, and readers aren't impressed this is *only* the "First Draft." More often than not, if you place "First Draft" on the title page they'll be concerned you haven't taken the time to send them a well-developed script. On the other hand, the words, "Final Draft" can indicate that you believe the play is finished and can no longer be improved. Rewrites occur at any time, even after the play is produced. If you need to indicate draft, then record the date you finished the draft under the copyright. This way you can quickly tell the draft without the reader's knowledge.

Your title page should look something like Figure 8.1.

THE CAST OF CHARACTERS PAGE

Following the title page comes the *cast of characters*. This is a listing of the characters' names, ages, and possibly a brief description (emphasis on *brief*) such as "The father," "Kim's niece" or "A quiet woman in her thirties." If your play uses double casting (using one actor to play more than one role) you will want to indicate this on the cast of characters page. Sometimes a playwright will get fancy and call this page the *dramatis personae,* which is also acceptable.

Figure 8.1

Play Manuscript Title Page

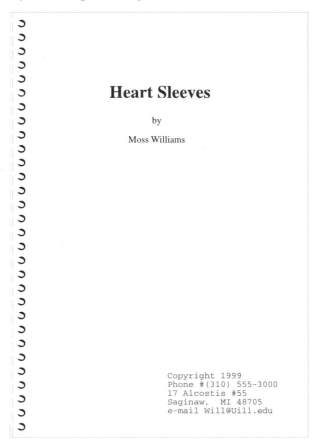

Heart Sleeves

by

Moss Williams

Copyright 1999
Phone #(310) 555-3000
17 Alcostis #55
Saginaw, MI 48705
e-mail Will@Uill.edu

SET DESCRIPTION

The set description is placed at the bottom of the cast of characters page. The set description should be well written, simple, and to the point. Describe only what will advance the characters within this particular story. Chekhov said, "[if you] describe a gun hanging over the fireplace of the set, then, by the end of the play, that gun had better be used." Give the essence of the location, the mood, and important details as you lead the reader's eye around the set. Don't go into such a detailed description that you totally design the set (leave that to the set designer). Avoid terms such as "stage right" or "down stage left" to place props, and set pieces such as windows or doors. Published plays from Samuel French might do this, but only because they want to help high school or amateur producer/directors who seldom have experienced designers. Here are a few examples of what your stage description might look like:

Time: Early evening—The present

Place: 130th Street, New York City

Setting: A skeleton set suggests the second floor flat of Acey Aldridge. It's older but clean. The living area has been converted into a study. In one corner is a desk and many law books. Borders suggest walls. The entrance to the flat is in the back. Other doors lead to a kitchen and a hallway—it's a makeshift apartment. Sparely decorated but comfortable. On one side are bars that indicate a window. Its sparseness suggests its infrequent use.

Time: Late afternoon in May—The present

Place: Galveston, Texas

Setting: A neutral playing area that can become several places. Most of the time it suggests various rooms in the house of Norman Sr. and Belle Burnand. The place is the product of minds shaped by the Depression, so nothing is too fancy or without purpose. Two playing areas are more permanent. One is the front porch where Indian summer hangs a skyline of bullion-tinted leaves over the rusted deck chairs and the entrance to the house. The other is a tiny section of basement. Bare light bulbs. Wet block walls. An ancient coal furnace that has been converted to oil. Its tentacle heating ducts make it look like an upside-down octopus.

Your cast of characters and set description page should look something like Figure 8.2.

SYNOPSIS OF SCENES

If your play has many scenes you may want to include a synopsis. This may be placed on the cast of characters page or on a separate sheet and looks like this:

ACT I

Scene 1—A rooming house, Chicago, 1973
Scene 2—Ben's living room, New York, 1994
Scene 3—A hospital waiting room
Scene 4—Ben's living room
Scene 5—Church, the next day

ACT II

Scene 1—Ben's boyhood home, Chicago, 1973
Scene 2—School room, Chicago, 1974
Scene 3—Ben's living room, 1994
Scene 4—Church, two weeks later

Figure 8.2

Cast of Characters and Set Description Page

```
                    Cast of Characters


      NORMAN SR..................The Father, 60s

      BELLE.....................The Mother, 50s

      NORMAN JR.................The Only Son, 23

      CASEY.....................The Older Sister, 30

      KAROLINE..................The Girlfriend, 25

      LARRY.....................The Paper Boy, 16



      TIME: An autumn afternoon

      PLACE: Flint, Michigan

      SETTING: A modest kitchen. A mix of 60s and
      70s. The old checkerboard green and off-
      white linoleum floor has been mopped. All
      that remains of the mess once here are the
      dead or dying plants in the window. Pushed
      against one pine paneled wall is a small
      Underwood typewriter. The floor is covered
      with books. In the corner is a pile of heavy
      cardboard boxes. Towards the back is a
      hallway (crammed with a washer/dryer) which
      leads to the back entrance. There are two
      doors, one leading to the basement, and on
      the other side, one opening to the rest of
      the house. Above the doors are mounted deer
      antlers. On the walls are hung rodeo
      posters, calendars and a dozen or so fishing
      poles.
```

CHARACTER DESCRIPTION PAGE

Plays don't have a character description page. The characters should be clear from the dialogue and not need detailed descriptions before the play begins. It's allowable to place a description of the character in the stage directions just before his or her entrance, but it should be brief. For more on character description, see the section on stage directions later in this chapter.

THE TEXT FORMAT

After the cast of characters, set description, and synopsis of scenes page(s) should come the first page of the script. Be aware that no two playwriting books give the exact same format, so small variations occur from one writer's script to another's. What follows is how most typical unpublished play manuscripts are formatted in the United States and Canada.

PAPER

Type on only one side of each sheet. Twenty-pound 8.5-by-11-inch paper is the standard. White (and *only* white) paper is acceptable.

FONT

A script is always typed. If you use a computer, only letter-quality or laser printing is acceptable. **Dot-matrix printing is unacceptable.**[1] If you can't afford a laser printer, check into the laser-quality printers such as ink-jet and bubble-jet. They produce laser-quality work at a fraction of the cost. If you can't afford one, put your script on a disk and pay someone to laser print it. If you shop around, you'll find a wide variation in price per page (be sure to check at your local university, they often give their students special rates).

The most commonly used font is 12-point Courier. Some writers prefer 13-point Courier as slightly larger and easier to read. Fourteen-point Courier is considered too big, and 11-point Courier is too small. If your computer doesn't have Courier, try to use something similar. Here is an example of the Courier font:

Courier 12

Courier 13

If you are using a typewriter, Pica (ten letters per inch) is standard. Elite is too small.

MARGINS

One inch on the top, bottom, and right sides of the page is the norm. The left margin should be 1⅜ inches to 1½ inches, to allow extra room for binding.

PAGE NUMBERS

Page numbers appear in the upper right corner. The title and cast of characters pages are not numbered. If your play has more than one act, the act number is indicated by spelling out "Act One" or with Roman numerals. Any one of the following is acceptable:

Act One 12.

Act One. Page 12.

I-12

---

[1] Only letter-quality dot matrix printers will suffice. Take a close look at the printing from your dot matrix printer; if you see any individual dots, it's not letter-quality and you will have to find a better printer.

If your play has scenes as well as acts, you'll want to indicate this with lowercase Roman numerals:

I-ii-50

II-iii-61

The page numbers don't start over each time you begin a new scene or act. A reader should be able to quickly look to the last page of a script for its total length.

Layout: What follows is the accepted format for a unpublished play:

IMITATING LIFE

ACT ONE

SCENE 1

           (THE LIGHTS RISE: NURSE
           WICKES, a malevolent nurse,
           folds sheets off the laundry
           line. In the house, we can
           see the feeble HARLEY WEAR
           lying in his Craftmatic
           adjustable bed. ART WEAR,
           his son, a thirtyish,
           professor type walks up
           holding a small bag of
           groceries and a pack of
           super-size bladder-control
           diapers. WICKES punches her
           stopwatch.)

           NURSE WICKES
Told you so.

           ART
They're a little late.

           NURSE WICKES
It's been two hours. They're dead somewhere on the side
of the road or they're not coming.

           ART
Nurse Wickes, you'll be amazed at what'll happen when
you develop a positive attitude toward people.

           (ART notices the pile of
           junk mail near the laundry.)

                              NURSE WICKES
Mail came. You got a rejection.

                              (ART inspects a ripped
                              letter.)

                              NURSE WICKES *(Cont'd)*
Thought it was one of his. Opened it. Read it. Was going
to paste it all back together but, what the hell, you
got a positive attitude, you can handle it.

                              ART
Wish you wouldn't open my--

                              NURSE WICKES
What's that, five rejections this week?

CHARACTER NAMES

Character names should be capitalized and indented four inches in from the left
side of the page.

DIALOGUE

Dialogue is single-spaced and runs from margin to margin. Note that there is no
space between the character name and the dialogue.

USES OF "CONTINUED"

When a character's speech is interrupted by a page break, the word "CONTIN-
UED" or "MORE" should appear parenthetically at the bottom of the page and
the speech should be finished on the next. Example:

                              HAZEL RUBY
So you're a year older than Harry and maybe a little
taller, who notices? You realize that you and Harry
remind me a lot of my second marriage. I was married
four times, wait, five, well, six if you count the
                         (CONTINUED)

_____

                                             I-2-67

                              HAZEL RUBY *(CONTINUED)*
one that was annulled when I was fifteen. But that
second one, not counting the one that was annulled, was
the best. Nothing ever topped it. If I had my way,
Dougie and I would still be married today.

DUAL DIALOGUE

It doesn't happen often, but if two characters need to speak at the same time, you should split the page in half and allow each line to occupy one side of the page. Example:

JOHN
Would you get your life together?
You make me sick, laying around
the house! Doing nothing!

MARCIA
You never listen to me. All you do
is talk about yourself. Well, I
matter.

STAGE DIRECTIONS

Stage directions describe the physical elements of the play and qualify the say-ings and doings of the characters. Stage directions are used to briefly delineate characters and convey important blocking (the movement of the actors on stage). They may even indicate how a line should be said or describe character's reaction.

There are three keys to writing good stage directions. First, make them uncomplicated and lean. George Bernard Shaw's habit of expanding his stage directions into essays was fine for him but not a good idea for a modern begin-ning playwright. Your script should be dominated by dialogue, not stage direc-tions. Second, stage directions do not go into details unless those details are significant to the story. Third, stage directions should be suggestions, not com-mands. Every production of a play is different. Actors, designers, and directors will bring their unique interpretations to scripts. Stage directions should invite collaboration rather than tell them exactly how to block, design, or interpret it.

Stage directions go in one of two acceptable places on the page. One is about three inches from the left side of the paper, the other is on the same margin as the character's name. Example:

> (JANE walks to the window
> and grabs the plant.)

Or:

> (JANE walks to the window and grabs
> the plant.)

Stage directions should be single spaced and enclosed in parentheses. If a char-acter is mentioned, the name should be capitalized. This helps actors quickly find the stage directions for their character.

DIALOGUE INTERRUPTED
BY A STAGE DIRECTION

Some playwrights borrow from screenplays and use "CONT'D" next to a character's name when that character's speech has been interrupted by a stage direction. Example:

HAZEL RUBY

When I was your age I let another five years go by before
it occurred to me that first marriages are always
failures. They were never meant to succeed.

> (HAZEL RUBY grabs a drunk
> and throws him out of the
> bar.)

HAZEL RUBY *(CONT'D)*

And all those successful first marriages you read about
are really failures in private. It's just a big joke
on everyone. If they really wanted first marriages to
succeed, they'd put a moratorium on marriage until the
age of thirty or thirty-two.

It's also acceptable not to use "CONT'D," in which case the same speech interrupted by a stage direction would look like this:

HAZEL RUBY

When I was your age I let another five years go by before
it occurred to me that first marriages are always
failures. They were never meant to succeed.

> (HAZEL RUBY grabs a drunk
> and throws him out of the
> bar.)

And all those successful first marriages you read about
are really failures in private. It's just a big joke
on everyone. If they really wanted first marriages to
succeed, they'd put a moratorium on marriage until the
age of thirty or thirty-two.

Stage direction should never contain dialogue. For example, don't include lines such as "They all say 'cheers.'" Instead, the word "cheers" should appear within the dialogue.

EVERYONE

Cheers!

DESCRIBING A CHARACTER
IN A STAGE DIRECTION

When introducing a new character, a playwright is allowed few words of description in the stage directions. You don't want to stop the read with a long delineation. For example, you could write, "Captain Barts is five-feet-nine, two hundred and twenty pounds, dark hair, blue eyes . . ." and bore to death everyone who reads it, or you could just state, "Captain Barts looks too fat to be a cop." Let the brief description be a stepping-off point. Give the reader a first impression, any further character information will come from the dialogue and action.

Here are several samples of character description:

```
(BELLE BURNAND, a flaky
fifty-year-old, always in
a quiet, personal hurry,
rushes in.)


(NORMAN enters. He's General
Patton in Hush Puppies.
Intense. Seemingly unhappy.)


(They are met by JERRY
SWANN, a sleazy young
executive known for his
lightning-fast ability to
kiss ass.)
```

An excellent example of character description is found in *A Streetcar Named Desire,* in which Tennessee Williams compares Blanche to a "moth." In a single word the playwright allows the reader to picture the character, the actor to understand the rhythm of Blanche, and the costumer an interesting place to begin the design.

STAGE DIRECTIONS TO AVOID

Don't include comments like "MARTHA is a charming woman with frank insights," or "BETH is fun to be around when she's had some wine." These characteristics should be clear in the action and dialogue. You also want to avoid unnecessary details of the character's physical description. Through the years, many different actors may play the part; if you write that the character has blue eyes and that detail doesn't tie directly into the story, you've eliminated all those wonderful brown-eyed actors from playing the part.

Obvious stage directions can also be eliminated. For example, if a character says, "Look at the view, aren't the city's lights wonderful tonight?" then it's unnecessary to have the stage direction read, "She looks out the window." Most stage directions should be implicit in the lines. The same is true with blocking. Painstaking details such as "He crosses down stage right" or "She takes a puff of her cigarette" are rarely necessary. Keep blocking directions simple and state only the most important movements. The vast majority of movements will be decided by the director and actors. Their decisions will depend on the set design (which will differ for every production) and information learned during the rehearsal process.

Stage directions should not reveal exposition about a character that cannot be played. For example:

```
                        (BETH enters, she is JOHN's
                        long-lost sister.)
```

Or:

```
                        (LUNDY and JILL were once
                        roommates. They have
                        remained close friends since
                        college days.)
```

If Beth is John's long-lost sister, that information should come out in the dialogue and not be openly stated in the stage directions. Nothing should be said in the stage directions that cannot be seen and played on stage. If Lundy and Jill are best friends, you might say they hug and treat each other like old chums. The fact that they were roommates and have remained close since college should come out in the dialogue.

Stage directions can clarify a character's reaction, but they do not tell what a character is thinking. For example, the following is unacceptable:

```
                        (JOHN thinks he should
                        apologize to JANE so he
                        mopes near the door for a
                        moment.)
```

But it is acceptable to state:

```
                        (Confused, JOHN mopes near
                        the door for a moment.)
```

The audience cannot read exactly what a character is thinking, but they can see the character's reaction to his or her thoughts. (The reaction in this case is that John mopes). In other words, just like dialogue, stage directions must work on two levels, the *page* and the *stage*. Working on the page means directions are lean enough that a reader, designer, director, or actor gets the needed information without taking away from the dialogue. Working for the stage means that whatever the stage direction calls for must be physically stageable by the actors and financially stageable by the theatre. Your unpublished manuscript will look different from most published plays, which often have detailed stage directions. Publishers such as Samuel French and Dramatists Play Service will greatly amplify the stage directions to include exact blocking. (These amplifications are often drawn from the first production and are not in the playwright's original script.) As with set descriptions, publishers do this to help high school and amateur directors.

We close this section with the worst stage direction ever written. It was penned by a student writer who, for some reason, wishes to remain anonymous:

> (The look on her face turns
> from horror to terror.)

PARENTHETICALS

Parentheticals are stage directions that help qualify or interpret a particular line of dialogue. They are helpful, descriptive words and indicate how a line should be said or point out an action that clarifies why a character says something. Unlike stage directions, parentheticals are placed right into the dialogue. To separate them from dialogue, parentheticals are enclosed in parentheses and italicized. The best time to use a parenthetical is when the line has a great deal of subtext and you want to ensure clear interpretation. Example:

> JOHN
> *(grimacing)*
> I love you more than life itself.

Or when a line is short and needs clarification:

> MARCIA
> *(loving)*
> Oh?

Placing the parenthetical beside the character's name is less often used but is also acceptable:

> MARCIA *(loving)*
> Oh really?

You may place the parenthetical directly beneath the character's name:

> MARCIA
> *(loving)*
> Oh really?

Parentheticals are also placed within the line of dialogue if it will help with the meaning of the line.

MARCIA

I've had about enough of this. You've got to take some responsibility. *(John holds out flowers.)* See what I mean? We can't afford these! *(Her heart melts)* God. I love you.

If possible, avoid constantly intermixing parentheticals with dialogue. This can take away from a reading. Whenever possible, the interpretation should be inherent in the line. If you average more than two parentheticals per page, more than likely something is wrong with your dialogue. Here's an example of what you want to avoid:

BETH
(Gets up and stares at FRED)

So? *(pause)* Is that what you're trying to say? *(No answer. FRED looks away.)* I bet that's not what Sally would say. *(She crosses to the chair.)* Am I right?

Also avoid parentheticals that don't directly affect the line. Example:

JOHN

It's just impossible. *(walking to the window)* We aren't meant for one other. Sorry.

OTHER PARENTHETICALS

A few other standard parentheticals indicate how a particular line of dialogue is to be said. The most common are: pause, off, beat, and O.S.

Pause: A *pause* is a temporary stop in the dialogue, but not a stop in the action. The characters may need a moment to consider a major revelation, or perhaps an important change of subject can only be motivated if the character has time to work things through.

Beat: The word "beat" is used in dialogue to indicate a brief hesitation slightly longer than a period but shorter than a pause. (In playwriting the word "beat" is used for several purposes; the beat/bit is covered in chapter 5.) In the following example, both pause and beat are used correctly:

BELLE

It's nice to meet you. What's your name?

                                    KAROLINE
Karoline Livingston.

                                    BELLE
Where did you meet my son?

                                    KAROLINE
At the Campus Suicide Prevention Center.

                                    (Pause. BELLE attempts a big
                                    smile to cover her shock.)
                              KAROLINE *(Cont'd)*
. . . I work there as a student counselor on the hotline.
I'm getting my master's in psychology. Norman used to do
volunteer work there.

                                    BELLE
                                 (beat)
My Norman did volunteer work at a suicide hotline?

                                    KAROLINE
Yes. It's very rewarding.

Off: The word "off" (short for "playing off") might also appear in a parenthetical to indicate that a line of dialogue is motivated by something the character is seeing or touching. This is used only when clarity is in doubt. For
example:

                                    JIMMIE
                             (off the dead body)
Are you trying to tell me this has been here for two
days?

                                    GILBERT
I haven't seen it.

                                    JIMMIE
For two days!

                                    GILBERT
It was behind the couch. I don't make it a habit to look
behind the couch.

O.S.:   This abbreviation means that the line of dialogue is to be spoken from
off stage. For example:

                                    SAM
How much longer are you goin' be in the bathroom,
Darling? I really have to go!

```
                          CHARLOTTE
                           (O.S.)
          I'll be out in a minute. Leave me alone!
```

WIDOW CONTROL

A widow is a character name or speech that is cut off at the bottom of a page and continued on the next. Widows make a script look unprofessional. Always check your script's pagination. If a speech is cut by the end of a page, use a "continued." If a character's name falls at the bottom of a page and his or her dialogue on the next, move the character name to the next page. Many word-processing programs can be set up to do this automatically.

TEMPLATE

A play format template is located in Appendix E.

THE END

The last page of a scene should have the words "END OF SCENE" in parentheses, and the end of an act should include the words "END OF ACT" in parentheses. The end of the play should include (THE END) or the more formal (CURTAIN).

BINDING

All theatres and contests require that your script be firmly bound. The best way to bind your script is to use a spiral or strip (also known as "Velo") binder. These require a special machine to punch holes in the margin and thread in plastic combs to firmly hold the script together. Most copy shops will bind your script for a nominal charge, but if you're sending out many scripts, it's time to invest in your own binder. They can be found at most office supply stores. The three-hole punch and metal brad method used with Hollywood screenplays is unacceptable, as are staples, folders, and three-ring covers.

PLAYWRIGHT VS. COMPUTER

Typing a play on an antique Underwood typewriter is a little old-fashioned. Today, most writers use computers. All modern word-processing programs have a *template* or *style sheets* that can be programmed to suit the needs of the playwright. Change the settings in your program to place the character names, stage directions, and dialogue in the proper location without having to tab in. Appendix F lists computer programs designed to help playwrights format their plays and screenplays. These programs can be expensive so try the template or style sheets first.

FINAL THOUGHTS ON FORMAT

Recently, an acquaintance was put in charge of selecting the winning script for a play contest. Facing the piles of scripts was a difficult task. At first he tried to give every script a fair chance. He read without judging the script's appearance, but quickly discovered that every play that failed to follow the proper format or was poorly typed was, without exception, also a boring, poorly written waste of time. After days of reading, he began rejecting scripts simply by their appearance. A playwright who doesn't follow the proper format or submits a script full of typos doesn't give herself a fighting chance. The old saying "You can't judge a book by its cover" doesn't apply to playwriting. Producers, directors, and readers always judge a script by its title page and format.

Chapter 9

READINGS, CONTESTS, AND SUBMISSIONS

There was a time when a playwright could enter production without first testing the script. This method often led to frantic overnight rewrites as

If it's good, it'll rise to the top.

Lew Hunter

the writer scrambled to correct unforeseen problems. Today, almost all plays are test-driven before they reach the stage. They get analyzed, tested, and double-checked through a series of cold readings, rehearsed readings, script-in-hand performances, and small workshop productions, sometimes called plays in progress (PIPs). Because plays are designed to be heard, the best way to test your writing is to have readings. Readings are a form of miniproduction. They can be heavily flawed, totally miscast, and still be a good first test for a playwright.

PRIVATE READINGS

Once you think your script is ready, make copies, invite a few friends over (preferably actors, but not necessarily), assign roles (including someone to read stage directions), and listen to the play as it is read aloud. Because the participants will be reading cold (without rehearsal), they'll stumble and misinterpret lines. Don't be concerned if this first reading doesn't go well. First private readings seldom do.

During a reading, a playwright must actively listen, take notes, and judge the play, so don't be tempted to read a role yourself. Even if you wrote the role for yourself, let someone else take it. You'll be too busy looking for sections that don't work, plot points and motivations that aren't clear, and story logic problems.

After the reading, take a break and then talk about the play. Get everyone's opinion. Friends will tend to phrase criticisms kindly, so don't allow them to only praise the script. Praise is good for the ego, but it won't help you on the rewrite. Ask everyone to be kind but critical. If you're thrilled about how things went and wouldn't change a thing, then you're most likely not listening. No playwright writes a perfect first draft. When the note session is done, you should be armed with pages of notes and ready to attack a new draft.

PUBLIC READINGS AND NOTE SESSIONS

Many theatre organizations offer an informal reading series in which new plays are read aloud to an invited audience. Not only is this an opportunity for the playwright to hear the script, but it can also be a playwright's audition if the theatre considers new work. This is why you need that private reading first. You don't want to discover basic flaws in public. Public readings are usually given cold, without rehearsal, or they may be *staged readings,* which have a short rehearsal process and sometimes even a director.

A playwright can take several steps to help ensure a successful public reading. First, make sure the theatre is *casting to type.* This means that the actors are playing characters close to their own age, race, and temperament. You don't want a nineteen-year-old kid playing a seventy-year-old man, or an easygoing gentleman reading a bar-fighting cowboy. Second, require the actors to study the play before the reading and talk to each of them about the role so they have a basic understanding. Third, read only those stage directions affecting the clarity of the play. Long, dry passages of stage directions will bore the audience. Try to cut at least 50 percent of them. You don't want the actors constantly interrupted with "She walks to the window" or "She takes a pause." Above all, cut parenthetical remarks such as *sadly,* and *proudly.* Let the actors play the emotions instead of reading them to the audience.

During the reading, the playwright should not only listen to the play, but also watch the audience's reactions. Those reactions may be subtle. If audience members shift or wiggle their chairs, it can mean they're bored. Audience members may cough or even close their eyes for a rest as they lose interest. We were at a reading of a new comedy in which no one laughed except the playwright, who enjoyed himself immensely. After a while the playwright's guffaws infected the audience and they began laughing at the playwright, which he then interpreted to mean that the play was a great success; he laughed even harder. A reading is a time for a playwright to be quiet and objective. Sit in back where your note-taking won't bother anyone. Be sure to listen objectively and have a copy of the script on which to make notations.

POST-READING DISCUSSIONS

Some readings are followed by an open forum in which the audience, cast, and theatre members can comment on your play. Empirically speaking, these open, "democratic" play critiques are often poorly handled. Group dynamic is a powerful and mysterious thing. These post-reading discussions usually contain half-thought-out ideas, brutal and unhelpful comments, or worthless phrases such as, "I enjoyed it."

The playwright can improve a note session in several ways. First, make up a list of questions you have about the play and ask your audience for specific answers. Even with a list, you'll find that the vast majority of the notes are general. Comments such as "I think the second act could be bumped up by five percent," or "That character got on my nerves," don't help a playwright. Ask for specific examples to support the stated point of view.

Second, after the reading and before the discussion, get up in front of everyone and make a statement about what you've learned and what changes you're considering. This can save precious time, allowing the audience to comment on less obvious points rather than stating what you already know.

Third, never become defensive! Even if you totally disagree, you can't dominate the discussion with justifications. The Circle Rep in New York once had a policy that playwrights couldn't talk during post-play discussion unless a question was directed to them. This forced the playwright to sit and listen. The play should defend itself. If it doesn't, there's something wrong, and if you listen, someone just might give you the answer.

Fourth, the audience has done you a favor by coming to the reading, so be certain they believe their point of view is valuable (whether it is or not). When audience members repeat a point of view or try to dominate the discussion, it's usually because they believe their point was glossed over. Give them a positive response: let them know you've made a note of it and will give it a great deal of thought.

The best way to hold a post-reading discussion is for the theatre to appoint a moderator. It's the moderator's duty to

1. Make sure that the playwright's questions about the play are answered. The moderator must understand that a play reading is primarily for the good of the playwright, not the needs of the audience to socialize, express endless opinions, or hear themselves talk.

2. Set a time limit. *All* critique sessions will turn negative if they go on too long. You don't want the notes to become a laundry list of minor problems. Set a time limit and end post-play discussion on or near that time.

3. Avoid redundant comments. No person or point of view should dominate the discussion. Limit the time each person is allowed to talk. Once a point has been made twice the moderator should ask for new points of view.

While at the Circle Rep in New York, I attended more than one hundred new play readings. One post-play discussion was particularly noteworthy. The reading had gone well and, as the note session began, the audience agreed that it was a good play. The first comment was, "Thank you. Because of your play, I'm going to call my mother and tell her how much she means to me." The next comment was, "Your play was brilliant. Thank you." This went on for about five minutes. Then, the tenth comment was "There was a very minor problem in the second act, . . ." and the audience member went on to elucidate the group on some small structural flaw. The next person suddenly jumped in, "You're right! There was a problem in the second act!"

The feeding frenzy had begun. The next note built on that thought, and the next agreed with him, and so on. One hour later, the majority of the audience had convinced themselves that the playwright had major rewrites ahead of her and the play did not "speak to anyone" in its present form. The audience had circled themselves into the opinion that the play they loved so much an hour before was a total failure. In the theatre, or with any work of art, majority doesn't rule. Playwright Lillian Hellman said, "Decision by democratic majority vote is a fine form of government, but it's a stinking way to create." Comments should be made about your play and not as a reaction to other comments.

After several such note sessions, a playwright learns that most people, sadly, don't know the intricacies of script writing. Look at the priorities of the people giving the notes. Most public readings don't go well. The audience knows this, and yet they still come. Why? People love giving notes to writers. They love to be part of the process. They thrill at the opportunity to critique, but their priorities often get mixed up. Their first concern is not to sound foolish. Their second is to say something constructive. Most people will sacrifice number two in order to fulfill number one. All note-givers fall into three types:

1. Spotlighters: People who love to hear themselves talk.

2. Instant Playwrights: People who give notes as to what *they* would do if they were writing your play.

3. Guides: People who try to understand what the playwright is attempting and give notes that might help the writer reach those goals.

The third type is obviously the most likely to help a playwright, but all three should be listened to. Even those who love to hear themselves talk will occasionally stumble onto a good idea.

Note session critiques fall into three general types:

1. Vague and evasive terms: Usually given by people who don't know what they're talking about.

2. Subjective evaluation: Whether it helps or hurts the playwright's ego, it's not much help in rewrite.

3. Precise analysis: What a playwright waits and hopes for but seldom gets.

Good criticism is exact. Even phrases such as "I loved it" should be followed by the exact reason. Precise analysis is always better than subjective appraisal.

TAKING SUGGESTIONS

The ownership of a play, unlike film and television, remains with the playwright. No one is allowed to make changes, alterations, or omissions without the consent of the playwright. Any changes made become the property of the playwright even if the changes are someone else's idea. If a director, producer, actor, or anyone should make suggestions on how to improve your script and you incorporate the suggestions, they cannot come back and demand joint authorship. Your work is your work, and you should never share authorship because someone makes a few good suggestions.

Several court cases have related to this situation. The courts ruled that the only way an individual can claim to be a collaborator is if his or her additions to your script are independently copyrightable and the two parties (you and the actor, director, producer, or whoever) intended to be joint authors at the time the play was created. This conflict doesn't arise often, but if an unscrupulous member of the theatre should confront you regarding sharing credit because of a suggestion (even if the individual's suggestion turned your play around), stand your ground. The law is on your side.

WHERE TO FIND A READING

First you need a list of all the theatres in your area that have readings. Get on the phone. Ask friends. Many theatre companies have some sort of reading series or will consider doing a reading. Next, you'll have to get your play to the person who decides if it's worth reading. Make sure the script is ready and looks professional. If they say "No" don't push it. Often a theatre needs to know you before they'll read your script. Attend other readings, let them get to know you, and then resubmit. If you can't get a public reading, or no theatres in your area have reading series, then stage your own. Rent a space, rehearse the actors, advertise, and do it all yourself.

SELF-PROMOTION

Too many playwrights treat playwriting just as an art, but it's also a business. Learn to promote yourself. Even a playwright who has an agent must manage and build a career. This means you should attend theatre conferences, join several theatre companies in your area, and keep detailed notes about all the people and theatres you mail to. Build up a clientele, a database of theatre groups, directors, actors, and producers who are happy to read your work.

CONTESTS AND SUBMISSIONS

Play contests are as old as playwriting. The ancient Greek poet Thespis is often called the first actor. His claim to fame is that he won a playwriting contest held during the Festival of Dionysus in Athens in 534 B.C.

Today, hundreds of playwriting contests are held each year. To win a contest, you need a well-written, polished script, one on which you've worked for months (if not years) writing, rewriting, and doing readings until the play is a work of art. Next, you want to make sure your script doesn't fit one of the reject categories. Ninety percent of contest submission scripts are rejected for one of the following reasons:

15% Scripts immediately rejected because they are poorly typed, not bound, or in some way failed to follow contest rules.

15% Plays that actually were disguised screenplays.

10% Crude or inappropriate material.

20% Didactic plays in which the author is preaching.

30% Obvious first scripts, written by total amateurs. Plays lacking consistent story and characters. Plays that are all emotion but no craftsmanship.

FINDING THE RIGHT CONTEST OR THEATRE

Once you believe you're ready, it's time to find a theatre or contest that's looking for a play like yours. Each year produces hundreds of diverse playwriting contests. Some offer the winners a reading. Others offer cash prizes and full productions. The best sources for contest information are:

The Playwright's Companion Feedback Theatrebooks 305 Madison Avenue, Suite 411 New York, NY 10165	*The Dramatists Source Book* Theatre Communications Group 355 Lexington Avenue New York, NY 10017	*The Dramatists Bible* Box 1310 Miami, FL 33153

Other sources are:

The Writer's Market Writer's Digest Books 9933 Alliance Road Cincinnati, OH 45242	*The Writer* (monthly magazine) 8 Arlington Street Boston, MA 02116	*The Dramatists Guild Resource Directory* The Dramatists Guild, Inc. 1501 Broadway, Suite 701 New York, NY 10036

Market InSights for Playwrights
P.O. Box 4863
Englewood, CO 80155

All of these publications list information about contests and agents, as well as institutional, amateur, and professional theatres. They often tell you what each theatre is looking for. Some specialize in writers from certain states or want scripts of a certain style or about particular subjects (for example, children's plays, experimental works, women's issues, or gay and lesbian themes). These books also list each theatre's submission requirements. Some have entry forms you must send for, and others have specific guidelines you must follow. Some theatres will not accept an unsolicited script. If you send a script to a theatre that doesn't accept them you will get it back, unopened. Get a copy of *The Dramatists Source Book* or *The Playwright's Companion,* and you'll save time and money by finding the right contest or theatre for your particular script.

QUERY

Many theatres don't want entire scripts, but instead a *query*. A query is a script sample. If the theatre likes the sample, they'll request the entire script. Queries can be good for both the theatre and the playwright. The theatre has fewer scripts to read, and the playwright saves on copying and postage. A query contains a cover letter, resume, synopsis, a sample of dialogue, and a self-addressed, stamped postcard.

COVER LETTERS

When you send a query, enter a contest, or send any script, you'll want to include a *cover letter.* Here is an example of how your cover letter might look:

```
Friedrich Schiller
Artistic Director
Bacchae Theatre
389 North Whizzer
Chicago, IL 60609


Dear Mr. Schiller,

Innocent Thoughts is a controversial work that deals with the
relationship between whites and blacks, and Jews and Christians.

Innocent Thoughts won the 1996 National Playwrights Award from the
Unicorn Theatre in Kansas City, MO and is the winner of the Playwright's
Festival at the 24th Street Experimental Theatre in San Antonio, TX.

It's a simple play (only two characters and a rudimentary set).

The action takes place in a jury room where Arlen Weinberg, a Jewish
anthropology doctoral student, has come to be interviewed as a possible
expert witness in a murder trial. The lawyer is Ira Aldridge, a black
man who is defending a white policeman accused of killing a black man.
When they discover that they both grew up in Lawndale (a suburb of
```

Chicago that was once an all-Jewish neighborhood but is now all black)
fireworks result. Their childhoods, cultures, and convictions come into
conflict.

I'm a BFA acting student who lives in windy Wyoming.

I've enclosed a few pages of the script, a resume and a SAS postcard.

Would you like a copy of the full script?

Sincerely,

William Seneca

This cover letter includes

- *(paragraph 1)* a pitch line
- *(paragraphs 2 and 3)* information that might help get the play read or produced
- *(paragraph 4)* a brief synopsis
- *(paragraph 5)* a little something about the playwright

We'll examine the elements one by one.

The Pitch Line (paragraph 1):   A pitch is a short sentence (or two) designed to create interest. A pitch is not a deep examination of the play but a quick summary designed to make the reader say, "What an interesting situation/conflict/character." This short pitch is placed in the cover letter only to get the script read and doesn't have to be a totally accurate accounting of the play.

You want the pitch line to be interesting, but don't hard sell the script. We once saw a cover letter in which the playwright wrote, "This is a wonderful script, which you must read. If you're the type of producer who loves to please an audience, don't let this script go by." A playwright is not a used-car salesperson. In a well-written sentence or two, attempt to create interest; don't jam *your* opinion down their throats.

A pitch can also be done orally. Years ago I was at Greenblat's Delicatessen on Sunset Boulevard, when I heard a deep, resonant voice I had heard many times before. I turned to find the actor Billy Dee Williams standing beside me ordering a sandwich. I seized the moment and said, "Hi, I'm a playwright and I just finished a new play." He gave a polite "go away" smile. He wasn't interested. Then I pitched, "It's a modern version of Othello using Chicago cops." He smiled and said, "I'm sorry, but I don't . . ." Then he stopped, thought for a second, and finished, "I'd like to read that!" The pitch opened the door. It created a possibility. It doesn't always work. In fact, most of the time it doesn't, but a playwright should always have one ready. In any case, a pitch is always better than saying, "I just wrote this, like, play, would you read it?"

Information That Might Help Get the Play Read (paragraphs 2 and 3):
Include in your cover letter any information that might help get your script read:
it's won awards, you know someone at the theatre, you've had a play read or
produced there before, or perhaps it has a small cast and simple set or other
elements that might make it inexpensive to produce. If the theatre is interested
in a particular type of play (women's issues, musicals, children's plays), you
should point out that your play fits their needs.

Synopsis (paragraph 4)   A synopsis is a brief summary of the play. You don't
want to tell the whole story; you simply want to whet their appetites. In the
cover letter example, the playwright includes the synopsis right in the text
of the letter. If the synopsis is longer, then it should be included on a separate
sheet of paper, but no more than one page! Here is an example of a longer
synopsis:

A View from the Light Booth

A Farce By
Moss Williams
1007 Oresteia Ave.
Drocnoc, NC 28025
(704) 555-9456

Synopsis

A VIEW FROM THE LIGHT BOOTH is a comedy about the technical side of the theatre.
The entire play takes place in the light booth of the Chicago-Ensemble-Repertory-Group-
Theatre-Project on the final night of the Company's questionable production of
HAMLET.

The story of HAMLET, unfolding unseen in front of the light booth, is mirrored
inside the booth as Ross, the technical director, comes face to face with the new board
operator: his stepfather Charlie. It's not a happy reunion; there are too many ghosts.

Charlie's presence is the last thing Ross wants to deal with tonight. Ross, disillu-
sioned with the theatre, has decided that tonight will be his swan song—he's giving it
up to become a lighting designer for a rock band. Charlie, the purist, can't understand
why his stepson wants to leave the theatre.

As stepfather and stepson attempt to work out their troubled relationship they
must deal with the crises befalling HAMLET below: the cast comes down with food
poisoning; Yorick's skull is missing; the police want to shut them down; and worst of all,
the critic from the *Chicago Tribune* chooses this night to review the show. The techies
decide there is only one way to prevent disaster: The critic must die.

In the end, Charlie—by helping Ross rediscover his dreams—reawakens his stepson's love for him. The play ends happily, other than the fact that the critic survives.

A VIEW FROM THE LIGHT BOOTH is the NOISES OFF of technical theatre.

A Little Something About Yourself (paragraph 5):   A cover letter can also
contain a short sentence about yourself. It's not necessary, but if something
about you might interest others in your script, include it, briefly, in the cover
letter.

RESUME

A query might also include your resume. Your playwriting resume should include information about the plays you've written, where they've been produced, and awards you've won. You might also include information about degrees or special writing classes you've attended. If this is your first play and you don't have any worthwhile writing credits, don't include a resume.

DIALOGUE SAMPLE

A query includes a sample of dialogue. A theatre usually wants five to ten pages of the script to show that you can write interesting, sustained dialogue. It's best to include the beginning of your script. If your script is ready to be submitted, the first five to ten pages should be a good read and a perfect dialogue sample. If you want to send a dialogue sample from later in the script, you'll need to write a short introduction to set up the scene and characters.

SELF-ADDRESSED, STAMPED POSTCARD

Include a self-addressed, stamped postcard (SASP) so that theatres can let you know if they're interested. The back of the postcard might look like this (almost all laser-quality printers can be set up to print postcards using the envelope setting):

```
From: Bacchae Theatre
389 North Whizzer
Chicago, IL 60609


WOULD YOU LIKE TO SEE A COPY OF:

INNOCENT THOUGHTS?

_____  Yes, send script.

_____  Thank you, but no.

NOTES:

_____

_____
```

You might also include a *brief* pitch of other plays you have written. The card would look like this:

From: Bacchae Theatre
389 North Whizzer
Chicago, IL 60609

WOULD YOU LIKE TO SEE A COPY OF:

INNOCENT THOUGHTS?

————— Yes, send script.

————— Thank you, but no.

I've enclosed a brief synopsis of several other
plays I've written. Would you like to see a copy of

————— ALL THE THINGS I SHOULD HAVE SAID

————— COMMA HAPPY

————— SMALL SACRIFICES

SENDING QUERIES ELECTRONICALLY

Sending a query via e-mail is in its infancy but it is growing. Each year, more and more theatres are accepting e-mailed queries. This method can be very helpful to a playwright because it eliminates postage and can speed up the response, but there are two important areas to consider before you electronically contact a theatre. First, never send e-mail queries to a theatre unless you know they accept such messages. Newsletters like *Market InSights for Playwrights* will tell you which theatres are open to e-mail queries. Second, sending an e-mail query takes a great deal of preparation. The dialogue sample is the problem. E-mail throws off the format, making your script look unprofessional, even unreadable, when it arrives. Using the "file attachment" feature that most E-mail programs have doesn't help because it will only work if you and the receiver are using the same word processing program. If the theatre has a different word processing program, your script will arrive as gibberish.

The best way to send an e-mail script sample is do a "save as" and change the script into an ASCII (text with line breaks) file. An ASCII file formats in text only, this makes it readable by all word processing programs. Because it loses its format (including tabs, underlines, bolds, and accents), you will need to change the format of your play. Theatres that accept e-mail queries understand that the proper format is impossible. The best format for a sample script e-mail query looks like this:

IMITATING LIFE

TIME - October - The present.

SETTING - The set is fractured. Many different locations are expressed with only a few props and few set pieces.

PLACE - Several locations around Los Angeles.

SCENE 1 - A THEATRE - WEST HOLLYWOOD

(Larry Finer, a man with the energy of a bumble bee, walks out in front of the set. It's almost like the previous scene was part of a play.)

LARRY
Lovely reading. Lovely choices. I want to thank our lovely actors and all you lovely, concerned people for staying after. Treat today: the actual playwright is in our presence. May I present Arthur Philip Wear. Applause?

(Art, the playwright, walks out on stage. Light applause. LARRY grabs two stools and places them center stage.)

LARRY
First, it's an honor and a splendor for our little black box to have you as part of our Monday Night New Plays Reading Series and Cook Off. Tonight Bob brought his fantastic pork tar tar. It sounds unsafe but it's lovely. Second, our playwright doesn't have a lot of time. Busy man. Very busy. (to Art) What is it you have to run off to? Important business?

ART
No. My father's dying.

LARRY
Family stuff. And we all know how tragic that is! Playwrights lead such tragic, obsessed lives. Look at O'Neill.

Once you have reformatted your script and saved it as an ASCII file, you'll need to e-mail the script sample and query to yourself. This is the only way to make sure the script will arrive in a readable form. Correct mistakes and send it to yourself again, until it arrives looking the way you want it to. Once you are satisfied, e-mail the query to the theatre.

The first time you do this, it may take several hours to make the pitch look professional, but after the initial effort you will have it ready to go on a moment's notice. Just think of the postage and photocopying you will save.

FINAL THOUGHTS ON QUERIES

A query might also include the cast of characters and information on the setting. If you are sending out many queries, you'll want to keep the number of pages to a minimum in order to save on postage. Above all, your query must be clean, well typed, and organized so that it can be quickly read. The reader will judge your ability to write by your cover letter and synopsis. A poorly written query can keep a well-written script from being read.

SENDING A FULL SCRIPT

When you submit a full script, not only should it look professional and follow the proper format given in the last chapter, but it must be neat and clean. You don't want to submit a script that looks as though it's been read and rejected by several theatres. When a script is returned from a theatre, inspect it before you send it back out. Check for pencil marks, bent pages, and general appearance. If you use a spiral binder, you can improve the look of the script by replacing the title page and cover.

SASE

When submitting a script, most contests and theatres require the playwright to enclose a self-addressed, stamped envelope (SASE).[1] Unfortunately, most theatres aren't exact about what they want. Some want a business-sized envelope to send the rejection letter. Most want a large envelope with proper postage to return your script once they've rejected it. Others want both.

If you don't enclose a large SASE, you won't get your script back. (As if the cost to the playwright isn't great enough, you must pay to have the script and rejection letter returned.) If you do not want your script back, then you should say in your letter that there is no need to return the script (better yet, ask

---

[1] Never send checks, cash, or money orders to cover return postage.

for the script to be recycled). In some cases *The Dramatists Source Book* or *The Playwright's Companion* will let you know exactly what type of SASE a theatre or contest wants.

REJECTION LETTERS AND GLUING PAGES

Rejection letters differ a great deal from one theatre or contest to the next. Some are short and to the point. Others try to give a few words of encouragement. Almost all are form letters.

You will seldom get comments as to why your script was rejected. Often, the most a rejection letter will say is, "Your script isn't right for our theatre at this time."

Never call a theatre demanding feedback or an explanation as to why your script was rejected. A kind letter, explaining that you're a beginning playwright and in need of feedback, may or may not get a reaction. Most theatres are understaffed and don't have time to explain their decisions. Many times they don't know who read your script and if they do, that person won't remember it.

One way of getting feedback without the reader knowing it is to glue pages. This is done by placing a slight, pin-drop of glue on certain pages (for example pages 5, 25, and 50). Place it close to the binding where it won't interfere. When the reader opens to that particular page, the tiny drop of glue breaks. Later, when the script is returned, the playwright can quickly see if the glue is broken. If it is, the writer knows that the reader made it at least that far into the script. If the glue is still sealed, she knows the reader became bored.

You'll discover quite a few scripts returned totally unread. Some theatres get so backlogged they simply have to return whole piles of scripts without consideration. We were once at a theatre that rejected a six-foot-high stack of scripts simply to make room for a new office copier. This is nothing but a waste of the playwright's time and money, but it does happen. Gluing pages will let you know if a theatre has such a practice, so you can avoid sending it your next effort.

SUBMISSION RECORD

Playwrights should keep a record of all submissions. This record includes date sent, date returned, contact person, theatre address, and reaction. Occasionally, a playwright will receive a rejection letter saying the theatre is not interested in this play but would like to see the writer's next effort. This should be noted in the submission record. A submission record can be kept in your computer by using database programs. A submission record might look something like this:

Name	Organization	Address	Notes	Date Sent	Result	Telephone & Notes
Bob Jones, Art. director	Mirror Repertory Company	352 E. 159th Street New York, NY 10002	Hated Script	1/1/96	Reject 2/3/96	212-555-6087
Jan Wright, Literary Con.	Mise en Scene Theatre Co.	11305 Cotillion Blvd. N. Hollywood, CA 90332	Would like to see next script	2/21/96	Reject 4/31/96	NA
Lynn Felicia, Director	Kansas Repertory Theatre	4949 Parsipany Street Kansas City, MO	Wants to see script!	10/4/96	Request script 1/3/97	NA
Bob Horton, Director	Morristown Theatre Guild	Box 1502-3 Morristown, TN 37814	No reaction	10/4/95	Rejected 1/4/96	615-555-9260
Ayette Sams, Art. Director	First Street Playhouse	423 Valerie White Ave. Ithaca, NY 14850		11/9/96	Waiting	NA
N. A.	Mountain View Cabaret Theatre	201 S. Cleese Ave. Mountain View, CA 94040		3/9/96	Waiting	415-555-MCVT
N. A.	M-Square Entertainment	26 Shatner Ave. New York, NY 10003		1/18/96	Reject 5/9/96	212-555-0990
Mark Wilber, Art. Director	Chocolate Bayou Theatre Co.	Box 130007 Houston, TX 77219		1/18/96		713-555-0070
Tommy Lawton Owner	The Theatre Scene	294 Stewart Street Bldg. F San Francisco, CA 94123		6/18/96	Returned Theatre out of business	415-555-8001
Bryant Wilson, Art. Director	Velvet Theatre Center	3636 Velvet Creek Blvd. Dallas, TX 75219	Interested in next script	12/2/96	Script request 4/3/96 Rejected 8/5/96	214-555-8210

See Appendix F for a list of computer programs that help a writer keep track of submissions.

HOW THEY WILL EVALUATE YOUR PLAY

Every theatre uses a different method when evaluating a play. On the following page are examples of evaluation forms currently used by the Utah Playfest Contest and the Mill Mountain Theatre New Play Competition are typical of forms used across the country. Put yourself in the reader's shoes and take the time to fill in these forms. Does your play pass the test? Would you recommend it?

THE HARSH WORLD OF THE CONTEST

Years ago, while putting myself through UCLA film school, I worked as a secretary for Interscope, a Hollywood production company. I was in charge of sending scripts out for *coverage*.[2] The banality of my job gave me time to concoct a wicked scheme. I took one of my screenplays and sent it to a reader under a pen name, so my boss wouldn't discover what I was up to. If the coverage came back good, I was going to show him the script, but the coverage came back, "This is the worst screenplay ever written." So I sent it to another reader, a female reader and gave my title page a female author. It came back, "Not bad. We ought to have her in and see if she has anything else." Finally I wrote on the title page, "A new screenplay by William Goldman *Jr.*" I was passing myself off as the son of the author of *Butch Cassidy and the Sundance Kid, Marathon Man,* and *The Princess Bride,* certainly one of the most popular, talented, and richest screenwriters in Hollywood. This time the coverage came back, "Some problems, but wonderful." Not one word of the screenplay was different.

Rejection is an integral part of being a writer. One reader will call you brilliant; the next will label you an amateur. You have to learn to deal with it and keep going. Set a goal: you'll enter one contest a week, or one every two weeks, whatever your budget will allow, but enter. It's the only way to win. When the rejection letters start arriving, remember they mean you're trying. If you win one contest for every fifty you enter, you're doing well.

SEVENTEEN SUREFIRE WAYS TO GET YOUR SCRIPT REJECTED

Linda Eisenstein is an award-winning playwright who for a decade was the director of Cleveland Public Theatre's Festival of New Plays. This meant she had

---

[2] Hollywood producers seldom have time to read, so they hire professional readers who report back to the producers. Their report is called coverage.

UTAH PLAYFEST
READER'S RESPONSE FORM

Short Play _____   Full Length _____

Title of play _____

Name of
Author _____

Name of
Reader _____

Date Assigned _____ Date Due _____

Recommended for Consideration _____

Not Recommended for Consideration _____

Here is an evaluation form you may consider using in reviewing the play you have
been asked to read. Please check items that you see as problem areas.

THOUGHT/PREMISE: _____ is not clear
                          _____ is too obvious, stated openly
                          _____ play centers on more than one thought
                          _____ characters do not suit it well
                          _____ plot does not suit it well

CHARACTERS: _____ read like unadulterated stereotypes
                          _____ do not grow on "discover" anything
                          _____ are not opposed to each other
                          _____ are unrealistic
                          _____ do not demonstrate conflict well

LANGUAGE/DICTION: _____ is unrealistic (stiff/poetic)
                          _____ is not suited to characters/mood
                          _____ exhibits little variety among characters
                          _____ some speeches are too long
                          _____ lacks foreshadowing/plants

CONFLICT: _____ is static
                          _____ no concrete objectives
                          _____ is unclear/unfocused
                          _____ focus of conflict changes during the play
                          _____ jumps

FORMAT: _____ actor or stage directions
                          _____ title page
                          _____ character names (capitalized, "cont'd")
                          _____ spacing (single/double)
                          _____ pagination

PLOT: _____ has no sense of urgency
                          _____ is cinematic (too much freedom with unities)
                          _____ is not coherent or logical
                          _____ is predictable/unoriginal (no twists)
                          _____ scenes are too long/short
                          _____ needs equilibrium/denouement

PRESENTATION: _____ Not typed or poorly typed
                          _____ not neat (e.g. smudges, correction by hand)
                          _____ typos, misspellings, bad grammar
                          _____ improperly stapled or bound
                          _____ length of play (too short/long)

COMMENTS:

written by Mark Damen copyright Utah State University

MILL MOUNTAIN THEATRE NEW PLAY COMPETITION
Reader Critique Report

Recommended to selection committee   YES   NO

Appropriate idea/treatment for MMT?   YES   NO

Ready "to Go"   YES   NO

Good idea but needs work   YES   NO

TITLE _____

AUTHOR _____

ADDRESS _____

TELEPHONE NO. _____

History of Play _____

_____

Agent _____

Address _____

Phone _____

Rights

Play number _____

Date Processed _____

Reader _____
On a scale of 1-10 what is
your rank of this play? _____

Received _____

SASE   YES   NO

PC   YES   NO

Returned _____

Standard refusal   YES   NO

Other _____

Forwarded to judges _____

NOTES: _____

_____

_____

Type of play:
Musical   Comedy   Farce   Sit-com   Melodrama   Drama   Tragedy
Memory   Monologue   Religious   Historical   Pseudo-historical   Satire

No. of Acts _____ Pages _____ Historical Period _____

No. of women _____ Ages _____   No. of men _____ Ages _____

Special characteristics _____

Costumes: Many   Few   Pull   Designer   Simple   Possible   Period
             Construct   Rent   Street wear   Transformational

Setting: _____

No. of Scene changes _____

I did (or did not) like this play. State opinions and give concrete examples.

_____

_____

In general the characters are: Stereotype   Prototype   Unbelievable

                                  Unusual   Interesting   Well-developed

                                  Undefined   Flat   Biographical

Reader Critique Report   Page 2

On a scale of 1-10 does this play have

Astonishment (immediate interest?) _____

Suspense _____

Satisfaction _____

Conflict _____

Counter conflict _____

Do I believe _____

Do I care _____

Am I interested _____

Main Idea or Theme (Author's intent) _____

_____

Imagery _____

_____

Plot line _____

_____

_____

Is there a permanent change in one or more characters? _____

_____

What is unusual about this play (different?) _____

_____

What is exceptionally good about this play? _____

_____

What is exceptionally poor about this play? _____

_____

I feel that this play would be sent to the selection committee because _____

_____

I feel that this play needs further work because _____

_____

I feel this play is worth the extra work because _____

_____

to read and reject hundreds of new scripts each year. She has come up with the following list of surefire ways to get your script *rejected:*

1. Write a play with nothing but unpleasant characters. This is an age of antiheroes, after all. Make sure no one is onstage whom an audience could possibly like or want to spend time with. If audience members wanted to be comfortable or happy, they should have stayed home.

2. Choose a topic that you think is marketable but you don't really care much about; after all, a playwright should be able to crank out something mildly entertaining without a strong point of view. Something like an episode of your favorite sitcom should go over well, don't you think?

3. Write a play that requires a realistic set change every three or four minutes. Or that has at least two or three insurmountable props, perhaps a driveable car that goes on and off stage. Or lots of cool special effects. If *Miss Saigon* can have a helicopter that hovers and lands onstage, why can't you?

4. Don't include a cast list at the front with the names and number of characters; after all, you wouldn't want the theater to be intimidated by the cast size right away. Let them discover the vast army of characters by reading the play. Make sure to include plenty of characters that have only one or two lines. After all, actors need work.

5. Don't number the pages, either. Let the theatre guess how long it'll take by hefting it. Anyway, 160 pages isn't all THAT long, is it? Especially when the play is in five acts and twenty-three scenes.

6. Leave the pages loose or stuck together with a paper clip that easily falls off. (This is especially effective when you've been diligent about rule 5 above.)

7. While you're at it, invent your own play format; the one from Samuel French or *Dramatists Sourcebook* is sure to be too confining. Be creative with your spelling and grammar, too. All of this will show an irrepressible original mind at work.

8. Open your play with several pages of stage directions, in long, impenetrable blocks. Describe the sets and furnishings in such numbing detail that the set designer will know exactly where to buy the priceless antiques you need for scrupulous authenticity.

9. Make sure that the first ten or fifteen pages are nothing but exposition or trivia by minor characters. Most audiences don't settle in or stop rustling their programs until fifteen minutes into the play. Don't give them anything meaty until their bottoms have conformed to their chairs.

10. Put in lots of stage directions for every speech, indicating exactly how you think an actor should say the line. Example:

```
                                    JANE
                                    (coyly)
          No.

                                    JOHN:
                                    (very angry, but holding it
                                    in)
          Why not?

                                    JANE
                                    (flirting more hesitantly now)
          Because.

                                    JOHN
                                    (swept away with passion)
          All right, then.
```

11. Be sure to include at least one three-page monologue, per character in every scene. And do keep all the characters onstage whether they have anything to do or say in the scene or not; after all, the actors need to practice concentrating on listening intently for a half hour without dialogue or stage business.

12. Make the dialogue as generic as possible. You might, for instance, write an absurdist play where all the characters are named MAN and WOMAN 1, 2, 3, and so on, and they all spout general philosophical abstractions until it's hard to tell their characters and dialogue apart. That way your play will be intellectually deep and universal, and everyone will be able to identify with it.

13. Alternatively, base your play on your own life, particularly your frustrations and how no one understands and appreciates you. Don't change ANYTHING; people need to experience unvarnished reality.

14. Print your script on a dot-matrix printer in which you haven't changed the ribbon in years. Use a "creative" font, such as all italics or cursive. Then photocopy it on the lightest possible setting to conserve toner. Even better, write your script in longhand. Anything to make it to stand out from all the others.

15. Send your script to every theater you ever heard of. Don't bother finding out what kinds of plays thcy usually do; they're bound to love your masterpiece, no matter what. After all, everyone, from a radical experimental company to a Shakespeare festival to a community theater that only does musicals, NEEDS to experience your gripping fifty-three-character historical play about Civil War amputees.

16. Diligently follow up by calling the theater every week or so until you're sure your script has been received and read. That way the staff will be sure to remember your name.

17. Leave your address and phone number off your script, and don't include a SASE (self-addressed stamped envelope, manuscript-sized) for return of your script either. That way, you'll never have to face rejection—because the theater won't be able to find you.[3]

SECOND-PRODUCTION BLUES

The playwright's struggle is not over when a play has been produced or has won a contest. Second productions can be harder to find than the first. Many theatres are not interested in producing a play once the cachet of being a "premiere" wears off. Second productions attract less publicity and fewer kudos than a first run. (hundreds of playwriting contests accept plays that have never been produced, but only a few are open to plays that have had one production.) Other plays are left in limbo because of an incompetent first production or bad reviews. Whatever the reason, playwrights often have trouble finding second productions. The key to success is exposure. You can't sit back and wait, you must continue to mail scripts to every theatre you can find (include the good reviews, throw away the bad), and push for that next production. *The Playwright's Companion* and other source books listed in this chapter also have information on theatres that are looking for new and previously produced scripts.

THE INTERNET AND WORLD WIDE WEB

The Internet and World Wide Web interconnect millions of computers, from personal laptops to huge main frames. Anyone can call up any particular Web site and download information on just about anything, including playwriting.

The Internet offers an incredible number of resources for playwrights and has many databases in which playwrights can list their work, get information about playwriting, read reviews, get tips from the pros, learn about workshops, take on-line courses and get information about theatres and theatre people. The problem is that it can be addicting. Surfing the Internet and visiting Web sites can be so much fun that it can interrupt your writing schedule. The Net is a great tool, but it won't write your next play. Appendix G lists playwriting Web sites.

BROADWAY

Broadway is in trouble. People have been saying that for years. Each new advent—movies, television, five-hundred-channel cable networks—has pushed

---

[3] First published in *Ohio Writer,* Volume IX, Issue 5; another version appeared in "Stage Directions," Feb. 1996. Reprinted with permission of the author.

Broadway one step closer to its grave. In 1965, forty new plays opened on Broadway. In 1995, there were fewer than ten. Even playwrights such as Neil Simon have trouble filling a thousand-seat house. This is a real problem for young playwrights, because the A-list of playwrights whose plays used to open on Broadway must now look to regional theatres for productions. This drives the lesser-known playwrights down to the small theatres and the unknown playwrights out of the picture entirely. It's a domino effect, and the loser is the beginning playwright. Until Broadway can solve its problems, the only solution for the young playwright is to become more aggressive. The age of the shy, sensitive playwright, who simply wrote the play and hoped someone would discover her, is over. The beginning playwright must now self-promote, advertise, and push herself into the spotlight.

THE DRAMATISTS GUILD

The Dramatists Guild functions as the playwrights' union, representing you in contract and royalty disputes, legal battles, and government issues. The problem is that the Dramatists Guild is an *open-shop* union, and therefore you don't have to be a member to get produced. Open-shop unions are not as powerful as *closed-shop* unions, in which you must be a member as a condition of employment. The Writers Guild of America, the union representing television and screenwriters, is a closed-shop union. Membership in the WGA is required to write for any major studio or network.[4] A closed-shop union can call meaningful strikes and therefore has the power to keep wages high.

The disparity of power in the two unions is a result of how screenwriters and playwrights market their work. As the Supreme Court sees it, a playwright rents a play to a theatre. The playwright retains ownership of the play (even years after death), so is considered a part of management. Managers cannot form unions, and therefore the playwright is left with a helpful but weakened guild. Screenwriters are considered writers for hire—that is, they can sell a screenplay, thereby relinquishing all future rights. Because screenwriters are considered employees, they can and have formed an airtight, powerful union.

Unlike the WGA, it's easy to join the Dramatists Guild. All playwrights, beginners to professionals, can and should join the Dramatists Guild. Established in 1920, the Guild provides its members many services, publications, and activities (although activities are limited to major cities such as New York, Chicago, and Los Angeles). The Guild's newsletter and quarterly magazine give members detailed information on contests, taxes, news bulletins, as well as interesting interviews with theatre professionals. It also offers its members a toll-free hotline to answer or refer business and legal questions, as well as advise on options, contracts, copyrights, and provide information on how to deal with

---

[4] For more information on the WGA, see chapter 12.

producers and agents. Members get reduced rates on theatre tickets, legal services, and health insurance. The Guild also maintains committees for women and
minority playwrights.

There are three levels of Dramatists Guild membership. *Student members*
are given a special low rate. *Associate* membership is for all playwrights
(whether you've been produced or not), and *active* members (who are allowed
to vote) must have had a major production on Broadway, off Broadway, or in a
professional regional theatre. To join the Dramatists Guild, call (212) 398-9366
or write:

Dramatists Guild, 1501 Broadway Suite, #701New York, New York 10036.

EXERCISES

Exercise #1
Write a short, well-constructed cover letter.

Exercise #2
Write one short pitch of your play (one to three sentences) and one page-long
pitch. Test-market each pitch on friends and classmates by having them read it.
You can't please everyone, but you can figure out whether your pitch stimulates
interest in 50 percent of the class. If you can't come up with an interesting pitch
for your play, your play may be unfocused and lack a central action or spine.

Exercise #3
Orally pitch your play. Can you come up with a short pitch that cuts to the core
of your play? Test the pitch on the class. Are people interested?

MARK TWAIN'S RULES OF WRITING

1. That a tale shall accomplish something and arrive somewhere.

2. That the episodes of a tale shall be necessary parts of the tale and shall
   help to develop it.

3. That the personages in a tale shall be alive, except in the case of corpses,
   and that always the reader shall be able to tell the corpses from the others.

4. That the personages in a tale, both dead and alive, shall exhibit a sufficient
   excuse for being there.

5. That when the personages of a tale deal in conversation, the talk shall
   sound like human talk, and be talk such as human beings would be likely
   to talk in the given circumstances and have a discoverable meaning, also a
   discoverable purpose and show of relevancy, and remain in the neighbor-

hood of the subject at hand, and be interesting to the reader, and help out the tale, and stop when the people cannot think of anything more to say.

6. That when the author describes the character of a personage in his tale, the conduct and conversation of that personage shall justify said description.

7. That when a person talks like an illustrated, gilt-edged, tree-calf, hand-tooled, seven-dollar Friendship's Offering in the beginning of a paragraph, he shall not talk like a minstrel in the end of it.

8. That crass stupidities shall not be played upon the reader as "the craft of the woodsman, the delicate art of the forest," by either the author or the people in the tale.

9. That the personages in the tale shall confine themselves to possibilities and let miracles alone; or, if they venture a miracle, the author must so plausibly set it forth as to make it look possible and reasonable.

10. That the author shall make the reader feel a deep interest in the personages of his tale and in their fate, and that he shall make the reader love the good people in the tale and hate the bad ones.

11. That the characters in the tale shall be so clearly defined that the reader can tell beforehand what each will do in a given emergency.

12. The author shall say what he is proposing to say, not merely come near it.

13. Use the right word, not its second cousin.

14. Eschew surplusage.

15. Not omit necessary details.

16. Avoid slovenliness of form.

17. Use good grammar.

18. Employ a simple and straightforward style.

Fenimore Cooper's Literary Offenses 1895
From *Greatly Exaggerated*
Edited by Alex Ayres

Chapter 10

STUDENT-WRITTEN PLAYS

Playwrights read plays. Published, professional plays are a good start, but sometimes it helps to read plays written by playwrights of your own age and level. This chapter contains three student-written plays. The first script is *Penis Envy,* a one-act written by Caroline Rule and a solid college-level first play that came in second place at a regional American College

> *Playwrights are not the creative force which governs the world; we are only second-rate creators who analyze, summarize by trial and error, who are happy and acclaimed as geniuses when we disengage one ray of truth.*
>
> Emile Zola

Theater Festival one-act play competition (region VII). The second, *Lemon 7-14,* written by Scott Pardue, took second place in the National American College Theater Festival. The last, *Acetylene,* by Erik Ramsey, won the American College Theatre Festival short play contest, the highest award a student playwright can win. The playwright received a $2,500 prize, publication through Samuel French, a production at the Kennedy Center, and an agent.

Evaluate each play. What are the problems and strengths of each script? Where has each playwright succeeded, and where is the script weak? Are the scripts formatted correctly? Do any of the plays follow formula? Which characters are well developed and why? How does your writing compare to these plays?

PENIS ENVY

A play in one act by
Caroline Rule

Cast of Characters

Julia................ 28

Kelly................ 28

Diedra............... 28

Siobhan.............. 29

Heather.............. 23

Time: Around 8:00 pm in April--the present.
Place: Denver, Colorado.
Setting: The living room of Julia Ramsey. It is tastefully decorated in a style that suggests comfort, but not wealth. The kitchen is directly upstage of the living room, separated by a breakfast bar/counter-type arrangement, so that the kitchen is separate, but visible. There are two doors leading out of the living room. The one on the right is the front door of the house; the one on the left leads into a hallway, which presumably leads to the bedrooms. There is a television in the DR corner of the living room, facing upstage.

1.

Penis Envy

ACT ONE

(At rise, JULIA is in the kitchen, preparing snacks. She is pretty, and dressed comfortably. She moves around, checking the oven, adjusting the temperature, etc. She goes into the living room and puts a CD on the stereo. The song ''Come On Eileen'' by Dexy's Midnight Runners comes on. She straightens the couch throw pillows, then moves back into the kitchen, takes a bottle of wine out of the refrigerator, etc. The phone rings, in the kitchen. She picks up the cordless phone and goes into the living room to turn the stereo down while talking.)

JULIA

Hello? Hi! What's up? . . . Uh-huh . . . Oh. Umm . . . Yeah. I don't mind, as long as everyone else doesn't . . . Sure. Okay. I'll see you in a little bit, then. Okay. Bye.

(She continues fussing in the kitchen, then moves into the living room and turns the stereo back up. The doorbell rings. She opens the front door to KELLY.)

JULIA

Hey, Kel! Come on in.

(They hug, general salutations.)

KELLY

Thanks.

(She takes off her coat. She is somewhat overweight, but pretty; she is expensively dressed. She has a small overnight bag on her shoulder.)

Can I just stick this in the bedroom?

JULIA

Yeah--put it in the big one, though. Alex is asleep, I hope, in his room.

KELLY *(Moving to the hallway)*

I thought your mom was going to take him tonight.

JULIA

She was, but this Bill guy asked her out again, so I said it was no big deal.

KELLY
(from hallway)

Is he the policeman one?

2.

                              JULIA
No, that's Dan. This one's a movie critic for channel four.

                                   (She moves back into the kitchen and
                                   checks the oven again.)

                              KELLY
                              (back in living room)
Bill Dobson? The red light, green light guy?

                              JULIA
I don't know. I guess so. Was he asleep?

                                   (KELLY samples from the tray JULIA has
                                   just taken out of the oven.)

                              KELLY
I didn't check. Do you want me to?

                              JULIA
No, that's all right. I'll do it.

                                   (She starts down hallway.)
Diedra called. I guess she's bringing some girl from the magazine with
her. Heather. Has she mentioned her to you?

                              KELLY
Huh-uh. Who is she?

                              JULIA
                              (Pause. She comes in from the hall.)
He's out cold, thank God. I have no idea who she is. She called right
before you got here, asking if she could bring her, so I said okay. I guess
she's an intern there, or something? I'm sure she's nice. I was just kind
of surprised. She knows this is supposed to be just us.

                                   (She offers hors d'oeuvre on a plate.)
Go ahead and sit down. Want some wine? It's Fetzer.

                              KELLY
                              (sitting on couch)
Sure. When did you get that bed? It's fantastic.

                              JULIA
                              (pouring wine, in kitchen)
Isn't it huge? Paul bought it for me last week. It was our 4 year and
3 month anniversary, or something like that. It was actually kind of
strange. I came home from Safeway at like three in the afternoon, and he's
already home, waiting for me. Said he wanted to show me something, and
there it is, this huge new bed. It's great, though. I guess. I feel like
I'm swimming in the damn thing, even with both of us in it.

                              KELLY
Wow. Must be nice.

                              JULIA
Yeah. He does this every now and then, you know? Just buys me something
for no particular reason . . . like when he got the water-jet things for

                         (CONTINUED)

3.

KELLY (CONTINUED)
the tub. Practically tore up the whole bathroom to turn the tub into a whirlpool, and now he hardly ever uses it. *(she smiles)* I guess that's just the type of guy he is.

KELLY
Yeah. God, remember this song? This is the greatest song. This is like, our entire freshman year, this song. What CD is it?

JULIA
One of those K-Tel collections. Biggest Hits of the Early Eighties, or something like that. $4.99 at Tower Records. That's why I put it on; to kind of set the mood. The whole thing's pretty good.

KELLY
(flipping through a Rolling Stone)
You'll have to let me borrow it. Where is Paul, anyway?

JULIA
Well, I told him we were having it here this month, and that he would have to disappear for the night, and he said no problem. I assume he's at work. He has some big contract due Monday anyway, so he said the extra time at work would do him some good.

(She brings two glasses of wine into the living room and sets them on the coffee table. She sits on the couch next to KELLY.)
I don't know. It's been weird lately. Last night, I asked him if there was something wrong, and he--

KELLY
(interrupts)
I saw Brian at the supermarket yesterday, in the Health and Beauty Aids aisle. He was buying corn removers. He said hi, but I just ignored him. I don't know what he thought of that. I hope it pissed him off, you know?

JULIA
(a little put out, still smiles)
Oh. Yeah.

KELLY
I don't know. What is the deal with all these men? I have the worst luck with guys. They're always real jerks. Well, at least he wasn't gay. For once. I swear, I have this infallible gay-dar.

JULIA
(has heard this before)
Yeah, I know.

(She goes back into the kitchen. The doorbell rings.)
Would you get that? It's probably Siobhan.

(KELLY opens the door. It is SIOBHAN. She is dressed very sloppy/artsy/ stylishly. She has one of those bohemian little Guatemalan bags and carries a bottle of wine.)

4.

                              SIOBHAN
Hi, guys.

                              (She comes in and walks straight over to
                              the TV, shedding her coat as she goes,
                              and taking a tape out of her bag,
                              leaving the bag on the floor.)
What time is it?

                              KELLY
                              (checking her watch)
Uh . . . Eight nineteen. Why?

                              SIOBHAN
My show is on at eight-thirty. I brought a tape so I could record it. *(an
afterthought)* If that's okay.

                              (JULIA comes in with the hors d'oeuvres
                              and sets them on the coffee table.)

                              JULIA
Of course. Is it the one on Sarah Bernhardt?

                              SIOBHAN
Yup. It should be pretty good. We got an interview with her niece, and
there's a nice collage of her stuff at the end.

                              (She turns on the TV and changes it to
                              PBS. It is currently on a show preview.
                              She puts in the tape and turns the
                              stereo off.)
I brought some Fetzer.

                              JULIA
                              (amused)
Oh good. I was thinking we might run out.

                              (She takes it and puts it in the
                              fridge.)

                              KELLY
It's a wonder you make any money at all . . . Friday nights at eight thirty
on PBS.

                              SIOBHAN
                              (a pause)
Well. Yes. I'm just glad it's on. *(pointedly)* Not everyone is lucky enough
to get paid for doing what they like to do.

                              KELLY
I like what I do.

                              SIOBHAN
I wasn't talking about you.

                              JULIA
                              *(coming in from the kitchen, clears her
                              throat)*
Can I get you a glass of wine, Siobhan?

5.

                              SIOBHAN
Sure, that'd be great. I'll get it, if you want.

                             JULIA
Okay. Glasses are above the sink.

                             (SIOBHAN heads into the kitchen. JULIA
                             picks her bag up off the floor and takes
                             it into the bedroom. When she returns,
                             SIOBHAN and KELLY are sitting on the
                             couch, intent on the TV, not saying a
                             word.)

                             JULIA
                             (hanging up SIOBHAN's coat)
Diedra called a little while ago. She's bringing someone with her.

                             SIOBHAN
Oh really? Who?

                             JULIA
A girl from the magazine. Heather. She's new.

                             SIOBHAN
That's weird.

                             JULIA
                             (sitting between them)
She didn't sound weird on the phone. She acted like it was no big deal, so I said it was fine. I'm sure it'll be all right.

                             (There is a pause. All three women are
                             watching the TV.)

                             SIOBHAN
Maybe they're lovers.

                             KELLY
What?!

                             JULIA
                           (dismissing it)
Oh, no. Diedra?

                             (SIOBHAN smiles and shrugs.)

                             KELLY
No way. Even if she was, she wouldn't bring her here. It wouldn't be the same. That'd be like bringing a guy.

                             SIOBHAN
How would that be like bringing a guy?

                             KELLY
Well, you know. If they were . . . lovers, if she was in love with a woman, it would be like having a guy here with us.

6.

                    SIOBHAN
Well, anyway, I'm just saying it's a possibility. *(to JULIA, a little
jokingly)* I seem to remember you two did a little bit of experimentation
back at school . . .

                    JULIA
Oh, please! We were drunk! We were only kidding around, Jesus Christ. And
all we did was kiss. *(she looks thoughtful)* Besides, she likes sex too
much. Sex with guys, I mean. Don't you remember that guy, what was his name
. . . we called him "Wonder Schlong," because that was all she could talk
about, the size of his . . . God, what was his name?

                    KELLY
                    (laughing)
I have no idea. We never called him by his real name.

                              (They are all laughing. The doorbell
                              rings again. JULIA opens the door, still
                              chuckling guiltily. It is DIEDRA, who
                              has HEATHER with her. DIEDRA is the kind
                              of woman who would wear baby-doll
                              dresses with combat boots.)

                    JULIA
Hi, babe! We were just wondering where you were.

                              (They hug. HEATHER stands a little off
                              to the side, looking very uncomfortable.
                              DIEDRA gives their coats to JULIA, who
                              takes them and goes down the hall into
                              the bedroom. DIEDRA brings HEATHER down
                              into the living room.)

                    DIEDRA
Heather, this is Siobhan Reese and Kelly King; guys, this is my friend
Heather Maxwell. She works with me in editing.

                              (They all shake hands.)

                    KELLY
Nice to meet you.

                    SIOBHAN
Hello.

                    HEATHER
                    (very quiet, almost murmuring)
Hello.

                              (General pause. Everyone is standing
                              there. JULIA comes out from the hall.)

                    DIEDRA
Heather, this is Julia Ramsey. Julia, Heather. Here, I brought some
Cuervo.

                              (She hands JULIA a bottle of tequila.)

                    JULIA
                    (taking bottle into kitchen)
It's good to meet you, Heather.

HEATHER

It's nice to meet you, too.

(Another pause.)

KELLY

So . . . where are you from, Heather?

HEATHER

Um, I'm from here. From Aurora, I mean. I just graduated from CU, though.
In December. So I just moved back. In January, I mean.

JULIA

Oh, CU? That's where we all went.

HEATHER

Yes, Diedra's mentioned it. I, um, I brought some wine.

(She gives JULIA the bottle.)

JULIA
(looking at the bottle)

Oh, great . . . thanks.

(As JULIA takes the wine into the
kitchen, she mouths the word "Gallo?"
to KELLY, and makes a face. Another
pause. SIOBHAN suddenly turns to the TV
set, turning up the volume.)

SIOBHAN

I think this is it!

DIEDRA

Oh, is your show on tonight? I almost forgot.

KELLY
(under her breath)

I would have liked to forget . . .

SIOBHAN
(checking her watch)

Oh no, wait, this isn't it . . . this is still the show before. Damn.

(They all watch the TV anyway. Everyone
sits or kneels on the floor in front of
the TV. It is a documentary on the life
of Sigmund Freud. A narrator is reading
from a passage by Freud. During this
speech, all of the women are thoroughly
entranced with the screen.)

TV NARRATOR

". . . One cannot very well doubt the importance of envy for the penis. . . .
As regards little girls, we can say of them that they feel greatly at a
disadvantage owing to their lack of a big, visible penis, and that they
envy boys for possessing one and that, in the main for this reason, they
develop a wish to be a man--a wish that reemerges later on, in any neurosis
that may arise if they meet with a mishap in playing the feminine part. . . .
The girl's recognition of the fact of her being without a penis does not by
any means imply that she submits to the fact easily. On the contrary, she
continues to hold on for a long time to the wish to get something like it
herself."

8.

        (There is a long moment of silence.
        SIOBHAN starts to laugh, at first just a
        chuckle, but then a real, large laugh.
        DIEDRA joins her. JULIA looks
        incredulous, not at them, but at the TV.
        She turns the volume down.)

            SIOBHAN
            (still laughing)
Oh, please.

            HEATHER
He really said that? I always thought it was sort of just an exaggeration,
that whole penis envy thing. I thought it was like a joke. He really said
that.

            KELLY
Lord knows, I certainly don't want one. Like I don't have enough floppy
body parts as it is.

            DIEDRA
Yep. He really said that. "All women want a dick!" I'm with Kelly. They're
so ugly . . . if I had one of those things on me, I think I'd have to have
it removed.

            SIOBHAN
Oh, I don't know, I think they're sort of cute, the way they're all
wrinkly. They're fun.

        (They all laugh again.)

            JULIA
That reminds me, you know, Alex did the greatest thing the other day . . .
so typically male. I was changing his diaper, and he's laying back on the
changing table, and you know, I'm wiping his little butt with the wipey,
and suddenly he reaches down and grabs his . . . you know, his penis, and
he says, all worried like, "Bubby? Bubby?" Like he's afraid it's not
going to be there one day.

            SIOBHAN
He named it Bubby? That's so great!

            KELLY
            (suddenly)
Steve!

            JULIA
What?

            KELLY
Steve!

            SIOBHAN
Steve what? You know someone who named his Steve?

            KELLY
No, "Wonder Schlong"! His name was Steve. Steve Mundy. Remember?

            JULIA
Oh yeah, Steve Mundy. Jeez.

        (She laughs.)

9.

DIEDRA
Steve Mundy? What brought that on? That was ages ago.

KELLY
(realizes she has just blurted that out)
Oh, you know. We were just talking about school and everything. Sex . . .
you know. Stuff.

HEATHER
Who's Steve Mundy?

DIEDRA
Oh God, he was just this guy. This guy I knew back in school. *(She smiles.)*
Well, I guess I didn't just know him . . .

KELLY
She knew him in the biblical sense.

(She and JULIA laugh.)

HEATHER
Oh.

DIEDRA
(shaking her head)
Wow. I'd forgotten all about him . . .

SIOBHAN
Did you know, women only have nerves in like, the first three inches of
their vaginas?

(A pause. The women look at her.)

DIEDRA
No way. Really?

SIOBHAN
Really.

KELLY
So?

DIEDRA
(to KELLY, in disbelief)
So?! *(to SIOBHAN)* That can't be right. I mean, why would size be such a big
deal?

SIOBHAN
Well the point is, it shouldn't be. I mean, it shouldn't matter, right? If
we can only feel the first three inches anyway, then anybody over three
inches should be the same.

DIEDRA
But they aren't. It does matter.

JULIA
(smiling)
It sure does . . .

SIOBHAN
I know. That's what I'm saying. Isn't that weird?

10.

JULIA
Maybe it's like big breasts . . . you know, it doesn't really matter, but
guys like them better anyway. Well, some guys do.

KELLY
What was the point of this again?

SIOBHAN
Don't you think it's funny that there's a panty liner and a chewing gum
both named "Carefree?" I mean, what does that tell you about American
society today?

JULIA
What?

SIOBHAN
You don't think that's a little weird?

KELLY
Siobhan, you are so . . .

HEATHER
Excuse me.

DIEDRA
Where are you going?

HEATHER
To the bathroom.

JULIA
Oh, it's down the hall, second door on the left.

HEATHER
Oh, right . . . thanks.

(She goes.)

JULIA
Did we offend her or something? She had a sort of odd look . . .

DIEDRA
I don't know. She's not real big on sex . . . talking about it, I mean. You
know, it makes her uncomfortable.

KELLY
Well what's she doing with you then? *(She laughs)* So, Diedra, how did you
two meet? *(realizes that sounds odd)* I mean, you know, who is she, what's
she like?

DIEDRA
She's an intern with us.

KELLY
She just graduated from college and she's just now an intern?

SIOBHAN
Well, not everyone can rocket right up to 50 thousand bucks a year, Kelly.

11.

                              KELLY
                              (glares at her)
I know, I just meant that that seemed kind of old, is all. To be an intern.

                              DIEDRA
She's only 23.

                              KELLY
Oh. Well, see? I thought she was older. *(to SIOBHAN)* So, no big deal, okay?

                              JULIA
                              (picks up the tray of hors d'ouevres)
Come on guys, let's cool it, okay?

                              (They all sit, except for KELLY.)

                              KELLY
                              (to DIEDRA)
Did you see Julia's new bed?

                              DIEDRA
Huh-uh. You got a new bed?

                              (JULIA nods.)

What for?

                              JULIA
Paul just got it for me. I don't know. It's huge.

                              KELLY
You should take a look at it. It's in the master bedroom.

                              SIOBHAN
Can I look at it, too?

                              JULIA
                              (looking at KELLY)
Yeah, sure. Go ahead.

                              (They leave. KELLY sits.)

                              KELLY
You don't really think they're lovers, do you?

                              JULIA
Do you?

                              KELLY
Well, why did she bring her?

                              JULIA
Maybe she's just trying to make her feel welcome at the magazine. You know,
show her around, introduce her to people.

                              KELLY
That doesn't have anything to do with us, Julia. We don't work at the
magazine.

                                                                    12.

                                        (HEATHER enters from the hall. She is
                                        very hesitant, and looks quite
                                        uncomfortable.)

                                        HEATHER
                                        (to have something to do)
Is it all right if I get a glass of wine?

                                        JULIA
Sure. I put it in the fridge.

                                        (She and KELLY smile at each other.
                                        Heather goes into the kitchen, gets a
                                        glass from above the sink, and pours
                                        herself a glass of wine.)

                                        HEATHER
Where's Diedra?

                                        KELLY
                                        (watching her for a reaction)
She's in the bedroom with Siobhan . . . they're looking at Julia's new bed.

                                        HEATHER
                                        (comes in and sits down on the chair)
Oh.

                                        (Dead silence. HEATHER sips her wine.)

                                        KELLY
So Heather, how did you meet Diedra?

                                        JULIA
                                        (quickly)
Heather, you don't have to answer that if you don't want to . . . Kelly's
just being nosy.

                                        (She smiles at Kelly.)

                                        KELLY
I am not being nosy! I was just trying to make conversation. *(a pause)*
Christ! Never mind, then.

                                        (SIOBHAN and DIEDRA enter from the
                                        hall.)

                                        DIEDRA
Man, that is a big-ass bed! When did he get you that?

                                        KELLY
Oh, you're so tactful, Diedra.

                                        JULIA
He just gave it to me last week . . . I guess it was Monday. Right after
that weekend Alex and I stayed at Mom's. I came home from the store and
there it was.

                                        SIOBHAN
                                        (sitting in front of TV)
How do you get into the closet?

JULIA

Um, well, you can only open the door part way now. I kinda have to squeeze
in there sideways. We had to order special sheets, too.

DIEDRA

What's the occasion? Did you guys get another marriage manual or
something?

JULIA

No. It's actually been strange lately. Awkward. Like we just met or
something.

(HEATHER is looking increasingly
uncomfortable.)

HEATHER

Um, you know, maybe I should go. You guys are obviously . . . well, I mean
I'm not really . . . um . . .

DIEDRA

No, you should stay.

KELLY

Yeah, stay. We don't even know you yet.

DIEDRA

Stay.

HEATHER
(resigned, but unhappy)

Okay.

(From the hallway leading to the
bedrooms we hear a baby/young toddler's
crying.)

JULIA

Oh, shit, there's Alex. Let me just go check on him.

(She leaves.)

HEATHER

She has a baby?

DIEDRA

Yes, she has a baby.

HEATHER

Is it a boy or a girl?

DIEDRA

Is that really important?

KELLY
(looking at them strangely)

It's a boy. Didn't you hear her say? His name is Alex.

HEATHER

Oh. Well, she just said Alex. That could be a boy or a girl.

14.

                              KELLY
No, she said "Let me go check on him." She said "him."

                              HEATHER
                              (suddenly loud)
Okay!! I'm sorry! I didn't hear her! What the hell is the big deal? I'm
sorry I'm intruding on your little group. I didn't want to come here,
anyway.

                              KELLY
Well, why exactly are you here, then?

                              SIOBHAN
                              (off the TV)
Oh, fuck! I got preempted!

                    (They all turn to look at her.)

                              DIEDRA
What?

                              SIOBHAN
My show! It's not on. There's some crappy old guy in a chair instead.

                              KELLY
                              (dryly)
I think that's Masterpiece Theater, Siobhan.

                              SIOBHAN
Well, whatever it is, it's on instead of my show. Fucking programming
director. That guy is such a shit. He hates me, I know he does.

                              KELLY
                              (as before, under her breath)
I can't imagine why.

                              DIEDRA
I'm sorry, Siobhan. I know this one meant a lot to you.

                              SIOBHAN
It drives me nuts. I do their crappy documentary on "Sage Chickens of the
Northern Plains," just so they'll let me do this one, and then they don't
put it on. Something that actually means something, and they don't show
it. I bet they didn't even keep the copy I brought in.

                    (JULIA comes in from the hall.)

                              JULIA
What's the matter?

                              KELLY
Oh, Siobhan's busting a gut because her show isn't on.

                              DIEDRA
Oh, you're so tactful, Kelly.

                              JULIA
It's not on? How come?

15.

SIOBHAN
I don't fucking know. Can I use your phone?

JULIA
Yeah, sure. Umm . . . you can use the one in the bedroom . . . if you want
privacy, I mean.

SIOBHAN
Thanks.

(She goes.)

JULIA
Yikes.

DIEDRA
Really.

KELLY
Anyway . . . Heather? You were saying?

DIEDRA
(interrupts)
What was the matter with Alex?

JULIA
Oh, his diaper was wet.

HEATHER
Um, excuse me again.

(She goes to the bathroom.)

KELLY
What is her problem? Why doesn't she want to be here? And how did she know
where the glasses were?

DIEDRA
What?

KELLY
She knew where the wine glasses were. When she got her wine. She just went
to the cabinet and got one. And what was that about Alex? Julia said
"him." How stupid can you be?

JULIA
Jeez, Kelly, what's your problem? You're acting like you're taking it
personally. Maybe she's just uncomfortable being with a new group of
people.

KELLY
She knew where the wine glasses were, Julia. She didn't ask where they
were, she knew where they were.

JULIA
So? What's the big deal about that? Maybe she heard me say where they were.

DIEDRA
Kelly--

16.

(The baby starts to cry again.)

                    JULIA
Dammit. . . . Let me see if he's okay.

          (She goes.)

                    DIEDRA
Kelly, listen to me. I have to tell you something really important.

                    KELLY
First tell me what is up with Heather. Why did you bring her?

                    DIEDRA
Well, they're both pretty much the same thing . . . Kelly, I brought
Heather because . . . because she knows Paul.

                    KELLY
                    (a pause)
So?

                    DIEDRA
Kelly, she knows him. She's met him. She slept with him.

                    KELLY
What?! She slept with Paul? When?

                    DIEDRA
I guess last weekend. She came to work on Monday, and we had lunch
together, you know, 'cause we've been talking a lot lately, and she told me
about this great guy she met on Friday night.

                    KELLY
Oh, god.

                    DIEDRA
I know. So she goes on and on about how she met him at Mingles, and he
asked her to dance, and how he was a great dancer, and she doesn't usually
sleep with a guy that she's just met, but this time she did. She told me
that they went home to his place, and they talked for a while, and drank
for a while, and then they ended up in bed.

                    KELLY
Holy shit. They came here?

                    DIEDRA
Yes, they came here. They did it in her bed, Kelly.

                    KELLY
Oh my god.

                    DIEDRA
Yes. I know.

                    KELLY
Oh, fuck.

          (HEATHER comes in from the hall. She
          stops and listens for a second.)

17.

                                    KELLY
How could you bring her here? You brought her back here?

                                    HEATHER
You told her?

                          (KELLY turns to look at HEATHER.)

                                    DIEDRA
Yes, I told her. That's why we're here, remember? Now we need to tell
Julia.

                                    KELLY
                            (completely incredulous)
Tell Julia?! You can't tell her! It'll kill her!

                                    DIEDRA
Kelly, that's why Heather is here. Julia needs to know about this.

                                    KELLY
Jesus fucking Christ, Diedra! Do you know what this would do to her? She is
completely devoted to Paul. This would ruin her life. And what about Alex?
You can't tell her!

                                    DIEDRA
Kelly, it's gonna end up being better for her to know. She needs to know
what Paul is really like. I've . . . I've been wanting to tell her about
Paul for a long time. I've seen what he's really like, Kelly, and she needs
to know.

                                    KELLY
Diedra, listen to me. She gave up her career for that man. She decided to
give up acting, and marry him, and be a housewife. And now you're going to
tell her she made the wrong decision? She'll go nuts! She agonized over it
for three weeks when he asked her to marry him, Diedra, and you're going to
tell her she was wrong. She will absolutely go nuts.

                                    DIEDRA
Don't you see? That's why we have to tell her! She has to know. Besides,
you always told her she never would amount to anything anyway. You treated
her career like a joke.

                          (HEATHER has been quietly miserable
                          throughout this whole exchange. SIOBHAN
                          comes in from the hall.)

                                    KELLY
I don't believe this. I can't believe you brought her here for this,
Diedra.

                                    SIOBHAN
Brought who here for what?

                                    KELLY
Oh, god.

                                    DIEDRA
Brought Heather here to tell Julia that she slept with Paul.

                                  (pause)

18.

                              SIOBHAN
Whoa. She slept with Paul? With Julia's husband Paul?

                         (DIEDRA nods.)
Wow. *(pause)* How was it?

                              KELLY
Oh for Christ's sake, Siobhan.

                              DIEDRA
Shut up, Kelly. We have to figure out how we're going to tell her.

                              KELLY
Well, I'm not going to tell her.

                              DIEDRA
Yes, thank you, Kelly, we figured that out.

                              SIOBHAN
I'll tell her. If you want me to, that is.

                              HEATHER
                              (suddenly)
Don't you think I should tell her?

                              KELLY
I thought you didn't want to. I thought she had to drag you here.

                              HEATHER
Well, she did. But I think I should. I mean, she has a kid.

                              KELLY
Oh, that's very noble of you, Heather. I can't believe you brought her
here, Diedra.

                              SIOBHAN
                              (casually)
You know, he tried to get me to sleep with him a couple years ago.

                              KELLY
What?!

                              SIOBHAN
At Brenda's wedding reception. You remember, at the Hilton? Julia was
pregnant with Alex. He asked me to dance, and he was hanging all over me,
saying we should go up to one of the rooms. I figured he was just really
plotzed, so I let it go.

                              DIEDRA
You're kidding. How come you never told me about that?

                              SIOBHAN
I don't know. Didn't seem all that important at the time.

                              DIEDRA
Didn't seem all that important? Siobhan, if you had just told me . . .

                         (JULIA comes in from the hall.)

19.

                    JULIA
God, sometimes it takes him forever to get settled down. He's gotten so
used to sleeping with Paul and me in that bed. . . . What? What's going on?

                    KELLY
Oh, nothing. We were just. . . talking.

                         (They all sort of look at each other,
                         but not at JULIA.)

                    JULIA
Oh-kay. *(pause)* Why don't we sit down?

                         (They all move into the sitting area.)
                    JULIA
Can I get anybody anything? Some more wine?

                    SIOBHAN
I'll have some of the tequila, if that's all right with Diedra.

                    DIEDRA
No problem.

                    JULIA
Oh! I almost forgot. I made a pea-pod salad for us. Does anyone want to try
it?

                    DIEDRA
                    (trying to be upbeat)
Sure. I'll have some. It sounds good.

                    KELLY
Diedra, you hate peas. You throw darts at pictures of peas.

                    DIEDRA
                    (hissing)
Will you shut up!

                    JULIA
What was that?

                    DIEDRA/KELLY
Nothing!

                    SIOBHAN
Christ.

                    JULIA
                    (coming back into sitting area)
Here you go.

                         (She sets a bowl in front of DIEDRA, and
                         a shot of tequila in front of SIOBHAN.)

                    JULIA
So what did the PBS guys say, Siobhan?

20.

                        SIOBHAN
Oh, the dickheads were all out. *(she downs the shot)* I got transferred from
line to line, but no one picked up.

                        KELLY
Imagine that, on a Friday night.

                        DIEDRA
Kelly!

                        HEATHER
So what is it you do, exactly, Siobhan?

                        SIOBHAN
Well, I'm sort of a free-lance film-maker. I do mostly documentaries and
public-interest kinds of things. The one that was supposed to be on
tonight was on Sarah Bernhardt.

                        HEATHER
Oh. Isn't she the one who had that weird lesbian thing with Madonna?

                        KELLY
Oh boy.

                        JULIA
                        (trying to suppress laughter)
Umm . . . no. That's Sandra Bernhard. Sarah Bernhardt was an actress--

                        KELLY
Never mind, Julia. Just . . . don't waste your time.

                        HEATHER
                        (attempting to be polite and pleasant)
And what do you do, Kelly?

                        KELLY
                        (patronizing)
I'm an engineer. Not the kind that work on trains. An electrical engineer.

                        (Smiles, turns to JULIA, sweetly.)
And what do you do, Julia?

                        JULIA
Cut it out, Kelly. She's trying to make conversation. *(to HEATHER)* I'm a
housewife, actually. But I used to be an actress. Well, I guess I still am,
really. But I decided to give it a rest when Paul asked me to marry him.

                        HEATHER
Oh.

                        DIEDRA
Listen, Julia, there's something I need to tell you . . .

                        KELLY
Oh, Christ.

21.

(HEATHER is as far away as is humanly
possible from JULIA without leaving the
sitting area.)

                    JULIA
What is it? Is something the matter?

                    SIOBHAN
Well, in a manner of speaking, yes.

                    DIEDRA
Let me tell her!

                    SIOBHAN
All right, sorry.

                    DIEDRA
Julia, you don't know how hard this is for me to tell you, but . . .
well . . .

                    (A very agonized pause. KELLY has her
                    face in her hands.)

                    DIEDRA (CONT.)
Julia, I slept with Paul.

                    (KELLY looks up. HEATHER, SIOBHAN, and
                    JULIA gape at DIEDRA.)

                    JULIA
What?!

                    KELLY
What?

                    HEATHER
Diedra, you don't have to . . .

                    DIEDRA
                    (cuts her off)
I'm not. I did sleep with him. About two months before your wedding. I was
drunk, but he wasn't . . . and we slept together.

                    SIOBHAN
Well, shit fire and save the matches.

                    (huge pause)

                    JULIA
(very quiet) I feel like throwing up. You're not making this up, are you?

                    DIEDRA
No, I'm not. I am so sorry, Julia. I didn't mean for it to happen.

                    JULIA
                    (on the verge of tears)
Why did you wait until now to tell me? Why are you doing this now?

22.

DIEDRA
I thought it was just a last little fling, you know? Sowing his wild oats, or whatever that crappy cliche is. I thought he got it out of his system, and there was no real reason to tell you. *(pause)* But there is now.

KELLY
Oh, god.

JULIA
What? You mean you slept with him again?

HEATHER
(meekly)
No. I did.

KELLY
Jesus Christ, am I the only one he didn't hit on? How come he didn't try anything with me?

JULIA
Oh, god. Oh my god. I can't believe this is happening.

HEATHER
It was last weekend. I met him at a bar, and he brought me home. I didn't know he was married, he told me that--

KELLY
Okay, okay, I think we can spare the gory details. She doesn't need to hear that.

HEATHER
Sorry.

JULIA
Oh god, the bed. The fucking bed.

DIEDRA
Julia, I am so sorry to have to tell you this. I wasn't even going to tell you. I mean, I thought it was just that one time, but then Heather told me what had happened and Siobhan--

(JULIA stands up and smacks DIEDRA
across the face in one motion.)

JULIA
You bitch! You fucking whore!

(KELLY and SIOBHAN jump up to hold her
off.)

KELLY
Whoa, whoa, whoa, Julia. Come on now, I know you're upset. Just calm down.

JULIA
How could you?! And how could you bring her here? *(she sits down hard)* Oh, god. I can't believe this. You were my friend.

DIEDRA
I still am, Julia. I know this is hard, but--

23.

JULIA
You don't know anything! You have no idea! You fucking cunt, you seduced my husband.

SIOBHAN
Hey, now Julia, come on. He wasn't totally blameless, either. I mean, I think that's pretty clear . . . he was part of it, too.

JULIA
(moaning)
No . . . no, he wasn't . . . he couldn't have . . .

KELLY
Julia, he did. You can't blame it all on Diedra. I mean, he lied to Heather about being married . . .

JULIA
No, he didn't! You're wrong! I won't believe you!

KELLY
Sweetie, come on now. This isn't like you. I think you need to face reality, here.

JULIA
(she laughs)
Reality?! I should face reality? The reality, Kelly, is that I gave up everything for him. I gave up Hollywood for him. I fucking stayed home and played housewife for him . . . oh god, Alex.

(She is crying. KELLY and SIOBHAN move to comfort her.)

SIOBHAN
I think you need to spread the blame a little more evenly, hon. I know it's hard, but you have to face up to this. I'm sorry. You can't just get mad at Diedra and not Paul. I mean, it's not all her fault. She just thought you should know.

JULIA
Oh god, I know. I knew there was something wrong. I just didn't want to know. I didn't want it to be what I thought it was. He just . . . he made me look like a fool. I feel like a fool.

(DIEDRA and HEATHER have moved toward the door. They are getting ready to leave. DIEDRA is still holding her face where JULIA has slapped her.)

DIEDRA
I'm going to take Heather home. I . . . I guess I shouldn't be around for awhile.

SIOBHAN
Okay, Diedra.

(They turn to go.)

JULIA
(standing up)
Diedra, wait. I . . . I'm sorry I hit you. I just . . . I just don't want to think that I could have screwed up this badly. That I was too dumb to see it.

24.

                    DIEDRA
Oh hon, it's not your fault. You didn't screw up.

                    JULIA
I'm so embarrassed. I feel so . . . stupid. Blind.

                    KELLY
Julia, it's not your fault. You couldn't have seen this coming.

                    JULIA
But I should have. He's my husband.

                    HEATHER
I am so sorry, I didn't know.

                    KELLY
(glaring at her) Thank you. I'm sure that makes her feel a lot better.

                    SIOBHAN
Oh, Kelly just stop. Quit getting all pissed at her. It's not her fault,
either.

                    JULIA
                    (to DIEDRA)
What were you going to say about Siobhan? to *SIOBHAN)* Did you sleep with
him, too?

                    SIOBHAN
Well, no. But he wanted me to. He asked me to.

                    JULIA
Christ. What am I going to do? I have to leave him. Where am I supposed to
go? What if he wants Alex?

                    SIOBHAN
I think you need to talk to him, Julia. Once he knows that you know the
truth, he'll get serious.

                    JULIA
I can't face him. I'll kill him. How could he do this to me? To Alex? I'll
kill him.

                    (There is a knock at the door.)

                    PAUL'S VOICE
                    (Off Stage)
"Ladies? I'm sorry to interrupt, I know I'm not supposed to be here for
this thing, but I just need to get my overnight kit. Julia?"

                         (The women look at each other. They look
                         at the door. They look at JULIA.)

                    JULIA
Heather, would you get the door?

                    BLACKOUT

                    THE END

Lemon 7-14

A Play in One Act
by
Scott Allan Pardue

© 1998
4170 South Helen Apt. #901
Laramie, Wyoming 89119
University of Wyoming
(307) 555-5435

Cast of Characters

Eugene Christian Scott: *Young man in his twenties*

Spring Theresa Locksley: Young woman in her twenties

*Clive: A very large bouncer wearing a leather jacket painted like a cow
with the word "Moo" on the back.*

The Set

A scrim divides up and downstage. Behind the scrim, upstage, are three
poles cut at different lengths extending from a platform two feet in
height. In front of the scrim, downstage, is a simple apartment setting.
Downstage right sits five two-by-two-foot blocks indicating a couch. One
of the blocks runs up the stage right wall and the other four on the
downstage wall. The configuration creates an L-shape. Center stage is a
small circular bar table with two chairs. Upstage left, sits a bar at an
angle. Behind the bar is a small sink area and counter-top with a coffee
pot. On the downstage left corner of the bar sits a typewriter. There are
three bar stools, one upstage at the typewriter and two downstage. Upstage
right is an exit to the bedroom and upstage left is an exit out of doors.
The bar area and the circular table double as the apartment setting and a
strip-bar setting. All furniture should be painted black so as not to
indicate any specific locale. Locations should be defined by what the
characters bring on and off with them.

Time 1981.

Lemon 7-14

(Darkness. Silence. Within the darkness
we hear typing. Warm lights saturates
the scrim dividing up and down stage. In
front of the scrim a man, GENE, sits at
the bar-counter typing on an antique
typewriter. Behind the scrim we notice
the naked silhouette of a woman who
appears to be inside a cage hanging on
to a pole. As she speaks, GENE stops
typing.)

THERESA
Look at me and I will dance for you And shed each article of spider threads
That hang between us like so many lies. Lies as soft as sheets on lonely
beds.

[The lights fade within the cell and the
scrim becomes opaque. After a brief
pause GENE looks up and addresses the
audience.]

GENE
Are you judging me? I hope not because I'm a playwright, not an actor. I'm
not trying to excuse the performance because acting does come between us,
but acting and writing are two very different forms of art and I'd feel so
much more comfortable if the emphasis was on the script and not the actor.
You see, it's an issue of control. A script is a lot easier to manipulate
than an actor. An actor can take a script, memorize it, and no two
performances will ever be the same. I would go so far as to say that an
actor changes a script more than the playwright. Just watch the words. I'm
a playwright, not an actor.

THERESA
[enters from outdoors]
I think you're Jesus. Isn't that what you want me to think? Jesus?

GENE
I'm busy, Theresa.

THERESA
You play Jesus, and I'll play Mother Theresa.

GENE
I'm thinking.

THERESA
I see.

GENE
You do?

THERESA
Yes.

GENE
[pause, Gene smiles]
You play the tot and I'll play St. Nicholas.

2.

                    THERESA
What?

                         GENE
Can you feel it?

                    THERESA
What are you talking about?

                         GENE
It feels festive, doesn't it? Yes . . . yes! An aura of Christmas in the
summer time!

                    THERESA
Maybe you spend too much time alone, Gene.

                         GENE
I think I might. Come here.

                    THERESA
I don't think I trust you.

                         GENE
Come on. Sit down. Come on, Theresa, sit. Now close your eyes.

                    THERESA
Oh, for Christ's sake.

                         GENE
Don't take the Lord's name in vain, now, it's Christmas. Are your eyes
closed?

                    THERESA
Yes.

                         GENE
                         [Gene lays a present in front of her]
Okay, now open them.

                    THERESA
Gene . . .

                         [THERESA opens present and holds up a
                         pair of pointe shoes]

                    THERESA
. . . Pointe shoes.

                         GENE
Yes.

                    THERESA
Gene, these are really expensive.

                         GENE
Do you like them?

                    THERESA
Well, let me put them on and see. I should stay on the floor with these.
Yes, these will work wonders for my feet.

3.

                                    GENE
Oh, my God! That's it!

                                    THERESA
What?

                                    GENE
Staying on the floor . . . staying grounded. I have to ground the action in
the text.

                                    THERESA
Gene, come on.

                                    GENE
What are a bunch of words if they don't indicate the idiosyncratic
behaviors of the characters. They're not personalized. I've just been
writing symbols.

                                    THERESA
Yeah? Well, I guess you better personalize them.

                                    GENE
It's a question of what really communicates. You know what I mean? What
does an audience relate to more, some abstract concept or shoes?

                                    THERESA
No, let me guess . . . shoes.

                                    GENE
Shoes.

                                    THERESA
                            [Theresa sits on top of bar]
Like, pointe shoes. C'est D'accord?

                                    GENE
That is exactly it.

                                    THERESA
Gene, I don't give a shit.

                                    GENE
I'm starting to run out of paper, can you believe that? I just bought five
reams.

                                    THERESA
I said I don't give a shit, Gene! *[pause, they stare at one another]* Thanks
for the shoes.

                                    [THERESA begins picking cotton balls
                                    from between her toes and setting them
                                    on the counter.]

                                    GENE
Go to bed. It's late . . . What are you doing?

                                    THERESA
What?

4.

                              GENE
What is this?

                            THERESA
Little tiny tampons for my toes. I keep losing my pinky nail. Look. *[pushes foot in front of his face]* Do you want to wash my feet?

                              GENE
No. Theresa, would you do me a favor and throw those in the garbage instead of all over the counter here. We eat off this and I don't want to stare at a bunch of disgusting cotton balls.

                            THERESA
You have your crap all over it.

                              GENE
My crap isn't all sweaty and bloody and gross.

                            THERESA
And I suppose your crap doesn't stink, either. Come to think of it, I've never heard of Jesus taking a crap, so maybe you don't have any crap at all to stink up the place.

                              GENE
Let it go, will you?

                            THERESA
Are you writing? Is that what you're doing?

                              GENE
Yes.

                            THERESA
It's so funny.

                              GENE
What?

                            THERESA
Oh, you, you write about this and that so casually, so clearly. You seem to have a lot to say about sex. Got some hang-ups, maybe?

                              GENE
You think so?

                            THERESA
I don't know. I'm not Jesus, you are. But you know what I hate?

                              GENE
What's that?

                            THERESA
You always start off with those long-winded monologues about theatre. Why not just start the damn play and say what you want to say. You always go off on tangents. You always do that. Are you listening to me?

                              GENE
Of course.

5.

THERESA

I think you ought to. You'll put people to sleep if you keep doing that. So what are you writing about this time?

GENE

A stripper.

THERESA
[pause]

Are you condemning me?

GENE

No. You are.

THERESA

He is meek, and He is mild; He became a little child.

GENE

Go to bed.

THERESA

Put that in your script.

GENE

All right. Now go to bed.

THERESA

Can't sleep.

GENE

Why not?

THERESA
[sarcastically]

Because I'm lonely. I'm ever so lonely. Do you ever get that way?

GENE

Usually when I'm not alone.

THERESA

Is it true what they say?

GENE

What's that?

THERESA

That you just walk around being holy waiting for the Romans to nail you to the cross? No. That's not true for you now, is it? No, our second coming here has Jesus trying to nail himself to the cross. And here I am at the foot of your cross like Mommy Theresa . . . or Mother Mary . . . or Mary Magdalene . . . I could be your lover and your mother both.

GENE

How's that?

THERESA

I could make your bed in the morning and sleep in it at night.

6.

GENE

You don't make my bed. I do.

THERESA

But you don't lie in it. Do you want a cigarette?

GENE

No.

THERESA

Are you sure?

GENE

I have my own.

THERESA

I know you want a cigarette so take one.

GENE

I don't want to smoke right now. I just had one.

THERESA

Testy, testy, testy. Feeling angry because you can only get one palm pinned? That's the way it is when you try to do it by yourself. It's like masturbation, you should get some help.

GENE

Theresa, would you let the Jesus thing go?

THERESA

Are you going to give me attention? I want attention mister, mister.

GENE

For what?

THERESA

I have something serious to discuss. *[to herself]* Shoes.

GENE

Do you now? I feel like our relationship is maturing.

THERESA

Good. That makes me happy. I am ever so happy. I haven't been this happy since you put that twenty in my G-string the night we met. Look at you, getting all embarrassed.

GENE

I'm not embarrassed.

THERESA

Now you don't look so happy. Feeling a bit pathetic you're dating a stripper? Maybe like you sold out, huh?

GENE

No. I don't feel like I sold out. Tell me why, but I don't like you stripping. You don't have to strip. You can do something else. Be a T.A for the dance department.

7.

THERESA
I'm happy with my job.

GENE
You're happy with a job like that? Why?

THERESA
Pays more than minimum. Lots of boys go puttin' bills in my panties. Lonely boys, like yourself.

GENE
Is that right?

THERESA
That's right. Got to pay for my education somehow. Think I'll let you lonely boys pay for it with your hormones. *[holds pointe shoes]* Oh, I have it. I could wear these when I do my routine. The regulars would love something different.

GENE
Why don't you go home. I really don't want to deal with you right now.

THERESA
Oh, yes you do. I know you do. Jesus! Jesus wants to save the stripper. Isn't that right? St. Nick in the summer time! Here's to you, Nick!

[She takes a drink]

GENE
Look, either go home or go to bed.

THERESA
Like I said, I have something serious to discuss.

GENE
Then by all means, talk. Please, open up. Let's discuss. This is a new aspect of our relationship, but I feel like we'll be the closer for it.

THERESA
Maybe. Maybe not. Oh, by the way *[Gene looks up at her]* . . . I burned your car down with a cigarette.

GENE
What? *[pause, Gene looks at her intently]* Are you serious?

THERESA
Maybe, maybe not.

[THERESA exits]

GENE
[to audience]
Regret is an acquired taste. It's like coffee. Those who drink it in the morning, drink it because they have drank it every morning since they can remember despite the fact it gives you bad breath that lingers on throughout the day. We are creatures of habit that way, hanging on to past mistakes out of routine. I suppose it's because we cling to them so fiercely that all of us, at one time or another, stand naked before an audience. We are all strippers. *[pause]* I met Theresa at a raunchy little tease bar called *The Shaft* in a small neighboring mining town. It had quite

(CONTINUED)

8.

GENE (CONTINUED)
a reputation at the university and those who were intrigued would make the
fifteen-mile trek to the basement of a .condemned building for a thrill.
They were supposed to close the place down, but in a small town with little
entertainment, it wasn't a popular idea.

> [Lights come up on the stage at *The
> Shaft*. As the music fades in we see
> THERESA's silhouette behind the scrim
> standing motionless inside the cage. She
> hangs onto the bar in the center of the
> cell and as the music builds she begins
> to dance. She goes through her routine
> with the sound of the audience getting
> wilder with each article of clothing
> stripped away. With nothing more than a
> G-string, we see GENE wander up to the
> stage mesmerized by her. The music
> slowly fades to *Fur Elise* and THERESA
> begins to suggest classic ballet in very
> simple, but very clean movements.]

GENE
[looking through the bars]
When I am alone I think to kneel Before a dream whose wanton piss-pore
presses To my tongue and swells with such a scent! And drools like stool
until the blood is spent.

THERESA
Look at me and I will dance for you And shed each article of spider threads
That hang between us like so many lies. Lies as soft as sheets on lonely
beds.

GENE
And where am I but in that very state, When the spit dries upon my empty
hands, When waters wrack the vessels in my brain With black-blown images
that flood the past.

THERESA
Let your eyes drift over me like lips That want to know the taste of every
curve For more than just the heave of breathing hips, For more than just
the pluck of tuning nerves.

GENE
Where am I? Alone and gasping in The vastness of the sea within my walls,
Miles of waves that want to pull me down Screaming, until I suck the salt
and drown.

THERESA
But you will feel my flesh becoming wet With more than just the surge and
swell of blood, You will drink the years of bitter sweat That pours with
the rush of a crying drug.

GENE
How like a virgin's love before she bleeds.

THERESA
How like a man when the soul concedes.

> [The lights fade inside the cell and the
> scrim becomes opaque. *Fur Elise* fades

9.

and the strip music resumes. The lights
shift to the bar scene as THERESA enters
and sits at the small table. CLIVE, the
bartender/bouncer, enters wearing a
leather jacket painted like a cow with
the word "Moo" on the back.]

[CLIVE begins wiping down the bar and
GENE approaches him.]

GENE

Rum and Coke.
[Clive motions that he can't hear]: Rum and Coke! *[Clive begins making it]*
You don't talk much, do you? *[Clive stares at him]* I said, you don't talk
much, do you? *[Clive hands him his drink]* Thanks! Do you know that dancer's
name? The one over there! Thanks! [approaches Theresa's table nervously] I
liked your act.

THERESA.
[looks him up and down and turns back to
her drink]

Most boys do.

GENE

I suppose you're right.

THERESA

Suppose?

GENE

You're right. Can I sit down?

THERESA

Whether you can or not has nothing to do with whether I'll let you.

GENE

May I sit down?

THERESA

Before you sit, I want you to look over there. Do you see that man there?

GENE

Yes.

THERESA

He can bench press a house, carries a thirty-eight, and just got out on
parole. *[she waves to bouncer]* His name is Clive. I tell you this because I
get hit on more than abused children. You see, a lot of boys think that
strippers are for sale. It's Clive's job to convince them otherwise.

GENE

Is that right?

THERESA

That's right.

[THERESA takes out a small white pill
and washes it down with a shot]

GENE

Do you have a headache?

10.

THERESA
That's funny. *[she laughs]* Have I got a headache. That's sort of like
asking permission to have sex. Are you asking whether I'll answer with an
excuse before you ask?

GENE
No. I was referring to the aspirin.

THERESA
Aspirin? *[she laughs]* That wasn't an aspirin, it was a Lemon seven-
fourteen. Takes the edge off the post-performance adrenaline rush. *[Gene
starts to sit down]* Ah-ah-ah. *[she waves her finger]* I haven't invited you
to sit yet.

GENE
Can I?

THERESA
If you're in good physical condition I'm sure you could, but whether you
can or not is inconsequential. I told you that before. Pay attention.

GENE
May I?

THERESA
No.

GENE
Why not?

THERESA
Do I have to give a reason?

GENE
I would appreciate it.

THERESA
You have to answer a question first. If you answer right, you can sit. If
you answer wrong, you can stand. If you decide to sit without answering at
all, you can talk to Clive instead of me. Understand?

GENE
All right, what's the question.

THERESA
It's the same one I always ask. No one's gotten it right yet, so I've made
it a policy not to accept lines from the patrons here at *The Shaft*. Most
end up talking to Clive.

GENE
Does Clive get hit on a lot?

THERESA
No, Clive usually does the hitting.

GENE
I see.

11.

THERESA
Good. I'm glad. Okay, here we go: What's a nice boy like you doing in a
place like this hitting on a stripper? Be honest, I've heard them all.

GENE
Two-dimensional photographs didn't scratch the itch.

THERESA
Were you thinking I might scratch your itch?

GENE
I don't know what I was thinking, but when I saw you dancing you didn't
seem like a stripper to me.

THERESA
Oh, yeah? What did I seem like?

GENE
A little ballerina in a cage.

THERESA
How so?

GENE
Your moves were choreographed very specifically, which tells me you want
to be an artist. But you're stuck in a cage so you can't express it fully.
I doubt most strippers rehearse their routines to such an extent, and I
doubt most strippers try to keep an edge on the image they create in the
minds of this kind of audience.

THERESA
[pause]
Have a seat. *[Gene sits]* You're pretty interesting for a pervert.

GENE
You're pretty interesting for a stripper.

THERESA
I'm not really a stripper.

GENE
I'm not really a pervert.

THERESA
What I mean is, I need the money for college.

GENE
Do you go to the university?

THERESA
Yeah. It's kind of a pain to drive fifteen miles to this red-neck mining
town every time I have to work, but the money is good and Clive takes care
of me. So what's your major?

GENE
English. What's yours?

THERESA
Dance.

12.

                              GENE
Dance. I should have guessed that. You know, I don't know your name yet.

                              THERESA
Theresa.

                              GENE
Theresa, my name is Gene. Glad to meet you.

                              THERESA
                              [smiling]
Shut up.

                              GENE
So how did you end up getting a job out here?

                              THERESA
I don't think you want to know.

                              GENE
Maybe you're right. Maybe not right now. Maybe now is not a good time.

                              THERESA
Maybe. Maybe not. *[Theresa gets up and begins to exit]* You may be right.

                              GENE
Do you want to go?

                              THERESA
                              [she smiles]
Maybe, maybe not.

                         [THERESA exits]

                              GENE
                              [to audience]
I've always wanted a fairy tale, to be a knight with arms emblazoned on my
shield, to have on my lance, a scarf, and to have in my heart a lady.
Anyway, Theresa and I began seeing each other . . . and while I do
entertain fantasies from time to time, with her it is extremely difficult
to walk on anything but the earth. There were moments, though. I remember
one time in particular. I was sitting in the living room and heard this
noise, like someone was drowning. *[Theresa enters gargling mouthwash, Gene
addresses her]* What are you doing?

                              THERESA
                              *[Spits the mouthwash out in the sink and
                              wipes her mouth with her arm.]*
I'm feeling inspired by God.

                         [She stares at him sexually]

                              GENE
                              [to audience]
She just kept staring at me. Not that I mind being stared at intently by a
woman, but when it's Theresa, the level of unpredictability can leave a
man searching frantically for some sort of shield. I did my best to ignore
the situation, but then she moved toward me and asked:

                              THERESA
Little lamb, who made thee? Dost thou know who made thee?

13.

                                    GENE
And who can ignore a woman who quotes Blake. *[to Theresa]* My mother, I
suppose. But does the child ever really know?

                                    THERESA
What were you like as a child?

                                    GENE
My mother would call my name, but I couldn't hear her beneath the surface
of my dreams. I had gills to take in the currents, there, and fins to find
my way.

                                    THERESA
You remind me of your plays.

                                    GENE
How's that?

                                    THERESA
You're always quoting yourself.

                                    GENE
Seems to me we spend the first half of our lives learning everything we're
going to say in the second half . . . if we make it that far. Who can ever
really quote themselves?

                                    THERESA
Well, I hope I can.

                                    GENE
Maybe you're just quoting me in some extended dream I'm having.

                                    THERESA
You wish I was in your dreams.

                                    GENE
Someone's making them wet.

                                    THERESA
Maybe you just have a wet brain.

                                    GENE
Maybe.

                                    THERESA
Tell me something.

                                    GENE
What's that?

                                    THERESA
Did you ever think you might drown?

                                    GENE
The water is very deep in places.

                                    THERESA
That wasn't the question.

14.

                              GENE
It can get very dark and cold. Sometimes I feel lost in the sea like the
light of the moon.

                            THERESA
Maybe your wet brain has iced over and you don't know which way is up.

                              GENE
What? You don't think I'm a good writer? I think I heard the voice. I
wouldn't swim if I didn't hear the voice.

                            THERESA
Maybe you should see someone.

                              GENE
Why?

                            THERESA
Most people don't hear voices.

                              GENE
You don't think so?

                            THERESA
I really don't.

                              GENE
I think they do. Everyone has a calling.

                            THERESA
Like me?

                              GENE
Yes, you. What about dance?

                            THERESA
It's true. I've been called by God to strip in front of a bunch of drunken
men. It helps his church by strengthening the traditional relationship
role play between men and women. I should get a Christmas card from the
Pope.

                              GENE
You know what I meant.

                            THERESA
I know. I'm sorry. I'm a little rough around the edges if you haven't
noticed.

                              GENE
So what were you like as a child?

                            THERESA
Oh, I was Miss Innocent. Straight A's and clean white clothes to match the
color of my stainless soul. It's like this though: you put a little girl
in a mold, a cage where she can't move, a cage where she's completely
dependent on how much she can please and she begins looking for some sort
of key to leave it all behind for a little while. I'm an amazing escape
artist. I'm like Houdini. You know what I mean?

                              GENE
I don't know.

15.

THERESA
I've been picking the lock with fifth positions and swan-like bows since I
was five. Since I was five! Now look at me. Can you believe it? Jesus, look
at me. I'm a Goddamn stripper . . . and I'm a little over-weight.

GENE
Are you all right?

THERESA
I'm fine, I'm fine. I'm sorry.

GENE
That's okay. Do you remember that poem I read you?

THERESA
Which one? Swear to God, I must have listened to three anthologies in the
past month.

GENE
We were up on the mountain and I had a copy of Blake. The wind was gently
bending pine trees somewhere in the darkness and their boughs seemed to
hush the rest of the mountain with a shshshshshshsh. I was staring into the
fire, somewhere lost in thought, watched it lick and spit at the night. And
then I felt you looking at me . . . And I looked at you and I said:

THERESA
Tiger, tiger, burning bright In the forest of the night-

GENE
What immortal hand or eye Could frame thy fearful symmetry? And then I
crept toward you, hungry. I was hungry to touch you and hungry to taste
you. Our eyes were riveted to one another as I crouched in front of you and
opened your shirt button by button. In what distant deep or skies Burnt the
fire of thine eyes?

THERESA
On what wings dare he aspire?

GENE
What the hand dare seize the fire? I ran my fingers through your hair like
the wind, then grabbed onto it as if you were something I might lose and
pulled you toward me. You clenched your teeth, but your eyes never left
mine. And I wondered. And what shoulder, and what art, Could twist the
sinews of thy heart?

THERESA
What the anvil? What dread grasp Dared its deadly terrors clasp? *[Gene
moves to kiss her]* Wait. Let me go change. Let me go . . .

[THERESA exits to her bedroom]

GENE
Theresa, wait . . . Come on . . .

[He hears sounds of THERESA tearing
apart her room. He pours himself a cup
of coffee, lights a cigarette and moves
to his typewriter.]

GENE
I know what you're doing in there. Do you hear me? Theresa?

16.

                        THERESA
What?

                        GENE
I said I know what you're doing in there. I'm psychic.

                        THERESA
You're what?

                        GENE
I said I'm psychic! I know what you're looking for!

                        THERESA
Is that right?

                        GENE
Yeah, that's right.

                        THERESA
Well, Gene, I bet I'm just as psychic. I bet you ran your fingers through
your hair, poured yourself a cup of coffee, lit a cigarette, and sat at
your Goddamn typewriter to write this play. --What did you do with the
Bacardi, Gene?

                        GENE
You're wrong.

                        THERESA
What?

                        GENE
I said you're wrong!

                        THERESA
You're lying. Where is it, Gene?

                        GENE
I didn't run my fingers through my hair.

                        THERESA
                        [enters frustrated]
What did you do with it?

                        GENE
I didn't run my fingers through my hair. You were wrong about that.

                        THERESA
Ask me if I give a shit about your hair.

                        GENE
Theresa, do you give a shit about my hair?

                                [THERESA grabs her purse and gets her
                                bottle of pills and takes a couple.]

                        THERESA
You forgot these.

GENE
So I take it you don't give a shit.

THERESA
Maybe, maybe not. *[grabs Gene's manuscript]* What have we here.

GENE
What are you doing? Give it back!

THERESA
So this is it, huh? The Oscar-winning play!

GENE
Come on, Theresa.

THERESA
Hang on, there, my little moca-mini, I just want to have a little look see. *[reads script]* "Darkness. Silence. Within the darkness we hear typing." OOOOH! That's good! That really sets the mood!

GENE
Would you stop it. Just give it back.

THERESA
[continues reading]
"Are you judging me? I hope not because I'm a playwright not an actor." Ain't that the truth! How new, how original for you to start off the play with a long-winded monologue about theatre! It's just not like you. Do you have street lights and poems in it, too?

GENE
You're making an ass out of yourself.

THERESA
Am I? Let's see exactly what I look like. *[thumbs through the pages, then stops]* Spring? My name is Spring in this? Oh, for Christ's sake, Gene, are you going for dramatic irony?

GENE
Yes.

THERESA
Well, let's see what little Miss Spring has to say--oh, and your name is Christian. That's very interesting. Spring and Christian. Don't they sound like a happy couple? Let's see . . . the innocent Miss Spring says in her . . . drunken stupor . . . *[recites]* "Testy, testy, testy. Feeling angry because you can only get one palm pinned? That's the way it is when you try to do it by yourself. It's like masturbation, you should get some help." I never said that. "Would you let the Jesus thing go," our stoic protagonist is intent on setting his little hussy straight . . . "Are you going to give me attention? I want attention mister, mister!" Our heroine tugs at his shirt. He throws her to the ground in a fury, slaps her across the face and kicks her right between the breasts, then screams . . . "For what!" She cries out in pain. Snot comes pouring out of her perfectly shaped nose as she wails all pathetic like, reaching, grasping, groping for her man! She falls to his feet . . . "I have something serious to discuss!" she wails and weeps. More snot comes pouring out of her perfectly shaped nose, belches quake out of her perfectly shaped lips, but her man doesn't notice. He is intent on abuse. He likes it hard. He

(CONTINUED)

18.

THERESA (CONTINUED)
likes it rough and dirty. He likes to be a man's man. He scowls at her,
grabs her hair roughly and yanks her head back . . . "Do you now?" he says
coldly, "I feel like our relationship is maturing!" Then he throws her to
the ground with the sensitivity of an ice pick, kicks her again between the
breasts, then walks away. He has won the day. *[Gene begins clapping]* Thank
you. I, you see, am an actress.

GENE
Very good. An Oscar-winning performance.

THERESA
For an Oscar-winning script.

GENE
Give it back.

THERESA
Have it.

[She throws it on the bar]

GENE
What is the matter with you? Jesus Christ.

THERESA
Talking to yourself?

GENE
Would you stop it. I know what it is, it's those damn . . . *things* you
take. Those . . . Lemon . . . *things*. If you wouldn't take so many you
might realize you're standing in reality without knowing it.

THERESA
Me?

GENE
Yes, you. What, you think I'm a drug addict drunk? Take a look at yourself.
You walk around in a bathrobe all day and night like you just got through
stripping for a bunch of lonely drunks. You don't eat, you don't sleep, you
just drink and drug like it's your only purpose for existence.

THERESA
Tell me, Jesus, what do you do in your spare time?

GENE
I work.

THERESA
You work?

GENE
Yes. I work. You think this is a hobby? You think this is a bunch of
dribble I lay down because I like it? It's work.

THERESA
Do you get paid for it?

19.

GENE

What?

THERESA

Do you get paid for it? If you get paid for it then it's work.

GENE

I don't have to get paid for it. It's work because it's my vocation.

THERESA

A vocation is a particular occupation in business. Occupations in business pay. If scribbling in a notebook is your occupation then you must be getting paid for it.

GENE

I'm not getting paid for it.

THERESA

Then it's not your vocation.

GENE

It's my vocation because it's my calling.

THERESA

Your calling?

GENE

Yes.

THERESA

And who, if you don't mind my asking, has called you to scratch ink all over perfectly nice sheets of paper?

GENE

God. *[pause]* Which is something you might not understand.

THERESA

And I'm not living in reality? I'm sorry, I'm sorry. Forgive me. My faith was shaken momentarily. You're Jesus and it slipped my mind just now. Of course you were called by God.

GENE

You may not like it, but that is the reality of the situation.

THERESA

And you would know it, wouldn't you?

GENE

I think I would know it better than you. My life isn't in the toilet. At least I have some sense of the outside world.

THERESA

You do?

GENE

Yes.

20.

THERESA

I've been trying to have a conversation with you for about an hour now, and I'm the addict? I'm the one who's not connected to reality? I'm not standing on Mt. Sinai spouting my connection to God. You say I walk around in my bathrobe all day not giving a shit about anything except drugs and a drink? Well, look in the mirror, Jesus, because the only thing you can think about is a Goddamn fiction for an audience. Like they give a shit! Your notebook is your Lemon seven-fourteen, this is your pill to pop! A fantasy! You think I can't live in reality? The only reality you can stand is your own warped imagination where you get to play God. Fine, Jesus, play me like a pawn to tell your Goddamn story, but tell me this: have I sinned? *[pause]* Come on, you're the playwright. Write the next line. Answer the Goddamn question!

GENE

I don't know what you mean, Theresa.

THERESA
                         [Theresa finds the liquor]
And look what I found. *[opens the bottle and takes a gulp]* Do, tell. Have I sinned because I fucked Jesus?

GENE

What are you talking about?

THERESA

What am I talking about? You have no idea, do you?

GENE

No, I don't. I don't have a Goddamn clue what you're talking about! Would you listen to yourself. You're not making any sense. *[Gene notices bottle of pills. Both he and Theresa run to grab them. Gene manages to grab them.]* It's these!

THERESA

Put them down, Gene. They're my only ones. They have to last me.

                              [GENE pours the bottle down the sink and
                              THERESA grabs his manuscript.]

GENE

Theresa, what are you doing? That's my only copy. Put it down!

                              [GENE lunges at THERESA, THERESA makes
                              her way to the sink and drowns the
                              manuscript in the water. Long pause.
                              GENE stares at the running water in
                              disbelief.]

THERESA

It is so pathetic that you can write about a woman getting raped by her stepbrother, a faggot refusing to leave his wife, and you can't even sense the tragedy in your own life. I hope that when this story is told you haven't warped reality to such a degree the listener hears a lie. And I hope you stop putting other people on stage for the thrill of a strip tease until you've stood there yourself and bared your own fucking self-righteous ass without the comfort of a cage.

GENE

Why should I strip when there's people like you around dying to do it for minimum wage? I'm surprised you sleep in my bed because I haven't paid a pimp! I'm surprised you make any tips at all! Have you seen yourself? Look at yourself!

21.

[GENE grabs her, holds her in front of a
mirror and rips open her shirt]
Can you imagine people paying money to see this? Look at yourself! This is
what you show people and you're proud of it? I want you out of here! Out!

[GENE exits to bedroom]

GENE

THERESA
If you could write reality down you would understand completely what a
joke you are. *[Gene reenters with a suitcase, exits again to bedroom]* I'd
say you are a comedy, but in comedies no one gets hurt. *[Gene reenters with
clothes, throws them in the suitcase]* The sad thing is, you hurt real
people without knowing it because you're so drugged up with your dreams.

GENE
Let go of me! I said let go!

[Gene exits again to the bedroom]

THERESA
You can't put real people on stage, just characters.

[GENE reenters with the rest of
THERESA's things, throws them in the
suitcase. THERESA pushes him aside and
zips up the suitcase awkwardly.]

THERESA
Theatre doesn't work that way. But if you could, you might understand the
kind of chaos you wreak as a real human being, you might understand that
you are the one pounding stakes into the palms of people and hanging them
up to suffocate. You might understand how little you really do care.

GENE
[Gene grabs her pointe shoes]
Take these, take all of your shit and get out!

THERESA
Give them to me! Don't touch them!

GENE
Like they mean a Goddamn thing to you!

THERESA
Give me my shoes!

GENE
You're not a dancer, you're a whore trying for tips!

[Pause. They stare at one another.
THERESA exits, GENE moves to the blocks
and sits. THERESA reenters. She neatly
places the pointe shoes on the table.]

THERESA
Fuck you.

GENE
What are you doing? Take your Goddamn shoes. Take them.

22.

THERESA

Can a character tell the playwright that? Fuck you. Why did you buy me the shoes, Gene? So I would dance for you in a little puppet show to impress your friends? I don't want you on my feet and I'm not here to impress your friends.

[THERESA grabs her suitcase and exits.]

GENE
[to audience]

I don't know where reality stops and the stage begins. Can you tell me? *[pause, Gene picks up the pointe shoes]* Someone told me once that if you went to the top of a mountain with a balloon, closed your eyes and poured all of your regret into it, when you let it go it would take the pain away. Well, I have gone to the top of a mountain, since then, with a balloon, a big red one. I sat down on a rock, closed my eyes, and clenched it, unpacking every skeleton of thought locked in my brain. I stood up and let it float away on the wind. I watched it until I couldn't see it anymore. I watched and waited and waited and watched. I felt like a fool. The other night I had a dream:

[The lights fade up on THERESA silhouetted behind the scrim. GENE picks up the pointe shoes and turns to THERESA.]

GENE

You were there and came up to me while I was writing at my desk. You held out a big red balloon and said:

THERESA

You see, I caught it.

GENE

Theresa . . .

THERESA

Shshshshhsh. Not now.

GENE

You know that song, *Fur Elise,* the one I always play when I write?

[pause, *Fur Elise* plays and THERESA begins dancing]

GENE

Isn't it like you and I? It seems to end where it begins going round and round and round and round: The song of futility.

[THERESA holds the pole and begins to suggest classic ballet.]

THERESA

Look at me and I will dance for you And shed each article of spider threads That hang between us like so many lies. Lies as soft as sheets on lonely beds.

GENE

I'm scared, Theresa.

23.

THERESA

Let your eyes drift over me like lips That want to know the taste of every curve For more than just the heave of breathing hips, For more than just the pluck of tuning nerves.

GENE

[walks closer to her] I'm scared that you will laugh at me.

THERESA

But you will feel my flesh becoming wet With more than just the surge and swell of blood, You will drink the years of bitter sweat That pours with the rush of a crying drug.

GENE

How like a virgin's love before she bleeds.

THERESA

How like a man when the soul concedes.

GENE

Theresa, what you're asking . . .

THERESA

Look at the both of us. We are like two drowning swimmers clinging to each other beneath the surface of the sea. It doesn't have to be like that.

GENE

I brought your shoes.

THERESA

I see that. So who is your play about, Gene? Me or you?

GENE

Open up the cage, Theresa.

THERESA

Why? Why, Gene? What's the point?

GENE

I want to come in.

THERESA

You want to do a strip tease for the audience? Is that it?

GENE

I would do it.

THERESA

From my perspective, it looks like you are in the cage.

GENE

I said I would. Didn't you hear me? I said, I would. I'm scared that you will laugh at me.

THERESA

I won't laugh at you.

GENE

Open up the cage.

24.

[GENE enters the cage and both he and
THERESA are silhouetted behind the
scrim. GENE begins to unbutton his
shirt.]

GENE

I'm scared.

THERESA

I know. So am I.

GENE

I feel like a whore.

THERESA

You're not.

GENE
[Gene begins taking off his pants]
Do you think people can see through me? I know what I am and what I look
like: A stripper on a stage who wants to be an artist.

THERESA

You are an artist.

GENE

The truth is you like the money and I like the applause. The truth is we
both need a fiction to function, we both need to suspend our disbelief
because belief in such a world as this is nothing less than frightening. It
is so much easier to strip with a thousand eyes that want to be entertained
than it is to strip with only two that want to love.

THERESA

What does it feel like?

[Gene stands before THERESA completely
naked]

GENE

Bare and raw and real.

[Lights fade.]

THE END

ACETYLENE

By
Erik Ramsey

Winner of the 1994
American College Theatre Festival
Student Written One Act

1812 Arnold
Laramie, Wyoming 82070
(307) 555-1713
University of Wyoming
Copyright 1998

CAST OF CHARACTERS

RUBY

PASTOR

WELDER

SETTING: The stage is divided into a "nursing home" section and a trailer house area. The "trailer house" is basically a small kitchen, with a table, a bowl of apples on the table, chairs, and a stove. The nursing home contains a hospital-type lounge chair.

ACETYLYNE

(The lights come up. Ruby is in the
nursing home; she is bandaged about the
face with gauze in her mouth and sitting
very still. The Pastor is standing
across from her.)

PASTOR

Look, I brought you something.

(The Pastor reaches into his pocket and
takes out an apple, extending it toward
Ruby. Ruby turns toward his voice, and
slowly, very slowly, reaches for it; but
before she grasps it the lights go out
again. In the darkness on stage, a
welding torch is lit. The lights come up
partially as if the flame is the only
light. Ruby is in her chair in the
nursing home, and the Pastor is gone.
We can see the Welder standing in
the trailer house, full mask down to
protect his eyes and wearing coveralls,
protective garb. He tunes the flame and
turns toward Ruby, slowly approaching
her. The torch is a symbolic one--a
handpiece without the hoses. Its
ignition and burning emit a menacing
roar. Just as the Welder reaches the
foot of her chair, the torch flickers
out. The lights go down and come up
fully; the Welder is gone. Ruby babbles
through the gauze an irate, incoherent
gibberish, which slowly calms and
becomes understandable once she begins
to unravel her bandages and pull the
dressings out of her mouth. The gauze is
not bloody or soiled.)

RUBY

Mah na blamp ma nan! . . . . Mah nu, mahnu weeno! . . . I blem mynans. . . .
I blame myself. . . . I blame myself. All I had to do was give him an apple
for his lunch. But he didn't check the lunchbox before he left and I didn't
remember until I got the phone call. I meant to tell him that we'd run
outta apples, but I forgot. I forgot. . . . It didn't matter what kind of
apple, Dutch liked all kinds. He used to tell me about when he was a kid
and he climbed into old man Dixson's yard and stole a bunch of crab apples.
Made him sick for three days. But he never lost his taste for them even
after that. Apple pie, baked apples, apple juice, carameled apples, apple
sauce with his porkchops. . . . His favorite story was Johnny Appleseed. He
even found a painting of Johnny Appleseed which he hung in the entry right
next to our painting of Jesus. I don't know if he meant to, but he hung it
so it seemed like Jesus' eyes were looking right up at it. I told him I
didn't think that was right and he got really angry with me. Every time I
walked in the front door I saw those two paintings together. It was like
the two was brothers, Johnny and Jesus I mean. They both had long blond
hair and blue eyes and a ray of sunshine coming down on them. . . . Dutch
got angry a lot but most of the time I deserved it. He was just trying to
help me be a better person. I worried about his heart, that's how my father
died, so I did my best not to upset him. I don't know where I'd be without
him. He taught me so much about how to do things right. . . . The phone
call reminded me we needed apples and I went to the market right then so I
wouldn't make the same mistake again. Granny Smith was all they had that
looked any good. . . . And then I set about making supper.

2.

(Ruby moves to the trailer house part of
the set, begins to prepare the meal, and
gets it all set up quickly, taking
things from the stove, etc.)

RUBY
Dutch liked it to be ready at six-o-clock sharp.

(A cuckoo clock strikes six just as she
finishes setting everything out on the
table. Right after the clock strikes,
the Welder enters (his mask is down in
every scene) and sits at the table. Ruby
loads his plate, and as she does, she
asks.)

RUBY
How was your day?

(Before the Welder can speak, there is a
knock at the door. Ruby moves to answer
it. It is Pastor Ellersby; as he enters
the house, the Welder exits the stage
opposite. The Pastor is dressed in a
cheap, ill-fitting suit and carrying a
worn Bible. He is Baptist.)

RUBY
Pastor Ellersby, what a nice surprise.

PASTOR
Hello Ruby. Can I come in for a minute?

RUBY
Yes, yes, come in, come in.

PASTOR
Larry Wilkens called me a little while ago and told me the news.

RUBY
How is Larry? He's Dutch's boss you know. I haven't seen him since the
Memorial Day picnic.

PASTOR
Uh . . . he's fine, just fine . . . um, Ruby--

(Ruby cuts him off.)

RUBY
We were just sitting down to supper Pastor, I'll set another place.

(Ruby turns and hurries into the
kitchen.)

PASTOR
Oh that's really not necessary. I just stopped by to make sure everything
was all right and give you my condolences. I'm truly saddened about
Dutch. . . .

(The Pastor notices the two plates at
the table.)

3.

PASTOR (CONT'D)

I'm sorry, I didn't know you had company.

RUBY

What?

PASTOR

You've two plates set out here. Were you expecting someone?

RUBY

Oh . . . I, uh . . . Dutch?

> (Ruby turns toward where the Welder exited.)

PASTOR

What? Ruby, I was told you were telephoned about the accident. . . . Who did you make supper for?

> (Ruby is blank for a long moment.)

RUBY

Why, I made it for you of course.

PASTOR

But how did you know I was coming?

> (Ruby ushers him to the table.)

RUBY

The food's getting cold, Pastor. Would you mind saying a blessing over it?

PASTOR
(They sit)

Of course. . . . Lord, we thank you for this food and ask that you bless it to the nourishment of our bodies. We would also ask that you be with Ruby now as she faces the difficult days ahead. Thank you for reminding us that we live not by our plans but thine, Lord. We know you have called Dutch to a better place. In Jesus' name we pray, amen . . .

> (The Pastor begins to eat. Ruby is distracted.)

. . . I still don't see how you knew I'd be coming.

> (He notices Ruby is staring.)

. . . Ruby . . . Ruby . . . Are you okay? You haven't touched your food. Ruby?

RUBY

I'm sorry about the apple.

PASTOR

What? . . . Ruby?

RUBY

How are the peas? Do they need more salt?

PASTOR

They're fine, they're good. . . . Maybe you should lay down for a little while.

4.

                    RUBY
Don't be silly, I'm all right. Do you need some ketchup?

                    PASTOR
No, thank you. This is an excellent meal--you're quite a cook. Mrs.
Ellersby would shoot me if she knew I had two suppers tonight.

                         (The Pastor continues eating for a
                         moment; Ruby watches him very closely.)
I'm sure this must be a very difficult time for you. Is there anything you
need?

                    RUBY
Need?

                         (There is an uncomfortable pause; the
                         Pastor clears his throat and wipes his
                         mouth.)

                    PASTOR
I don't know . . . I just thought maybe you'd like me to make some
calls . . . to relatives I mean.

                    RUBY
(Distracted.) No . . .

                    PASTOR
You can lean on me you know, that's what I'm here for. That's my job . . .

                         (He waits for Ruby to respond, when she
                         doesn't, he continues.)
Ruby I want to help you. Will you let me? . . . Are you worried about what
life will be like without him?

                         (Ruby begins to play with a cigarette
                         lighter. The Pastor pauses for her to
                         respond, then continues.)

                    PASTOR
It's not good to hold back your feelings. If you let them out you'll feel
better. Let out the sadness and the anger and give them to the Lord. He'll
take care of you if you allow him to.

                    RUBY
Oh-my-gosh! I completely forgot the rolls!

                         (She rushes to the oven, but there are
                         no rolls inside. Confused, she returns
                         to the table and sits.)

                    PASTOR
Ruby, denying your emotions will only make things worse. It's okay to have
them as long as you don't dwell on them, and give them to God. . . . You
see, we don't need to suffer, Christ did that for us on the cross. He has
promised to take all our torments away.

                         (Again the Pastor pauses for a long
                         moment waiting for Ruby to reply. She
                         avoids his gaze and lights a cigarette.)
You must come to terms with this. It may take a little time, but I want you
to understand something: the pain is unnecessary to hold onto . . .

                    (CONTINUED)

5.

> PASTOR (CONTINUED)
> (He continues to eat, often speaking
> with his mouth full.)

I learned a great deal about grief a few years back when my wife's mother
died. She had been living with us for two years because her eyesight was
failing; but she was still strong as an ox, especially for eighty-seven.
She cooked and baked and she was wonderful with the kids. We all became
quite attached to her. . . . She was always the first one up in the
morning, making the coffee and setting the breakfast table. She said she
didn't need much sleep anymore, but then she'd often doze off during the
day, wherever she was. One Saturday morning, she got up like usual and had
the coffee percolating, this was when Jenny and Tom were still pretty
young, and then she sat down in her chair and must have had a stroke. The
kids used to get up real early to watch their favorite cartoons, and when
she didn't respond to their good mornings, they figured she'd nodded off,
and so they just kept the volume low on the TV and fixed their own bowls
of cereal. Jenny played dolls at her feet, and Tommy tried to steal one
away from her--as they wrestled around he accidentally hit her chair and
Grandma slid out of it. They tried to wake her up, and when they couldn't,
they came and got me. . . . We all had gotten so used to her being around,
and we all took it very hard that she was gone. I did some real soul
searching then, the family was in terrible pain. Even the kids, as young as
they were, understood and were hurting. It was then that the Lord helped me
understand that the pain was unnecessary, that he could take it from us. As
a family, we prayed for God to cleanse us of the despair. And we all felt
better almost immediately. Even little Tommy, who was confused and thought
he had killed her, forgot all about it then. . . . The sooner you release
it into the hands of the Lord, the sooner you can get on with your life and
be happy and fruitful.

> (He pauses again; Ruby flicks the
> lighter on and off, over and over.)

It is a natural thing to indulge in your emotions at a time like this. I
don't believe it's a sin to feel them, unless you learn how to hide in
them. But I hope you can pray with me and release them. I just want to help
you avoid unnecessary pain. There will be times when you fall back into
despair--but God can take any amount you can give to him. Will you pray
with me?

> (Ruby is still playing with the lighter.
> After he realizes she isn't going to
> respond, the Pastor reaches over gently
> and takes the lighter away. Ruby jumps
> back at his touch and stands up.)

> RUBY

Can I get you seconds on anything? Is the meat done enough?

> PASTOR

At least pray with me for strength. I know it is very hard for you to admit
what has happened today. These things take time. But I also know you
understand in your heart what I'm talking about.

> (Ruby turns away from him and fiddles
> with pots and pans.)

> RUBY

Maybe you're right Pastor. Maybe I should get some rest.

> (The Pastor stands up from the table.)

> PASTOR

Think about what I said. You know you can call me any time, night or day.
And thank you very much for the supper.

> (He moves to exit.)

6.

                    RUBY
You're welcome Pastor. Say hello to Mrs. Ellersby for me and tell her not
to worry, I'll have the brownies done in time for the bake sale.

                              (The Pastor smiles and exits. Ruby turns
                              and clears the table as she addresses
                              the audience again.)

                    RUBY
Dutch was a good man. He took good care of me and he only wanted what was
best. He didn't ask much, only that I do things right. He wasn't mean to
me, I deserved to be scolded when I forgot to do stuff. Dutch was a kind
man, he was trying to help me better myself. He never raised a hand to me.
Sometimes I wish he had; I might've remembered then. I might've remembered
and then he would be. . . . I was a burden to him and even though he
yelled, he could be very gentle too. I am clumsy, I mean, I drop things
sometimes, and burn myself. Whenever I burned myself, he would always fix
me up. Once I caught the stove on fire and tried to flap it out with my
arms. He got the burn ointment from his truck and smoothed it over my
hands. "I doubt if those will scar," he said, "I've seen enough burns in
my time. I can't tell you how many times I've seen careless welders torch
their own fingers like sausage. It's a good thing you don't have to do my
job." And all the other times too, spilling boiling water or ironing. He'd
come home from work and find me crying and bandage me up and he'd say:
"Burns are a part of work, shows you been workin'. Fire is a tool. Tools
are meant to be used right, use them wrong and they make things worse, but
they teach you a lesson."

                              (A robe over her clothes, she sits at
                              the table, lights a cigarette, and
                              drifts off leaning on one hand. After
                              she has fallen asleep, the Welder
                              enters and lights his torch. He turns
                              slowly and begins to weld on Ruby
                              directly, and she doesn't wake up
                              immediately. When she speaks, the Welder
                              stops welding her.)

                    RUBY
Dutch? . . . Oh, Dutch, I was so afraid. I'm sorry about the apple, honey.
Really sorry. I went and bought some right after they called. I promise
I'll never forget again. I know how important it is you have an apple in
your lunch. Pastor Ellersby was by for supper and it reminded me, I ironed
your trousers for church. And I saw some new shoes in the Wards catalog I'd
like for spring, if we can afford them. Oh, I'm so glad you're here. . . .
Why don't you come to bed now . . .

                              (The welder turns and moves to a far
                              corner of the trailer house where he
                              stands motionless for the rest of the
                              play, until he becomes involved in the
                              action again.)

                    RUBY
Dutch? . . . Dutch? . . .

                              (Ruby addresses the audience.)
Dutch had a right to be particular. He worked hard to make a living for me.
If I'd've only done things right. He used to quote his favorite Bible verse
to me all the time: "If it's worth doing, do it right." I learned from him
that there's a right way and a wrong way to everything. Once you start
doing things wrong, everything falls apart. Time and again he tried to
show me that, but I didn't listen close enough. There's a right way and a
wrong way to everything. There's a right way to make peas.

7.

(Ruby shifts back to the kitchen and
begins furiously making supper. She sets
it out on the table and the cuckoo clock
strikes six. As she finishes putting
things out, Ruby continues to address
the audience.)

RUBY

He never talked much before he ate. Sometimes I'd ask him how his day went,
but if he answered it was usually just a word or two. While I finished
dishing everything onto his plate, he'd say grace, always the same one:
"Our Heavenly Father, we thank Thee for Thy day of blessing, and for
the bounty which Thou hast spread before us. It is in Christ's name we
pray. . . ." And then he'd pick up his fork and start eating. . . . He was
really a good man. I mean, he had a heart of gold and he really was trying
to help me. Almost every time, when he took his first bite of vegetables
he'd say: "Goddammit Ruby, how many times do I have to tell you to salt
the vegetables?" I didn't mind that he was a little bit gruff about it. I
thought I did salt them, but I guess I must not've. But he wasn't really
angry with me, I knew that, and I didn't take it personal. I can't blame
him for wanting things just so. He worked hard and deserved to have
his peas cooked right. He was tired and shouldn't have to think about
vegetables. Working is okay for some women, but growing up all I ever
wanted to be was a wife and a mother. . . . Dutch wasn't holding me back,
I wasn't barefoot and pregnant. He always made sure I had good shoes. In
fact, he liked to show me off when we went anywheres together. He bought me
nice things so I could be respectable in church, or when we went out for
Sunday dinner. He took good care of me and all he asked was me to do the
same for him.

(There is a knock at the door; Ruby
answers and the Pastor enters.)

PASTOR

Hello Ruby, we missed you in church today. I'm sorry, I didn't even think
about it, but if you need a ride in for the services, I could put you on
the van route.

RUBY

That's okay Pastor. Please, sit down. Can I get you some coffee?

PASTOR

Yes, that would be nice. . . . I just stopped in to see how you were
getting along, and discuss a few things about the funeral.

(Ruby doesn't reply, moves to get the
coffee.)

Mr. Tooney at the funeral home called me today and said he was having some
trouble getting ahold of you. Have you been home?

RUBY

Yes.

PASTOR

Oh. . . . Well, he just wanted to straighten out a few details, which
coffin you wanted . . . and, well he needs to know if Dutch had any life
insurance. It's sad, but even dying costs money.

(She pauses. The Pastor reaches for the
coffee, but she drinks it herself.)

RUBY

Did Mrs. Lofton wear her pink hat again?

8.

                              PASTOR
I'm sorry, what?

                              RUBY
Did Mrs. Lofton wear the pink hat to the service again today?

                              PASTOR
I'm not sure . . . I, uh . . . Ruby, about the--

                    (Ruby cuts him off.)

                              RUBY
Not that I don't like her pink hat. I think it's very smart. But if she
wore it again, it'll make the eleventh service in a row.

                              PASTOR
I didn't notice whether she wore it or not.

                              RUBY
It is a wonderful hat, but we're well past spring now, Pastor. It's almost
fall.

                              PASTOR
Yes, well I--

                    (She cuts him off again.)

                              RUBY
A scarf is best for fall, if you're gonna wear something on your head at
church. Of course men can't wear hats in church at all. I wonder why it is
women can and men can't.

                              PASTOR
I really couldn't say.

                              RUBY
Maybe it's because men are taller and if they wore hats, the folks behind
them wouldn't be able to see.

                              PASTOR
That could be, but I--

                              RUBY
I seen a Jewish service once on TV and those men wore hats, but they were
little ones like the kids used to wear, but without a propellor--

                    (The Pastor cuts her off this time.)

                              PASTOR
Ruby, we have to settle a few things. Is there anything special you would
like me to mention in the eulogy?

                         (The Pastor takes some notes from out of
                         his Bible. When she doesn't respond, he
                         continues.)
Why don't you listen to what I have so far. Then if you think of anything
to add we can put it in.

                    (CONTINUED)

9.

PASTOR (CONTINUED)

(He assumes a dramatic voice and begins to read.)
Every man has that in him which makes him stand out, rise above the rest.
Some are gifted with their hearts, some with their heads and some with
their hands. In this way, our friend Dutch was no different. He was given a
talent from God to use his hands to make things; to join things; to bring
them together. . . .

(The Pastor stands up and continues the
sermon addressing the audience as if he
were actually giving it. Ruby stops
fiddling with the lighter and remains
perfectly still staring at it.)
However, Dutch was more than just a welder--those who knew him well
remember that he was meticulous, a perfectionist who took great pride in
his work, in everything he did, and demanded nothing less from those
around him. Every seam he torched held because he took the time to do it
right. With fire and purpose he was able to make what were two things into
one. In a world that promotes the pursuit of money and sensual pleasure
above all else, what a rare thing it is to have known a man whose passion
lay in workmanship, in creation rather than the destruction which brings
short-term satisfaction. . . . We all have something to learn from him:
that there is honor and righteous fulfillment in doing whatever it is you
do to your utmost. Often we forget that we are to do everything to the
glory of God. Everything! A shabby job and carelessness do not glorify
God. This means our jobs are more than just something to provide money:
they are a form of praise. A form of praise every bit as important as
singing in this church on Sunday. Dutch's life should be an example to us
in the proper way to glorify the Lord. . . . Now, in this time of despair,
we must let God be our welder. We must let his holy fire weld our hearts
together where they are torn asunder by the loss of our loved one. David,
the Psalmist, has written the perfect prayer for us to send up to Jesus,
showing him we are ready for his healing fire: Psalm 23--"The Lord is my
shepherd, I shall not want. He maketh me to lie down in green pastures:
he leadeth me beside the still waters. He restoreth my soul." . . . He
restoreth my soul! David is telling us that God has the power to take away
our despair and restore our souls. We need not remain in a torn and broken
state. . . . "Yea, though I walk through the valley of the shadow of
death, I will fear no evil." . . . This is the truth, Ruby. God will
restore you if you ask it of him.

RUBY
I know who's to blame.

PASTOR
What? . . . Blame?

RUBY
I know whose fault it is.

(He pauses waiting for her to continue.)

PASTOR
It was an accident. . . . There's no one to blame here. . . . And we
absolutely must not blame God if that's what you mean. He doesn't operate
in a way we can understand Ruby. God is not at fault, he has a higher
purpose. . . . Even if it is a cliche, its true--Dutch is in a better place
now. Really, it's an honor to be called home, though I know how difficult
it is to look at it that way sometimes.

(The Pastor pauses again. Ruby stubs out
her half-finished cigarette and lights
another one.)
There isn't anyone to blame for death. When Adam and Eve were banished from

(CONTINUED)

10.

PASTOR (CONTINUED)
Eden, having to die was one of the things they were cursed with. We can't
change that. But like I've been saying, we can let God take away the pain.
Sometimes those left behind feel guilty for getting to go on living when a
loved one has passed. But there really is no blame here. We must realize
that it's all a part of a plan beyond our comprehension and live out the
rest of our lives.

RUBY
I don't feel guilty for being alive. That's not what I'm guilty of.

PASTOR
Ruby, God knows your heart, and he knows that it is innocent in this
matter. You must not punish yourself for something you didn't do,
something you had no control over. That's the devil speaking to you. Ask
God to cast him out.

RUBY
It wasn't the devil, Pastor, it was me.

PASTOR
I'm afraid I don't follow you.

RUBY
Why did Eve give Adam the apple?

PASTOR
What?

RUBY
Why did Eve give Adam the apple?

PASTOR
What does this have to do with what we're talking about?

RUBY
It has everything to do with it.

PASTOR
Uh, well she gave him . . . she . . . the Bible doesn't really say why she
gave it to him, only that she was tempted by the serpent into eating it
because he said it would make her wise like God. After she ate it, she gave
it to Adam.

RUBY
But there must be a reason why she gave it to him.

PASTOR
I don't know exactly. Some things we are given to understand and others we
must simply trust God for.

RUBY
I'll tell you why she did it; because if she didn't she would be lonely.
She would be alone. God would take Adam away from her because she ate the
apple and he didn't. She had to give him the apple. She loved him and she
couldn't stand to lose him.

PASTOR
I don't know if we should interject so much of our own meaning into the
Word, Ruby. We should be content with what we are told in it, and not worry
about what we aren't. But I still don't see what this has to do with the
situation.

11.

RUBY

I made a mistake, and I have to pay for it. God took Adam away from me
because I didn't give him the apple. We ran out, but it was still my fault.

PASTOR

Adam? You said God took Adam away from you.

RUBY

No, I said God took Dutch away from me just like he'd've taken Adam away
from Eve if she hadn't've given him the apple.

PASTOR

What do you mean? What does *original sin* have to do with you and Dutch?

RUBY

Original sin--the apple. Don't you see? I didn't give Dutch his apple, and
God took him away!

PASTOR

Are you speaking metaphorically? What do you mean by apple?

RUBY

What's *metaphorically*?

(Ruby grabs an apple from the table and
holds it up.)
An apple, an apple like this! All I had to do was give it to him!

(Ruby hands him the apple. He looks at
it, confused, then hands it back. She
looks at it, takes a bite, then
continues to hold it as she grabs a
broom and violently sweeps.)

RUBY

Right after we was married he laid it all out, how things was to be
done. . . . It wasn't no surprise, I seen my mother do most the stuff
for my father all my life, and the way Dutch wanted things wasn't too
different. Men like to have things ready for them when they come home so
they can relax and forget about work. Everything has to be just so. My
husband had a very stressful job, and he needed his rest. He needed things
done exactly right so he didn't get distracted and make mistakes. Mistakes
kill, he told me. And he was right; I learned firsthand he was right. I
remember it was the morning after the honeymoon, and he had to get up and
go to work. He was tying up his boots and he said: "Ruby, the courtin's
over now. There's certain things I expect outta a wife." He said: "I work
very hard and I don't expect much, but what I do expect is for things to be
done right so I don't have to come along behind you and re-do them. I don't
want to have to think about what's for breakfast and is my lunch made
'cause I have more important things to think about. If I don't keep my mind
on my work, that's how accidents happen." And then he said: "There should
always be eggs for breakfast, over easy, and there should always be a
sandwich and an apple in my lunch box. For supper I need some kind of meat
and bread and vegetables and a potato. Don't mess around with trying no
Chinese or spaghetti foods. Whatever else you want to fix alongside my
eggs or to go in my lunch box is fine, as long as there's eggs for
breakfast and an apple in my lunch." . . . Eggs for breakfast and an
apple, he said. An apple. Mistakes kill. . . .

(She has swept herself to the corner
near the Welder, her back to him. The
Welder comes to life, placing his gloved
hand on her shoulder. She jumps, turns

12.

(and backs away. The Welder lights the torch and advances toward Ruby. She speaks to him wildly, but the Pastor, unable to see the Welder, thinks she is speaking to him.)

RUBY

What do you want with me?

(She continues to back away from the Welder. The Pastor stands up.)

PASTOR

Calm down Ruby. . . . Easy now. . . . I'm sorry if I don't understand about the apple--

(Ruby cuts him off.)

RUBY

Why are you here?!

PASTOR

Ruby! What's wrong? Did I say something to upset you?

RUBY

I know it was my fault!

(The Pastor approaches her, hands out, trying to soothe her.)

PASTOR

Easy, easy now. . . . Everything's going to be okay.

RUBY

Go away! Please! Go away!

(The Pastor retreats a step at her vehemence.)

PASTOR

Okay. . . . Okay. . . . Why don't you lie down for a bit?

(At this point the Pastor and the Welder are standing side by side. Ruby is almost convulsive with pent-up fear and confusion; she drops the broom and winds up and flings the apple still in her hand at the Welder, but hits the Pastor.)

PASTOR

(He edges toward the door.) I'm going! I'm going! But I think you should consider seeing a doctor--

RUBY

Leave me alone!

(The Pastor exits as she picks up a cup and appears ready to throw it. The Welder closes in on Ruby and she drops the cup and covers her face with her hands.)

                                RUBY
I'm sorry about the apple.

                                        (The Welder grasps her forearm and tries
                                        to force the torch into her fist. Ruby
                                        struggles free and screams "No!"
                                        repeatedly as he again pursues her. He
                                        finally corners her, and horrified, she
                                        submits, taking the torch from him. He
                                        guides her arm in welding her own mouth
                                        until, obediently, she does it on her
                                        own. Then the Welder exits. Ruby
                                        continues to weld her lips and mouth,
                                        unaware the Welder is gone. The lights
                                        go down sharply for a brief moment. When
                                        they come back up, Ruby is in her chair
                                        at the "nursing home" again. She begins
                                        to bandage her face back up slowly.)

                                RUBY
I know there isn't no one to blame but myself. I killed him. . . . He
always said, "If it's worth doing, do it right." . . . I am paying for my
sin with fire . . . Hellfire . . . I blame myself . . . Mistakes . . . I
blame . . . Mistakes kill . . . I blame . . . Manna gabba hee . . .

                                        (As Ruby stuffs gauze into her mouth and
                                        slips back into gibberish three men are
                                        heard laughing off stage. Their muffled
                                        conversation mingles into a gibberish
                                        that matches Ruby's for a few moments.
                                        Then the Pastor enters speaking over his
                                        shoulder.)

                                PASTOR
Thank you, Doctor.

                                        (He moves next to her chair and stares
                                        down at her for a moment.)
And how are we feeling today, Miss Ruby? . . .

                                        (Ruby is silent.)
Would you like to go for a stroll in the garden? . . .

                                        (The Pastor looks behind himself,
                                        glancing around to make sure no one is
                                        watching. He reaches into his pocket and
                                        holds an apple out to her.)
. . . Look, I brought you something.

                                        (Ruby slowly reaches for it and the
                                        lights go out.)

                                THE END

Chapter 11

PRODUCTIONS AND AGENTS

Production depends on collaboration. Unlike any other artist in the theatre, a playwright must first work solo, then make the transition to collaborative artist. Collaboration is often a playwright's downfall. This happens for two reasons. First, in their lonely struggles playwrights seldom learn the techniques they

> To be a playwright you not only have to be a writer, you have to be an alligator . . . a playwright lives in an occupied country. He's the enemy. And if you can't live that way, you don't stay.
>
> Arthur Miller

need to participate in an ensemble. Second, most members of the ensemble (actors, designers, and the director) aren't used to having the playwright's input. Too often, playwrights are left behind, their hard work unnoticed, when in fact they have lavished more time (and perhaps even creativity) into the finished product than the actors, designers, producers, and director combined. To help with the transition, playwrights must learn to work with other theatre professionals. They need to understand the established norms and chains of command. In turn, the ensemble must learn to encourage the playwright's participation. In order to do this, the playwright must walk a tightrope, standing up for the play, while stepping on as few creative toes as possible.

PLAYWRIGHTS AND DIRECTORS

For hundreds of years, playwrights directed their own work. In ancient Greece the playwright instructed the actors, staged the play, and even performed in the productions. Later, actors took control of staging. Then, a little more than a hundred years ago, directors came into being. Directors take on heavy loads: they are responsible for interpreting the play, developing a concept, staging, and supervising the work of actors and designers. If the play flops, directors certainly take their share of abuse. One director wanted to replace the words "directed by . . ." in the program with the words "blamed on. . . ." In the Hollywood film industry, directors have almost total control and can tell the writer what to write. In television (sitcoms and hour-length shows), the directors are almost unnoticed and are subservient to the writers. In theatre, the playwright–director relationship is different for every production and must be defined before the rehearsal process begins. Technically, the playwright and the director are equals, and so should reach a compromise as to exactly how they will work together.

Directors must understand the playwright's legal rights. When rehearsals begin, some directors think the playwright's work is done. This isn't true. A playwright can be a major ongoing contributor to any production. The director must understand that the playwright has the right to be actively involved with the production. Playwrights may attend all rehearsals and performances. They are allowed to be present during auditions and help with the selection of the cast. The playwright is part of management, just like the director, and cannot be excluded from the rehearsal process or production meetings.

Directors can put a great deal of pressure on a playwright. After all, they must influence and control or they can't do their job. If roles are not defined, a passive playwright will most certainly be manipulated, yet a demanding playwright will alienate the director and creative ensemble. The playwright should be eager to take suggestions and correct flaws in a play, but there is a difference between the playwright's obligation to make revisions and an obligation to make specific revisions demanded by directors, producers, and actors. **As a playwright, you are not a writer for hire;** you own the script and don't have to make changes unless you believe they will improve your play.

Just as the director must understand the playwright, so must a playwright understand the director. An often heard comment from new playwrights is "I'll leave that for the director to figure out." A playwright leaves nothing troublesome for the director to solve. Directors may well interpret, but don't add to their load by writing impossible entrances, massive set changes that add nothing to the story, or a character that is so open to interpretation that anything is possible. It's the playwright's job, not the director's, to make a play playable.

The playwright's dilemma is to remain in control of the play without overtly challenging the director. The best way to do this is to discuss questions and artistic differences with your director away from other artists. Many directors are more than willing to compromise, accommodate, and even admit they're wrong, if it's done *in private.* A playwright who publicly disagrees or fights for power with a director won't win and, more often than not, causes division within the ensemble.

To avoid problems, the playwright should communicate her notes, thoughts, and criticisms of the creative team through the director. Never give notes to the actors or designers without the director's knowledge and approval. Even if the playwright and director are in total agreement, let the director give the notes. No two people will communicate the same thought the same way, and even slight changes in a concept can confuse actors and designers.

Playwrights *do* have a say in who will direct their play; too often new playwrights are so thrilled to have a production that they don't take time to learn about the director. Directors come in two models: *interpretive directors* have a deep respect for the playwright's words and use their imaginations to serve the playwright's voice. Accurately staging the original intention of the script is the interpretive director's goal.

Creative directors change the playwright's work in order to come up with a "refreshingly original production." Most playwrights would rather work with an interpretive director. Before working with a new director, investigate her past production history. If she is famous for doing a new version of *Hamlet* set on Mars, or if his last production was a clown version of *I Never Sang for My Father*, you might want to sit down and have a long talk or find another director. It's the director's job to work with you, to understand, develop, and stage your play as you see it. Here are some questions a playwright might want to ask before agreeing to a particular director:

1. Does the director listen? Can I talk with this person? Is he interested in my opinion?

2. Does the director have a clear concept that's consistent with my intentions?

3. Is the director creative or interpretive?

4. What is the director's history? If he is combative about his past, it's more than likely that he's the wrong guide for your play. She or he should be specific and proud about past productions.

5. Are the director's concepts flexible? After talking with you, does the concept change?

6. Did she choose to direct your play, or was it assigned to her by the artistic director?[1]

7. Does the director understand the Dramatists Guild's rules concerning the playwright's rights?

The playwright–director relationship is one of the most important within the theatre. You don't have to agree to *any* director. You hold the blueprint; make sure the contractor sees the play as you see it, understands it as you understand it, and has creative, interesting ideas on how to stage it and improve it. Above all, avoid the director who sets out to "save" or "fix" your play. If it's "broken," or needs "repair," it's not ready to be produced and you have no need for a director, at least not yet.

---

[1] An artistic director manages and supervises all artistic aspects of a theatre company.

A playwright enjoys power, too. Yet, the power of ownership marks the defeat of many playwrights. Although it's true the Dramatists Guild and copyright laws prohibit anyone from changing even a letter of a playwright's work without permission, a playwright must be inherently aware of what battle is worth fighting and what is best left open to another artist's interpretation. The original vision is yours, but you can't have so much control that you turn the director, designers, and actors into puppets. Playwrights who have all the answers, who never compromise, who are not willing to rewrite, who believe that their creative power is being challenged when someone makes a suggestion are not interested in producing the best play possible.

DIRECTING YOUR OWN WORK

If you're just beginning, directing your own play is not advisable. Unless you've been trained in directing and have directed several plays, the chances of successfully staging your own work are small. The common reason given for not allowing playwrights to direct their own work is that they lack "objectivity." But, as playwright/director Steven Deitz (who has directed many of his own plays) points out, just as many directors lack objectivity as playwrights. The real problem with directing your own play is technique. Playwright/directors are less likely to compromise. They seldom take into account the unique point of view and insights each member of the ensemble brings to the production. Instead, they try to stage the play exactly as they imagined it. The result is a rehearsal process spent "bringing everyone up to speed" with the playwright/director's vision, rather than making new and interesting discoveries.

Before you set out to direct your own work, try to find an experienced, understanding director who has great passion and respect for your play. If you can't find such a director, if you believe you can direct your own work, and if you have directing experience, then learn to wear two hats. Don't allow the playwright facet of your personality to direct. Split yourself into two people, a playwright who writes the best script possible and a director who won't allow the playwright's ego to become more important than the audience.

PLAYWRIGHTS AND ACTORS

Actors and playwrights have always had a special relationship. Actors depend on playwrights for their characters and words. Playwrights need actors to bring their creations to life. No two productions of a play are alike, and no two actors will play a role in exactly the same way. Thousands of actors have played Hamlet, and every Hamlet is different. This is because the final character that appears on stage is a combination of the playwright's creation, the actor's own personality and talents, and the director's vision.

To make this playwright–actor relationship as strong as it can be, the playwright must let the actor act. Actors aren't marionettes; allow them to explore, experiment, try, fail, and try again. The surest way to hurt the actor–playwright relationship is to step on the actor's right to explore. Through the director, you may guide the actors; never command them.

Actors need one consistent, unified voice, the director's. Certainly this is not to say you shouldn't speak to actors. Sometimes the director thinks the playwright can communicate the idea more clearly and will ask the playwright to give the note directly to the actor. Then, and only then, you may speak to an actor directly about the performance.

Be positive, open, and helpful around actors, but don't give them *line readings,* in which you tell them exactly how to act or say the line. To have a playwright read his or her lines with prescribed intonation is an actor's nightmare. Remember, the actor can teach you about the play. Keep an open mind.

Occasionally, a production must deal with a difficult actor. When an actor's demands get in the way of production, let the director take care of it. After all, that's part of the director's job, not yours.

A U D I T I O N S

A good director is interested in the playwright's ideas and wants the playwright present during the audition. Even so, the playwright should remain in the background. Let the director run the audition. Someone once said casting is 90 percent of directing. Get the right actor and you'll save yourself a lot of rehearsal time. As you look at each actor, consider the following: Does the actor have the vocal clarity, intelligence, energy, and stage presence the part requires? What was your first impression? Is the actor the right type for the role? After the audition, meet with your director. You have a say in casting. Be strong, yet understanding.

P L A Y W R I G H T S   A N D   D E S I G N E R S

Costume, set, and lighting designers have a great deal of work to do and little time to do it. Unlike an actor, who can grow, discover, and change up until opening night (and even after), the designers must set the design long before the opening in order to have time for it to be built. Receiving mixed signals from the playwright and director is the surest way to make designers' lives hell.

When dealing with designers, a playwright should always be helpful and friendly. But, again, notes, concepts, or critiques should be relayed through the director. If the designer doesn't follow your concept, your problem is with the director, not the designer. Also take into account the designer's point of view. As with directors, don't put the designers into impossible situations and leave them to figure out how to make it work. It's the playwright's responsibility to write plays that can be designed and staged.

PLAYWRIGHTS AND DRAMATURGS

The *American Heritage Dictionary* describes a dramaturg as a playwright, but that's not always the case. A dramaturg is a theatre's literary adviser. Sometimes they are playwrights, but more often they are experts in particular areas of theatre history, literature, or criticism. A dramaturg may help a production by assembling appropriate background material on a script or advising a director on a particular period. Dramaturgs may be responsible for editing or adapting old scripts or developing new scripts.

Few theatres have dramaturgs, but if you should be assigned one, know that he will be working with you to develop your script. The dramaturg is not a writer, but a script doctor who makes suggestions and comments that are supposed to help you improve the next draft.

There is a popular notion in the theatre today that playwrights do not have a great deal of insight into what they've written and need an outside voice to guide them. Why playwrights in particular lack insight has never really been explained to us. We have met just as many directors, actors, and dramaturgs who lack insight. The truth is, almost as many scripts have been hurt through development as have been helped. Like it or not, today's playwrights are being treated more and more like Hollywood writers for hire rather than the independent voices that create and own the scripts.

If you want to be produced, working with a theatre and perhaps a dramaturg is necessary. Refusing to make changes in the script will more than likely cause the theatre to lose interest. The key is to treat the dramaturg much like a director. Make sure the dramaturg has an understanding of your script and that his or her suggestions help you take the script where you want it to go. The dramaturg should be a colleague who assists the playwright, not a taskmaster.

It's not as bleak as we make it sound. Most theatres and dramaturgs want only the best for the playwright and the script. The keys are listening and respect. Playwrights who are open to and constantly listening for a good idea will not sacrifice the production to their own egos. All plays are rewritten. Becoming defensive and refusing suggestions is the end for most playwrights. Also, the dramaturg who has a deep respect for the playwright's words will be able to make only those suggestions that help playwrights realize their goals. (For more information on development and taking suggestions see chapter 9.)

PLAYWRIGHTS AND THE AUDIENCE

Today's theatre seems plagued by a feeling that the playwright and the audience are at odds with each other. Just listen to some playwrights complain about how misunderstood they are or denounce the audience as wanting only "entertainment." Many playwrights seem to be saying, "If the spectators would only follow me, I would lead them unto enlightenment, education, and my deep, secret pain." Good playwrights should never think of themselves as better than their audiences. A play has no meaning except in relation to an audience. A playwright is a communicator. **Failure to communicate is the playwright's fault.**

Some playwrights believe they shouldn't write for the masses. They think that if a play is "popular," if it interests and pleases a large audience, it's somehow less worthy than a play that appeals to a small, select group. *Entertainment* is a dirty word to many playwrights, yet it only means keeping an audience interested for two hours. It doesn't mean you have to write popular amusement. For a playwright to hold an audience throughout the play, there must be more than just amusement. A playwright must attempt to find and communicate truth. In this sense, *Hamlet* is an entertaining play.

Euripides, Shakespeare, and Williams all wrote for the masses, and they were some of the greatest playwrights of all time. Popular doesn't imply shallow. On the other hand, beware of giving the audience total control. If the playwright's only desire is to please the audience, there will be no growth, for no new ideas or points of view will be staged. Challenge, educate, and entertain your audience. A playwright is a guide. If the audience doesn't follow, the playwright must reexamine her techniques and not blame it on the spectator.

One student playwright wrote about the gay experience and was quite disappointed when a conservative, mostly heterosexual audience didn't understand or appreciate his play. He immediately condemned the audience as closed minded, announcing that he had written the play for a select group of people who had experiences similar to his. In doing so, he had unwittingly defeated the purpose of writing the play. A playwright takes no great joy in preaching to the converted. A playwright attempts to communicate with a diverse audience. Whether separated by race, gender, sexual preference, experiences, age, or time, audiences will always be diverse. It's the playwright's duty to attempt to communicate with all members of an eclectic group. By doing so, the playwright allows that group to find rare common ground and, at least for a moment, understanding. William Archer said it quite nicely: "The skill of the dramatist, as distinct from his genius of inspiration, lies in the correctness of his insight into the mind of his audience."

PLAYWRIGHT VS. CRITICS

Playwrights will never be free from critics. As long as there has been theatre, there have been critics. One of the oldest records dates back to 3000 B.C. when the Egyptian actor I-kher-nefert recorded his opinion of a play. Jean Racine, the French neoclassic playwright wrote, "They [critics] always look forward to some successful work in order to attack it—not out of jealousy, for on what grounds could they be jealous?—but in the hope that they will force someone to take the trouble to reply to their criticism, and that they will thus be rescued from that obscurity to which their own works would have everlastingly condemned them."

No matter how secluded playwrights may be, they still have a deep desire to please, and because of this, brutal critics have been the undoing of many of them. Director Rich Burk points out that "Critics seem to think that in order to impress their readers (or just their parents) they must cut their subjects to the very heart with a fatal blow. They are self-appointed keepers of social culture and not part of the arts community."

Often a playwright will win the critics' hearts with a first success only to have the next play panned. For example, Tennessee Williams could do no wrong according to the critics' in the fifties and yet could do no right in the sixties.

It's sad to think that years of hard work can come down to one performance. Will the critics like it? More than likely they won't. The vast majority of plays, according to the critics, fail.

There are some things that a playwright or theatre can do to help chances of getting a good review. First, make sure you know the names of the critics in your area. Their names should be in the box office, so when they call for tickets they don't have to relay their life history. Critics think they're important and feel everyone should know who they are. Play along. "Oh, Mr. Reardon! We have complimentary tickets waiting for you!" They'll eat it up. Next, make sure to offer them tickets only for the nights you want them there. Be certain the play is ready, pad the audience if necessary, and pray. Above all, never challenge a critic. They think their authority is absolute, so allow them that luxury.

When the review comes out, try not to put much weight in it. If you're overjoyed by a good review, you will be all the more saddened by the pan. Above all, don't let the critics destroy your desire to write. In some ways it's better for a playwright to be a failure for many years and succeed only late in life after the body of her work is done. In this way the critics can do little harm to the writer's desire to create.

FINAL THOUGHTS ON PRODUCTION

The play must be actor-proof, director-proof, and designer-proof. This means that the play is so well written that even an average actor, director, or designer can do it justice. You don't want to write a play that can be staged only by artists of extraordinary imagination and talents.

Plays are written to be performed, so a playwright must be two personalities: the lonely writer who creates and the public member of an ensemble who knows how to gently influence other artists. Playwrights are not employees, they are a part of management and have every right to be included in production. Be supportive, understanding, and give other artists a chance to be creative and fail. Let their opinions count, but make sure it's your play they're producing and not someone's loose interpretation.

AGENTS

The old joke concerning agents goes like this: One day a young writer comes home to find his house in flames. He runs up to a policeman and asks, "What happened?" The officer tells him, "Your agent came by, killed your whole family, took your car, and set fire to your house." Stunned, the writer smiles dreamily and says, "My agent came to my house! There's hope!"

Beginning writers often concentrate too much on trying to find an agent. If you're just starting out, you would need one only to help with contracts and to get your play to those few theatres and producers who won't accept unsolicited scripts. About 5 percent of all theatres demand that an agent submit the script, and the Dramatists Guild will help beginners (if they are members) with contracts, so even without an agent, you've got help. Spend your time writing great plays, win a few contests, get some productions under your belt, and then you'll be ready for your first agent.

If you're ready for an agent, then it's time to get an up-to-date list. You can find lists of agents in the *Dramatists Source Book* and *Playwright's Companion,* but the most complete list is in the Dramatists Guild's annual *Resource Directory* that you will receive when you join. Contrary to the thinking of most beginning writers, it's not that difficult to get an agent. The hard part is to write a script so good that an agent will want to sign you. Concentrate your efforts on making your script the best it can be and finding an agent will become much easier.

Contact an agent in much the same way you look for a production: send a query with cover letter, resume, synopsis, sample of dialogue, and a self-addressed envelope or postcard (S.A.S.E. or S.A.S.P.). Your letter should concisely state something about you and your new play. Your letter should not be too formal; you can let the reader know you're human and perhaps have a sense of humor. Any information on your other plays, awards, and honors should be included in a one-page resume. If you have no other plays, awards, or honors then chances are you aren't ready for an agent. Don't send a full script to any agency not familiar with your work or one that has not requested it. Begin by sending a query.[2]

First, send a mass mailing of query letters (including dialogue sample and resume) to as many agents as possible. Make sure the script sample is your best. Once an agent rejects it, it's going to be a while before they'll be willing to read additional submissions. Also, do not try to impress an agent by sending her more than one play. Agents are overwhelmed with scripts. They generally want to begin with one script and only your best. If you've written a good letter and your synopsis and dialogue are excellent, maybe two or three will write back inviting you to send the script. Some playwriting agents refuse simultaneous submissions. In other words, they want you to wait until they reject your script

---

[2] Chapter 9 includes information on and examples of queries and cover letters.

before you mail it to the next agent. Generally, if the agent doesn't mention anything about refusing simultaneous submissions, it's acceptable to submit to any and all agents who request a script. This process can take months, so keep a record. This record should include the dates, the secretary's name (if you've contacted the agent by phone), and any reaction (written or verbal).

If an agent invites you to send a script and you don't receive a response for a few months, it's perfectly acceptable to call. More than likely you'll speak with the secretary. Get the secretary's name and *write it down* for the next time you call. Be sure to be polite. Secretaries have been known to help polite beginning playwrights. They can move your script to the top of the reading pile or they can remind the agent about you. By the time all the agents reject your script you should be well on your way to a new play. Finish the next script, make sure it's good, and try again.

If an agent does ask you to sign with him or her, then it's time to do your homework. Unfortunately, no codes or laws determine who can be an agent. They don't need a license or have to pass a test, so get on the phone to the Guild, ask around, try to find as much information about that agent as possible. What's his reputation in the industry? Is she respected? It's also perfectly acceptable to ask the agent who he represents. Any big names? What successes has she had?

When you decide to sign with an agent, be sure to read the contract carefully and get the Dramatists Guild's reaction. Last, but not least, make sure the agent is excited by your writing.

A playwriting agent's standard fee is still 10 percent (some may take as much as 20 percent for amateur productions). Larger agencies will copy your script for you, smaller ones will ask you to send them copies. If your agent answers her own phone, you know you're with a small operation. There's nothing wrong with that. A small agent is better than no agent. Finally, never sign with an agent who demands an up-front fee. Some unscrupulous agents have been known to ask for a "signing fee" with the promise to refund the money when the script is produced. This is a scam. Agents get paid only when they succeed in getting you a production.

CONTRACTS

When it comes time for a production, beginning playwrights who don't have agents usually think they have to negotiate their own contract. This is not the case. Writing your own contract with a theatre can be difficult for someone who doesn't understand basic "legalese," so the Dramatists Guild has a preapproved standard contract that covers all the bases. It's available to members for a nominal charge. These contracts include small theatres, showcase productions, and options, as well as contracts for major productions and collaborations. It's beneficial to demand that a theatre use a preapproved Dramatists Guild contract. Never allow your play to be produced on a handshake. Always get a contract and always have a lawyer at the Guild look it over. Whatever happens, don't go it alone. It may look fine, but save yourself a lot of trouble; call the Guild, use their contracts, and follow their advice.

Even with a contract, some theatres attempt to avoid paying the playwright—sad, but too often true. Perhaps it's because the playwright's hard work is usually over by the time rehearsals start, or perhaps it's because the playwright is too willing to compromise. Our first major production was by a famous theatre in San Francisco. We were to receive 3 percent of gross, according to the contract, to be paid every Monday. The play opened and several weeks went by. No payments. Finally, when we called to inquire where our checks were, the baffled accountant said, "Oh, you want to be *paid?*"

If a theatre does not honor the contract, turn to the Guild. Their legal department can lean on a theatre. They'll write the theatre informing it of its responsibility and can publish that theatre's name in their newsletter, thus announcing to all playwrights that this theatre doesn't honor its contracts. If that doesn't work, take them to court.

FURTHER REMUNERATION

If a theatre company is staging your play's world premiere, they may ask that further productions have an announcement in the program stating that they were the original producing organization. It's a sort of free plug for them. These theatres or producers may also want a percentage of the profits should your play be produced again. That's right, they want a royalty paid to *them*. You may or may not be amenable to this. Call the Guild, only they can tell you if a particular theatre's demands are reasonable.

OPTIONS

Sometimes a producer or a theatre will want to *option* your play. There are two types of options, exclusive and nonexclusive. An *exclusive option* gives that producer or theatre sole rights to produce your play for a given length of time (usually a few months, perhaps a year). A playwright who grants a theatre an exclusive option is agreeing not to allow any other theatre to produce the play for that set period of time. In return, the writer should receive an advance payment as insurance that the production will take place. If the set period of time expires and the theatre or producer has not staged the play, the playwright keeps the money and is free to market the script elsewhere. The payment to the playwright may be small if the option is for a short time or much larger if the option time is longer. To get a ballpark figure of how much money should change hands, call the Dramatists Guild. If the producer or theatre does produce your play during the option period, then the advance payment is sometimes deducted from the playwright's royalties.

A nonexclusive option means that the theatre or producer forgoes sole rights to the script. For example, the nonexclusive option may cover only one city or geographic area for a set amount of time.

If you are offered an option, treat it just like any other contract; seek advice from your agent, lawyer, the Dramatists Guild, or all three. Don't allow a theatre or producer to sweet talk you into optioning your play without some sort of payment. Demand payment. Demand a contract that states the length of the option, exact effective dates, and how much money you'll be paid up front.

ROYALTIES

Royalties are a share of the proceeds or a set fee paid to playwrights for the right to perform their plays. Hundreds of years ago, plays were bought outright and the author had no further financial or artistic control over them. This is no longer the case. A playwright never gives up the rights or control of the script. A playwright rents a script. The rental fee is called royalty.

Royalties can vary widely from one type of theatre to the next. The smallest productions—most colleges, high schools, and community theatres—will only offer playwrights the amount they would normally pay Samuel French or Dramatists Play Service (about thirty-five to fifty dollars per performance). For amateur productions, the playwright should insist on being paid no less than these minimums.

An *Equity waiver production* is one in which Equity[3] actors act for free but with limitations (for example, the theatre must seat fewer than one hundred). Equity waiver productions usually happen in major cities and are a great way for a playwright to be produced with professional actors, but they have their drawbacks. If you're offered an Equity waiver production, insist on signing a Dramatist Guild–approved contract—it will state exactly how much you should be paid.

When playwrights succeed at getting major productions, they begin to make real money. In this case, the playwright's royalty is often a percentage of gross. *Gross* means the total amount of money the theatre takes in at the box office *before* paying bills, actors, or anyone else. Five to ten percent of gross is not uncommon. Occasionally the producer will offer the writer a flat dollar amount. This allows the writer to be paid per performance, per week, or per run and not have to gamble on the box office receipts. There is no rule stating what you must be paid one way or the other. It's a matter of personal preference.

STAGE WRITERS HANDBOOK

Playwrights have many questions concerning their rights. The only book that offers detailed answers to these questions is *Stage Writers Handbook* by Dana Singer. Ms. Singer, a copyright lawyer, has many years' experience helping playwrights navigate the murky waters of contracts. Her book also gives detailed

---

[3] Actors Equity is the union that represents professional stage actors.

information about copyrights, collaboration, underlying rights, representation, royalties, and publishers. The handbook is published by Theatre Communications Group and is a must-read for all playwrights. (ISBN 1-55936-116-6)

TAXES

Playwriting is a business. Playwrights can usually deduct their home office expenses as well as a portion of rent, mortgage payment, utilities, and phone bills. Remember to document the extent of work done in your home office and the exclusivity of its uses. Keep detailed records of how much you spend. The laws on having an office in your home are changing all the time, so be sure to check with the Dramatists Guild and your tax preparer about what deductions you are allowed. Some *business-related* expenses you may be able to deduct include

> Attorney and accountant fees
>
> Books and periodicals
>
> Business telephone
>
> Business telephone calls
>
> Clerical fees
>
> Commission to agents
>
> Computer hardware, software, and repairs
>
> Copying
>
> Dramatists Guild dues
>
> Office equipment, supplies, and paper
>
> Postage
>
> Professional education (nondegree classes)
>
> Publicity
>
> Research for a specific project
>
> Research materials
>
> Theatre tickets
>
> Traveling expenses (hotels, airline tickets)

For help with taxes get *The New Tax Guide for Performers, Writers, Directors, Designers and Other Show Biz Folk: From How to Get Organized to What to Do If You Are Audited, Including a Monthly Travel Expense Diary* by R. Brendan Hanlon (Limelight Editions/Proscenium Pub. NYC, 1994, ISBN/ISSN 0-87910-178-4).

THE STORY OF THE CONTRACT FROM HELL

We finish this chapter with the story of the worst contract ever written. Years ago we were visiting New York City when a friend from graduate school told us that he wanted to do an Equity waiver production of our first play. We were honored, even thrilled.

He met us at a restaurant on the East Side and showed us the contract. Seven pages of single-spaced legalese. To be honest, we didn't know better, so we didn't think anything of it when the contract stated that he, the producer, was going to get 60 percent of the royalties for the next five years. It also stated that he owned the rights to any television or movie version for the next ten years. In return he promised us twelve performances of the play somewhere in one of New York's many small black-box theatres[4] sometime within the next two years, but the contract also stated that, if for some reason he failed to fulfill his side of the bargain, the contract would still be valid. Our fee for all this was to be twenty-five dollars. He told us that "It's a tough contract, but if you want to be produced in New York, you really have to give up any rights the first time around."

He hauled out a pen for us to sign. We stalled. We suspected something was wrong when we had to pay for our own lunch. After the meeting we walked over to the Dramatists Guild and dropped off a copy for the legal department.

When we arrived home, the phone was ringing. It was the president of the Guild. He didn't even say hello, but shouted, "Have you signed this contract?" We told him we hadn't. "Thank God," he said. "This is the worst contract we have ever seen. We're thinking of asking Stephen Sondheim to write music for it so we can sing it at our annual Christmas party." I called my "friend" and told him no deal. He argued. Still no deal. I lost a friend, but gained self-respect. Never be so desperate for production you're willing to sell your soul. Stand up for your rights, get paid, and always check with your agent, a lawyer, or the Dramatists Guild before you sign.

---

[4] A black box is a small theatre that usually seats fewer than one hundred. Most larger cities have theatre companies that operate out of these little stages, which frequently are stores, basements, and warehouses converted into theatres. They are often square and painted black, hence the name.

Chapter 12

THE ALTERNATIVES: SCREENPLAYS AND TELEPLAYS

Life for the playwright is difficult. Driven by low pay and lack of respect, some playwrights will turn to screenwriting or television writing. There's hardly a famous playwright who hasn't, at least once, been seduced by Hollywood and "sold out."

> *Millions are to be grabbed out here and your only competition is idiots.*
>
> Herman J. Mankiewicz
> (in a telegram to Ben Hecht, 1925)

The Hollywood temptation has become so common that every playwright must have knowledge of this closely related field. Because there are many fine books on screenwriting (several are listed at the end of this chapter), we'll concentrate on screenwriting from the playwright's point of view. The major differences between screen/television writing and playwriting fall under the categories of environment, unions, pay, creative rights, structure, format, medium, and agents.

THE HOLLYWOOD ENVIRONMENT

Hollywood requires that most writers subjugate themselves to directors, producers, actors, and "current trends." In Hollywood, everything is a commodity. They will tolerate a work of "Art" as long as it can make a profit.

Even if you accept the Hollywood environment, it can still take years of writing and hard work to sell a script. Deciding to sell out is one thing, finding a buyer is another. Few Hollywood writers manage to capture the big money.

Only 393 writers sold a script for more than a million dollars between 1985 and 1994. At the same time, 1,333 people won more than a million dollars in the California State Lottery. The average Hollywood writer makes just over $50,000 dollars a year.[1] Yet, between twenty and thirty thousand so-called writers live in Los Angeles, trying desperately to break into the entertainment industry. Doctors, lawyers, waiters—everyone seems to have a screenplay or sitcom script. It's been estimated that three hundred screenplays are finished every day in Hollywood. Of those, some 10 percent are optioned; of that, only 10 percent are purchased and only 30 percent of those are actually made into movies. Even the talented writer in Hollywood faces an uphill climb.

U N I O N S

A significant difference between playwrights and screenwriters are their unions. As we mentioned, the Dramatists Guild (DGA) is an open shop. The Writers Guild of America (WGA), sometimes referred to as the Screenwriter's Guild, is a closed shop. This means that you are *required* to be a member in order to write for any one of the signatory companies.[2] Unfortunately, you can't just pay a fee and join the WGA. To become a member, you must sell a script (or be hired to rewrite a script) to one of the signatory companies. It's a Catch-22. You can't write for them unless you're a member of the union, but you can't become a member unless you sell. Once you've succeeded in selling a script, you'll receive a bill from the WGA for $1,500. That's your membership fee, and from then on you'll pay 1.5 percent of your writing income to the union. It's expensive, but worth it, for the union keeps wages high, looks out for the writer's interests, and can provide free health insurance and pension plans (if you meet wage and time requirements).

The Writers Guild has about nine thousand members. Almost half of those writers are retired or sold perhaps one script and never worked again. This means that Hollywood has relatively few full-time, working writers. The vast majority of films, sitcoms, soap operas, and dramatic shows are written by about four thousand people. Around twenty-five hundred write for television, fifteen hundred for the movies. It's an exclusive club.

The WGA is still dominated by men. As of 1994, 87 percent of its membership were white males, 10 percent women, and 3 percent minorities. But that's changing. Producers, agents, and film schools are looking for talented female and minority writers.

---

[1] *WGA Journal,* December/January Issue 1996.

[2] A signatory company is any film or television company that has signed a contract with the WGA. The list of signatory companies is long. It includes NBC, ABC, CBS, Paramount, Columbia, and any of a hundred other studios or film companies. Only very small film companies are not signatory.

WGA JOURNAL

If you are interested in screenwriting you'll want to subscribe to the *WGA Journal,* the union's monthly magazine. It contains interviews and articles on writing, copyrights, the networks, computer programs, and screenwriting workshops, as well as an up-to-date list of which television shows are currently in production. Call or write the WGA for a subscription. (The address is given at the end of this section.)

WHEN THE WGA STRIKES

We close this section with a warning. The WGA is a powerful union, and they come down hard on strikebreakers. If the WGA is on strike, a playwright shouldn't accept any offers to write for a signatory company. If you write for these companies during a strike, you'll be blackballed from membership in the WGA. There have been stories about talented college writers who crossed the picket line only to find that, once the strike was over, they could never again write for Hollywood.

For more information about the WGA, call or write the office in your area:

The Writer's Guild of America (West)
7000 W. Third Street
Los Angeles, CA 90048-4329
(213) 951-4000

The Writer's Guild of America (East)
555 West 57th Street
New York, NY 10019

Writers Guild of Canada
35 McCaul Street
Toronto, Ontario
Canada M5T IV7
(416) 979-7907

Writer's Guild of Great Britain
430 Edgware Road
London, England W21EH
44-71-723-8074

Writers Guild of Australia
60 Kellett Street
Kings Cross, N.S.W. 2011
011-61-2-357-7888

The New Zealand Writers Guild
P.O. Box 46-018
Herne Bay
Auckland 1030, New Zealand

WAGES

Because of the WGA, screenwriters' and television writers' wages are considerably better than those of most playwrights. A writer of a half-hour sitcom can expect to make at least seventeen thousand dollars per episode. This includes story money and payments for first and second draft. Additional money can be made on residuals, both foreign and domestic. Guild minimum for an hour television show is about twenty-three thousand dollars per episode. Staff writers for sitcoms and hour-length shows can earn anywhere from four thousand to fifteen thousand dollars (sometimes more) a week. Selling a movie can earn a writer anywhere from forty thousand to millions of dollars. **But when you sell your script to Hollywood, you lose all creative control.**

CREATIVE RIGHTS

Unlike playwriting, when a Hollywood company buys your television or movie script, they own it and can rewrite or significantly change the script without your permission. It's not uncommon for writers to tune in to one of their episodes and not recognize it, because the rewrites have been so extensive. Screenwriter Rita Mae Brown summed it up when she said, "You sell a screenplay like you sell a car. If somebody drives it off a cliff, that's it." Only the most powerful Hollywood writers, or writers who direct or produce their own work, have creative control.

Many writers attempt to play this down by pointing out that the check is still good, but for most, the art of writing becomes only the business of writing. Hollywood writers are driven to write not what they need to say, not what they want to say, but what will sell. Yet, ironically, if your only purpose in going to Hollywood is to write what will sell and cash in, you'll most likely fail. You'll end up chasing the elusive market, trying to find that hidden shaft of gold rather than writing a good screenplay. Good screenplays sell. Even if it's turned into a bad movie, the original screenplay was probably pretty good or it wouldn't have sold.

SCREENPLAYS

A common saying in Hollywood is "The three most important elements of a screenplay are, structure, structure, and structure." Character in Hollywood almost always takes second place. The Hollywood structure is melodrama. Ninety-five percent of all television shows and movies are pure formula melodrama.[3] Often writers attempt to break with the Hollywood tradition and write something *different,* only to learn the hard way that few in Hollywood are interested. Most television and movie producers want new and innovative scripts as long as they fit the strict guidelines of the formula. There are exceptions, but they are few. Movies such as *Tender Mercies, Diner, Pulp Fiction,* and *Remains of the Day* are wonderful Hollywood films that didn't follow the formula, but they're not the norm.

DETERMINING CREDIT

Unlike a play, movies are usually written and rewritten by several different writers. When you see a movie's credits, they'll list one or maybe two writers

---

[3] Chapter 2 has a detailed outline of the formula Hollywood uses.

(no more than three), but in reality, many more were probably hired to rewrite, make revisions, or "punch it up." These ghost writers are well paid but often receive no credit. The WGA determines (through arbitration committees) which writers will receive credit and which won't. They have strict guidelines to determine credit, but it comes down to which writers had the most to do with the finished product. Those whose writing had the most influence on the final cut get credit; those whose rewrites didn't, don't.

PRODUCERS, STORY EDITORS, STORY BY, ETC.

Writers are identified by a confusing array of titles in movie and television credits. As we have already pointed out, just because a movie lists "written by Jack Smith," it doesn't mean other uncredited screenwriters weren't involved. "Story By" generally means that the writer made a substantial contribution to the narrative, idea, theme, or story. Guild rules state that only two writers can receive a "Story By" credit, so only the ones who made the most substantial contribution are credited. "Based on Characters By" means that the source material of the screenplay is based on a different play, novel, or another movie. The title "producer" may also indicate a writer. Some screenwriters get tired of their lack of control and insist on taking on the additional capacities of a producer. This is sometimes just a puppet position, other times it is a writer with a real say in the finished product. Normally producers, associate producers, and executive producers are the money people, not writers. They are top dogs who are in charge of everything, including the writers.

Sitcoms or hour-length television shows are different. The head writer is called the executive producer. In television, unlike movies, the writers are in charge. Below the executive producer, the next writer is called producer, associate producer, executive story editor, story editor, and finally staff writer (though staff writers are seldom mentioned in the credits). This means that the story editor you see listed in sitcom credits is not someone who edits the stories, but just another writer (in this case, one who is at least third or fourth in the pecking order).

TREATMENTS

A *treatment* is a narrative (five to twenty-five pages long) that tells or pitches a movie idea. Writers still sell treatments to Hollywood production companies, but it's less common than it was twenty years ago. The problem with selling a treatment is that the writer not only loses creative control, but can lose all credit as well.

When we first arrived in Hollywood, we went down to a local bar where a guy was buying everyone a round. He had sold his treatment for five thousand dollars. We asked him why he didn't just write the script, and he answered that he didn't think he was a good enough writer. That is no excuse. Learn to be a good writer and write the script. If you have a good idea for a movie, don't give it away for pennies (yes, in Hollywood five thousand dollars is pennies). Write the script and sell it for real money.

BUILDING A SCREENPLAY

The process of writing a screenplay is very much like a play. Many of the same dramatic rules and principles apply, with two major differences: scope and cinematic thinking.

A play has one to perhaps a dozen scenes and few characters. A screenplay's scope is far greater. It can have more than a hundred scenes and dozens of characters, and so requires more organization. You might be able to write a play with only a few preliminary notes, but screenplays require a detailed scenario.

The best way to build a screenplay's scenario is with *scene cards*. These are three-by-five-inch index cards on which a screenwriter notes brief descriptions of each scene, one scene per card. The cards are then pinned on a bulletin board and arranged and rearranged until the full structure of the movie is realized. Before most screenwriters write, they have the entire story worked out. When crafting a serious drama, a screenwriter might have 60 to 80 scene cards. A more action-oriented screenplay may have as many as one hundred cards that look something like this:

SCENE

CARD

ONE

> *INT. ROW HOUSE-DAY*
>
> 1. Konigsberg comes out on his porch to find a note
>   drilled into the railing with a knife.
>
> 2. The note reads, "Get out or you're dead."
>
> 3. Runs inside.
>
> 4. Dark figure is waiting for him.
>
> 5. He's killed.

SCENE

CARD

TWO

> *EXT. ROW HOUSE (several weeks later)*
>
> 1. Nick and Wife consider buying the house.
>
> 2. Buddy and Amelia want them to take it.
>
> 3. Talk of the history of the house.
>
> 4. Can they really live where someone was murdered?
>
> 5. They don't like the idea of row housing, everything
>   looks the same.

<table>
<tr><td>SCENE</td><td rowspan="3">

Int. Nick & SALLY'S BEDROOM-NIGHT

1. A hot night.

2. The noise from the neighbors is too much.

3. They've made a mistake buying the house.

4. Through the wall they hear Buddy and Amelia fighting. They never realized that their best friends' marriage was in trouble.

5. They feel guilty for listening in.

</td></tr>
<tr><td>CARD</td></tr>
<tr><td>THREE</td></tr>
</table>

Some screenwriters prefer simple scene cards that have only a few words of description, others need detailed cards. Figure 12.1 shows an arrangement of finished scene cards that create a story board.

Several computer programs can help create and arrange scene cards. A list is included in Appendix F.

ACT I, ACT II, AND ACT III

In Hollywood, screenwriters and producers use the word "act" differently from playwrights. To a screenwriter, the words "act 1, act 2, and act 3" are simply a different way of saying "beginning, middle, and end."

If a movie producer says that your second act is weak, he means the middle of your story (the complications, obstacles, and conflicts) needs work. To a screenwriter, the word *act* is a structural term used to divide a screenplay into workable units, not a division marked by an intermission (or indicated in the script). The problem is that no two Hollywood producers or writers use the term *act* to mean the exact same divisions.

To add to the confusion, sitcom and hour-length television writers define acts in the same way as playwrights—a formal break in the story marked by an intermission or, in their case, a commercial.

CINEMATIC THINKING

Cinematic thinking is a problem for many playwrights, but the opposite is true in screenwriting. In a film, the majority of the story is told through pictures and images. Here you want to think cinematically. As you write a screenplay, try to see the action in your mind's eye, as if it were happening in real life and not on stage. You want to lead the reader's eye, make her see the movie and feel the mood of the location.

SHOW, DON'T TELL

Not only do you want a reader to see the scenes, but you want to tell the story visually. For example, rather than having a scene in which two characters sit at

Figure 12.1

Scene Card Story Board

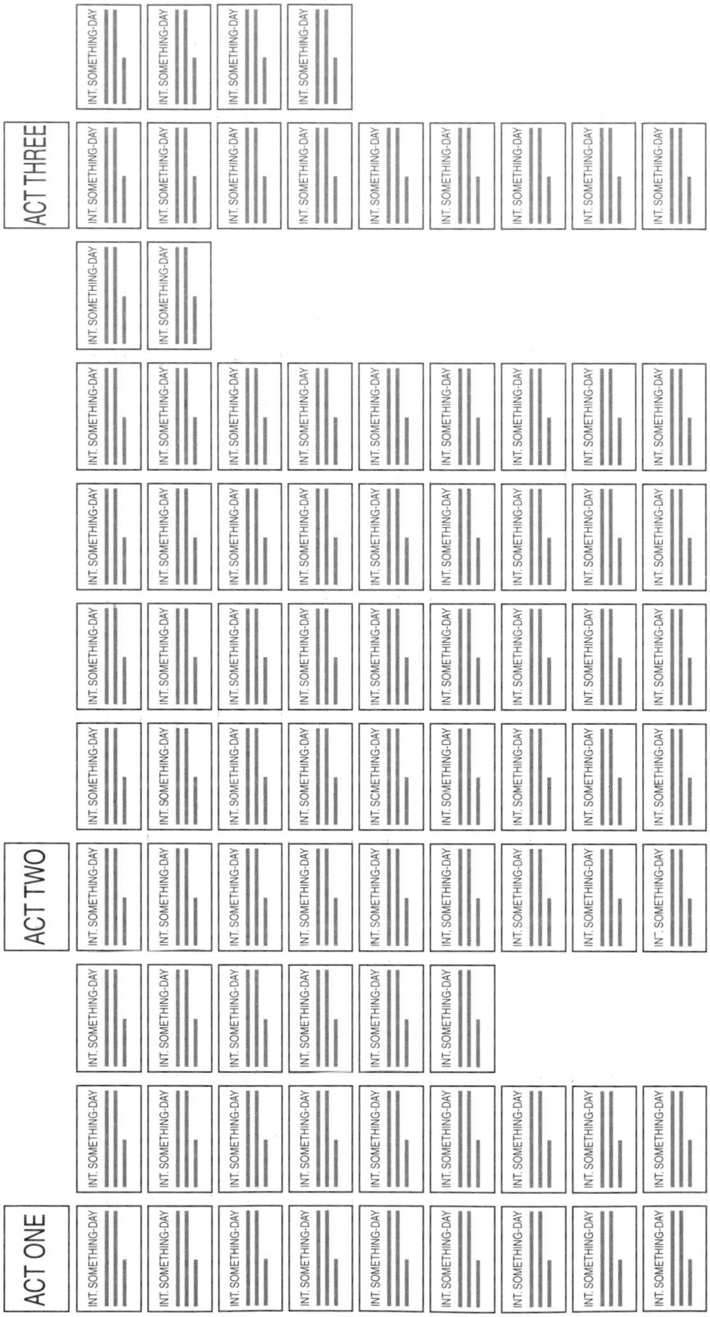

a bar talking about the time machine they found in an old professor's basement, *show* your reader the time machine; create a scene in which the characters discover it. Let your audience see the action rather than talk about it.

ADVICE FOR PLAYWRIGHTS TURNED SCREENWRITERS

Screenwriter Robin Russin offers eight bits of advice to playwrights who yearn to be screenwriters:

1. DON'T USE THREE WORDS IF TWO WILL DO THE JOB. This applies to dialogue, too. Even if you have a character who is meant to be long-winded, make every word meaningful.

2. IF YOU CAN'T SEE IT OR HEAR IT, DON'T WRITE IT. Internal moods, smells, tastes, dreams, and such must be described in a visual or audible way that a director can direct or an actor can act.

3. EVERYTHING THAT HAPPENS BETWEEN PLOT POINTS IS JUST AS IMPORTANT AS THE PLOT POINTS THEMSELVES.

4. IF YOU HAVEN'T HOOKED THE READER IN THE FIRST TEN PAGES, YOU WON'T.

5. ALL DRAMA IS CONFLICT. No conflict means no interest. Talk shows are the lowest level of this, the louder and angrier the better. The highest level is *Hamlet* or *Schindler's List*—sometimes devastatingly quiet, but boiling with conflict nonetheless.

6. THE PROTAGONIST AND ANTAGONIST WANT THE SAME THING. Both want love. Both want the Maltese falcon. Both want the Grail. Both want to win the race. Both have become, at the end, almost equally powerful, with the protagonist winning because she has the power of virtue on her side.

7. WRITE SOMETHING YOU'D ACTUALLY LIKE TO SEE YOURSELF. Don't write something you think you ought to write, for whatever noble intention. Write something you'd pay money to go see. That's what you're asking other people to do.

8. NO SCRIPT IS EVER FINISHED. Do not delude yourself that your first draft is good enough. It almost certainly is not, and you will ruin your chances with it if you send it out prematurely. Let it sit for a week or so, reread it carefully, get the opinions of people you trust, and rewrite it. Twice. Then move on, because it still isn't perfect, but nothing is, so get on to the next one. Trust me, if you sell the script, fifteen people will tell you why it needs to be rewritten again, anyway.

SCREENPLAY FORMAT

Just as in playwriting, if you don't follow the proper format, you'll be considered an amateur. The problem is that most beginning playwrights-turned-screenwriters use the format they find in a published screenplay or in *shooting scripts*. These contain several elements unneeded in a *spec script,* sometimes called a *show script* (spec is short for speculation). These are scripts a writer creates on speculation and hopes to sell.

Title Page: The title page of a screenplay is much the same as a play. The only difference between the two is that a screenplay requires a plain white sheet of paper (the same weight as the rest of the script). This may seem rather informal, but it's typical for a Hollywood screenplay. Never use a folder or clear plastic cover.

As do some playwrights, a few screenwriters attempt to make their scripts appear more legit by including on the title page statements such as "Property of Johnson and Associates" or "Owned by Johnson Films." No one is going to believe you own a film company. Leave such statements to the amateurs.

Binding Bind your script by using a standard three-hole punch and placing a metal brad in the first and third holes (no brad is placed in the middle hole). Don't buy the cheap, flimsy brads sold at department stores. Go to a good office supply and get the heavy-duty ones strong enough to hold a 120-page script.

Paper Just like a play, a screenplay is printed on only one side of each sheet. Twenty pound, 8.5-by-11-inch paper is the standard. White (and *only* white) paper is acceptable.

Font and Printers **Dot-matrix printers are unacceptable.** The most commonly used fonts are Courier 12 and 13.

Margins One inch on the top, bottom, and right sides of the page is the norm. The left margin should be one and three-eighths inches to one and one-half inches, as this allows extra room for brads.

Page Numbers Page numbers appear in the upper right corner. The title page is not numbered.

COPYRIGHT OR WGA REGISTRATION

You copyright a screenplay just as you do a play.[4] **The notice of copyright on the title page must be small and unassuming** (some screenwriters leave it off entirely).

The WGA offers screenwriters and television writers a registration service that is often faster than a Library of Congress copyright. If you write to the WGA Registration Department, they'll send you a registration form. Fill it out and send

---

[4] See chapter 8.

it back to the union with your screenplay or teleplay. In return you receive a WGA registration number. Place this number on the title page in place of a copyright notice. Example: Registered WGA #29543. Union members pay ten dollars for this service, nonmembers pay twenty dollars, the same as the Library of Congress charge.

You can register with the WGA scripts, treatments, synopses, outlines, ideas, even interactive media scripts, but not plays. A Guild registration lasts five years and can be renewed for an additional five. This service is set up to assist writers in establishing completion dates of a particular screenplay or piece of literary property. It is a record of the writer's claim to authorship, not a true copyright.

Just as with a play, there's no need to recopyright a screenplay or teleplay each time you make changes. Only when the script has been significantly altered should you bother to recopyright or get a new WGA registration number.

The Guild's registration office is open to the public from 10 A.M. to 5 P.M. Monday through Friday. It's located at 7000 West 3rd Street, Los Angeles, California. For more information on registration call:

Recorded Information (310) 205-2500
Fax (310) 550-0850
Main number (310) 205-2540

Or write:

The Writer's Guild of America *(West)*
Registration Department
7000 West 3rd Street
Los Angeles, CA 90048

CAST OF CHARACTERS PAGE

A screenplay contains no cast of characters page or list of scenes. The script begins after the title page.

FADE IN:

Screenplays begin with the words "FADE IN:," "FADE UP:," or the less common, "OPEN ON:." These words are capitalized and placed on the far left margin.

SLUG LINES

Before each scene is a slug line (sometimes called a master scene location or master scene heading) which identifies where and when the following scene takes place. This line begins with either "INT." meaning interior or "EXT." for exterior. Then it states the location, followed by a dash (-) and time of day, usually DAY or NIGHT. Slug lines are always in caps and followed by a double space (hard return). Here are examples of various slug lines.

```
EXT. GENE'S BEDROOM - NIGHT

INT. DOG HOUSE - DAY

EXT. AN OLD GAS STATION - NIGHT

INT. HOLIDAY INN - CONFERENCE ROOM - NIGHT
```

NARRATIVE

After the slug line comes narrative. Narrative in a screenplay is very much like stage directions in a play, only the writer is allowed to go into far more detail. Movies are a visual medium, and so the writer must be precise about what the audience sees. The narrative describes the physical action as well as location, mood, and character reactions. **The purpose of narrative is to make your reader see the movie.** Narrative is always written in present tense. Narrative in a screenplay is single spaced and flows from margin to margin. For example, here is a slug line followed by narrative.

```
EXT. ROW HOUSE UNITS - NIGHT

A chain of old Chicago row houses, shackled together
with common walls and porches. A solid sequence of Sears
siding and shutterless windows stretches to the horizon,
a dank cutout of the city's skyline.
```

MINI SLUG LINES

Once you have established the location, you may jump around to several locales within that location without using a new slug line. For example, if the slug line and narrative state:

```
INT. THE HOUSE OF JOHN DOW - DAY

The place is the product of minds that were children
during the Depression - nothing is too fancy or without
purpose.
```

You can now jump into, let's say, the bedroom without using a new slug line, but you must identify that we are now in the bedroom with a mini slug line:

```
BEDROOM - Larry slams the door. He throws himself on his
bed and stares at the bare ceiling.
```

Mini slug lines can also be used to identify what each character is doing within a given scene. For example, instead of writing long narrative paragraphs like these:

```
FADE UP:

EXT. KONIGSBERG'S HOUSE - NIGHT

Konigsberg steps outside to find the fuse box has been
smashed. Its simple metal walls have buckled from a
```

massive blow. A muffled click. It came from behind. He
turns to find a DARK FIGURE in a ski mask, surgical
gloves, and holding a Louisville slugger. Konigsberg
jerks back and dives for the house.

INT. KONIGSBERG'S HOUSE - NIGHT

He locks the back door and frantically searches the
kitchen drawers. He pulls out a silver semiauto handgun.
Then, silence. Only his hard breath. He slowly
approaches the door and peers through the curtained
glass. SMASH! The baseball bat shatters the window. A
surgical glove reaches in and unlocks the door. The DARK
FIGURE, bat raised, coolly enters and walks toward Mr.
Konigsberg. The broken glass twinkles on his ski mask.
Konigsberg closes his eyes and with a flinch, squeezes
the trigger. Click! A dud.

A screenwriter will use mini slug lines to lead the reader's eye and break the
action into easy-to-read-and-visualize bits. Here is the same scene using mini
slug lines.

FADE UP:

EXT. KONIGSBERG'S HOUSE - NIGHT

KONIGSBERG'S P.O.V. - The fuse box has been smashed. Its
simple metal walls have buckled from a massive blow. A
muffled click. It came from behind. He turns to find . . .

A DARK FIGURE - Ski mask, surgical gloves, holding a
Louisville slugger.

KONIGSBERG - jerks back and dives for the house.

INSIDE - He locks the back door and frantically searches
the kitchen drawers. He pulls out a silver semiauto
handgun. Then, silence. Only his hard breath. He slowly
approaches the door and peers through the curtained
glass.

SMASH - The baseball bat shatters the window. A surgical
glove reaches in and unlocks the door.

THE DARK FIGURE - bat raised, coolly enters and walks
toward Mr. Konigsberg. The broken glass twinkles on his
ski mask.

KONIGSBERG - closes his eyes and with a flinch, squeezes
the trigger. CLICK! A dud.

The narrative should not be static description. It is perfectly acceptable to let
your personality show. After all, the narrative is the writer speaking to the
reader. Here is an example of a less formal narrative in which the author is

having a conversation with the reader. It is perfectly acceptable as long as it fits the mood of the screenplay.

INT. DAVE'S ROOM - NIGHT

Dave is a tall, owl-faced kicker with heart. He is our protagonist. People like him, and so will you.

DAVE's P.O.V - Okay, the place isn't messy; Dave knows where everything is, but it could be cleaner. The three-day-old sandwich is a bit much. Dried tomatoes. Gross.

CUT TO:

At the end of a scene, it is common (but not required) to place the words "CUT TO" followed by a colon on the right margin. Like this:

CUT TO:

"CUT TO:" simply means that the movie is now changing to a new location or time. The master scene heading accomplishes the exact same thing, and so some screenwriters leave out the "CUT TO:." If it will help your reader see the movie and understand the mood, you may also use "FADE TO:" or "DISSOLVE TO:." This means that the end of a scene melts into the beginning of the next rather than a hard cut.

MONTAGES

A montage is a rapid sequence of brief scenes or images that underscore the story or tell the viewer that time in the story has passed. For example, if the character decides to become a skier and the screenwriter wants to show the process of him learning, she might use a montage. A montage in a screenplay would look like this:

MUSIC MONTAGE:

1. Larry stands on the skis for the first time. He falls.
2. He is now able do a few simple movements.
3. He plows into a woman. He isn't happy about it.
4. He is getting better. He can now turn. He smiles with his success. A four-year-old girl passes him doing much better.
5. Larry brags in the bar about how fast he went today. Then he sees the woman he hit. She's unimpressed.
6. He is now getting much better. He flies down the hill.
7. He makes a perfect turn, just missing a tree.
8. He talks over his style with a trainer.
9. He tries a tentative jump. He makes it.

CONTINUED

On some screenplays you may have seen the word "CONTINUED" at the upper left and lower right sections of almost every page. This is done on shooting scripts to let people know that whatever scene is happening on this page continues on the next page (as if you couldn't figure this out for yourself). This practice isn't necessary on a spec script. Leave it off; it wastes time and adds nothing to the read.

FADE OUT

The last line of a screenplay is usually "FADE OUT." This is capitalized and hugs the far right margin.

THE DON'TS OF SCREENPLAY FORMAT

There are two major *don'ts* on a screenplay: camera angles and numbering scenes.

Camera Angles.   In older screenplays you will see camera angles such as "CLOSE SHOT," "CLOSE ON," "WIDE SHOT," "MEDIUM SHOT," and "NEW ANGLE" listed. This is now considered old-fashioned and no longer done. It is the writer's job to tell the story, but not to direct the movie. Where a screenwriter twenty years ago would have written "CLOSE SHOT—A tear drips down her cheek," a modern screenwriter would write simply "A tear drips down her cheek." Inherent in the line is the fact that it's going to be a close shot.

Numbering Scenes: Spec scripts do not use scene numbers. Only shooting scripts have numbered scenes.

CHARACTER DESCRIPTION

Unlike a play, where the characters' names are always capitalized in the stage directions, in a screenplay narrative the characters' names are only capitalized the first time they enter. On that first entrance it's also acceptable to include a brief description. Just as with a play, the stress is on brief. If the character is minor, the description should be even shorter. If the character doesn't speak, there is no need to capitalize the character's name on the first entrance.

DIALOGUE

Screenplay dialogue has narrow margins. Example:

> WALTER CRONKITE
> *(on Television)* Today the U.S. Court of Appeals set aside the conviction of Dr. Benjamin Spock, author of *The Common Sense Book of Baby and Child Care*. Dr. Spock was arrested and convicted of conspiracy to counsel draft evasion . . .

All rules concerning dialogue in plays apply to movies. The only major difference is that movie dialogue must be short and to the point. As Vincent Canby, chief drama critic of the *New York Times,* points out, "One of the great things about the theatre is that you can have all the language you want. You don't have somebody telling you the characters are talking too much, as happens in the movies." There's an old saying in Hollywood, "Enter a scene as late as possible, exit a scene as early as possible." This means you should cut right to the heart of the scene. This also applies to dialogue. Screenplay dialogue is lean and to the point. As Richard Walter of the UCLA screenwriting program says, "Write headlines."

MOVIE MONOLOGUES

Monologues seldom occur in Hollywood movies. If you do have a long monologue, it's important to ask yourself what the audience looks at during the speech. The language may be wonderful for the stage, but what works for the stage is often boring in a movie. We once had a producer take out a ruler, slap it down on a speech and say, "That speech is four inches long, cut it to two."

PHONE CONVERSATIONS

Playwrights often use stage phone calls to bring in information and deliver news, but this seldom occurs in a movie. Phone calls are physically boring. What is the audience looking at during this conversation? Try to cut such conversations. It's a screenplay, you're not limited by a single location—let the characters meet face to face.

DUAL DIALOGUE

Format the same as a play (see chapter 8).

SOFTWARE PROGRAMS THAT FORMAT

A list of software programs designed to help screenwriters with formatting is found in Appendix F.

EXPOSITION

All the rules concerning exposition in playwriting apply to screenwriting (see chapter 5), although screenwriters use one form of exposition that playwrights seldom consider. Nonverbal exposition allows the camera to focus in on one physical action, one image or object that tells the viewer about the back story. For example, the camera may focus in on a newspaper article, show a particular scar, or follow the smoke from a hidden gun. In a movie, it isn't necessary for the exposition to be conveyed with dialogue. Consider physical action to tell the back story. What people do can be more powerful than any words they say. The old saying "action speaks louder than words" is true when it comes to nonverbal exposition.

PARENTHETICALS

Parentheticals in screenplay dialogue are almost the same as in a play (see chapter 8), with one major exception. The word "pause" is seldom used in a screenplay. This occurs because a pause should be filled with some sort of action, which should be described in the narration.

ABBREVIATIONS

Screenplay writing uses a number of standard abbreviations. "O.S.," which means "off stage" in the theatre, now becomes "off screen." This means that the line of dialogue is said in the next room, comes from a phone, or from somewhere off screen. You can also use "O.C.," which means "off camera." "V.O." means "voice over." This is used when you have a narrator. Example:

```
                NARRATOR (V.O.)
     I grew up in a Norman Rockwell painting. Well,
     almost. Our postman was a homosexual. But you
     couldn't tell from the outside, so no one
     really cared.
```

The only acceptable camera angle is P.O.V., which stands for point of view. This is used sparingly and only when it will help visually tell the story. Example:

```
GEORGE'S P.O.V. - Counselor Johanson looks like some
giant extinct species of bird, of which he is the last
surviving member.
```

LENGTH

Most screenplays are between 110 and 120 pages in length. Many producers and agents shy away from scripts that are longer or shorter.

TEMPLATE

A screenplay format template is located in Appendix E.

THE MEDIUM

Many basic playwriting concepts will work for screenwriting, but in addition to the fact that one is written to be performed live and the other for the screen, there are other important differences. First, as we've pointed out, screenwriting is much less confined. Playwrights who feel comfortable with one simple set and a small handful of characters may have trouble making the transition. Playwrights are often set free by the tight constraints and feel lost when an almost unlimited number of sets and characters are available.

Second, movies are a more popular form of entertainment, and in Hollywood, there is pressure to come up with material that pleases a wide audience. Although a playwright has the freedom to examine limited issues and smaller stories, the screenwriter who appeals to the masses will stand a better chance of selling.

Next, television and films are a visual medium. Physical action and spectacle are often more important than what is said. Hollywood is almost antilanguage. It doesn't have to be that way, but it is. On the stage, language is the major medium. Images are created through words; spectacle often takes second place.

Last, although we live in a free country, television and movies are still censored. There's no formal organization that fills this role, now that the Hays Code (a priggish "morality" code the Hollywood studio heads and the U.S. government imposed on the industry from the '30's to the '60's) is dead. Today, self-censorship controls the medium. Screenwriters and television writers know Hollywood will never say or do anything that will insult its following. Too much money is at stake. The theatre has a better chance of achieving true freedom of speech, for there is little money to lose.

To emphasize the many differences between a play and a screenplay (both in medium and format), here is the same scene in both play and screenplay forms. Note the screenplay has a different scope. It has been expanded to several scenes and is far more visually oriented. First, the scene as a play:

THE SCENE IN PLAY FORM

(KAROLINE LIVINGSTON enters. She's an attractive businesslike woman in her mid-twenties.)

KAROLINE
Hello.

CASEY
Hiya.

NORMAN JR.
Karoline, this is my sister. She's older than me.

CASEY
Thank you, Norman, for that wonderful introduction. *(to Karoline)* Name's Casey. I work for a living. Nice to meet you.

KAROLINE
Before Norman tells you, I'm older than him too.

CASEY
Whopper?

KAROLINE
I'm a vegetarian.

                              CASEY
No problem.

                              (CASEY digs her thumb
                              between the buns and probes
                              out the saucers of pretend
                              meat.)

                              CASEY *(CONT'D)*
There you go.

                              NORMAN JR.
Casey, forget about the Whoppers!

                              CASEY
How 'bout a beer?

                              (CASEY runs off to the
                              kitchen to retrieve a
                              Hamm's.)

                              NORMAN JR.
Look, I've been thinking, this may not be the right
weekend for you to be here.

                              KAROLINE
You've met my parents.

                              NORMAN JR.
That was different.

                              KAROLINE
How?

                              NORMAN JR.
Your parents are normal.

                              KAROLINE
At your rate, I'd be lucky to meet your parents at their
funerals.

                              NORMAN JR.
At least then they couldn't embarrass you.

                              KAROLINE
Nothing your parents could say would embarrass me.

                              NORMAN JR.
Maybe we could stay at a hotel.

                              (CASEY enters just in time
                              to hear this last remark.)

                              CASEY
Good start. You're already having to apologize for our
parents.

                            KAROLINE
Casey, would you tell Norman that it's perfectly natural
to think your own parents are strange or different.

                              CASEY
Norman, our parents are perfectly natural. Speaking of
nature, Karoline, there's something I have to warn you
about, you have to ask permission to go to the bathroom
at night. You see, our father has been in charge of an
assembly line his entire life . . .

                            KAROLINE
Buick, right?

                              CASEY
Right. What you got to understand is that in order to go
to the bathroom on the assembly line, you have to ask
permission. Our father is the one who grants permission.

                           NORMAN JR.
He does more than that. He's an executive.

                              CASEY
To understand our father, you must see the logic in
installing this quaint little custom at home. In order
to go to the bathroom at night, you'll have to first
yell, "I Have To Go To The Bathroom."

                            KAROLINE
You're kidding.

                           NORMAN JR.
Casey's not telling it right.

                              CASEY
When we were young, he was afraid we'd fall in. It's
twenty years later, his hearing is shot, so in order to
get permission, you have to stand out in the hall and
yell, at the top of your lungs, "I HAVE TO GO TO THE
BATHROOM!"

                            KAROLINE
                         (remaining positive)
All families have their idiosyncrasies.

                           NORMAN JR.
                         (to Casey)
Mom home?

CASEY

Hell! You missed the story of the week! Remember Hamblin Kerr? He had that awful accident back in high school? Got both legs taken off at the factory.

NORMAN JR.

I hardly remember the guy.

CASEY

Doctors put them back on, but they just sort of hung there. You'll never guess. He taught himself to walk.

NORMAN JR.

That's nice. Where's Mom?

KAROLINE

Shhh, Norman. I love human interest stories.

CASEY

Only thing is, he didn't tell anyone. He was going to save it for just the right moment. So, last week was Mama Kerr's sixtieth birthday, and he decided to give her his little gift. He got out of his wheelchair and walked into the living room. When she saw him, she was so shocked, she had a heart attack and died.

(Beat.)

NORMAN JR.

Why did you tell us that?

CASEY

You asked where mom was, she's at the funeral.

NORMAN JR.
(disgusted)

Great. Just great.

CASEY

Speaking of funerals, you're not going to believe this, Mom's gone religious on us! She even went to church!

(NORMAN JR. waves CASEY off.)

CASEY *(CONT'D)*

I'm sorry, Karoline, you're not particularly . . . ah . . . you know?

KAROLINE

Religious? A little.

                              CASEY
Yeah, well, sorry. *(beat)* So you two really going to get
married or is this just a fling?

                              KAROLINE
We've been dating, on and off, for almost two years.

                              CASEY
Two years! My marriage lasted only three weeks, what's
the secret?

                              NORMAN JR.
Don't bring them home to meet the family.

                                        (KAROLINE politely laughs.
                                        Then there is an uneasy
                                        beat as CASEY seems to be
                                        studying KAROLINE. Karoline
                                        takes it upon herself to end
                                        it.)

                              KAROLINE
Why don't I freshen up.

                              CASEY
You need to go to the bathroom?

                              KAROLINE
Yes.

                              CASEY
Well?

                              KAROLINE
Well what?

                              CASEY
Well?

                              KAROLINE
Oh. I have to go to the bathroom.

                              CASEY
Permission granted. Down the hall and to the right.

                                        (KAROLINE grabs her shoulder
                                        bag and exits.)

                              CASEY
Nice person.

    Now here is the same scene in screenplay format. Notice that, unlike a
shooting script, the scenes are not numbered and it includes no camera angles
such as "close up, medium shot, long shot."

THE SCENE IN SCREENPLAY FORM

FADE UP:

EXT. BURGER KING - DAY

NORMAN AND KAROLINE - drive up to the ordering mike.

NORMAN - a typical college football player, is having a
bad day.

KAROLINE - is a contrast to Norman. More cerebral.
Opposites attract.

ORDERING MIKE - The voice is barely audible. The static
reads like rapid machine-gun fire - as if a massacre
were occurring inside.

> VOICE
> *(broken English)* Yello . . .
> *Yelcome to the home of the Yopper.*

NORMAN - isn't paying attention.

> NORMAN
> I can't do it.

> KAROLINE
> You've warned me. I know what to
> expect . . .

> VOICE
> *(broken English)* Yello . . .
> *Yelcome to the home of the Yopper.*

> KAROLINE
> There is no such thing as an all-
> American family.

KAROLINE - gives him a reassuring kiss. It doesn't help.

> VOICE
> Yaven't got all hay.

> NORMAN
> Yeah, a Yopper, I mean, a Whopper,
> a dinner salad, and two Diet Cokes.

DRIVE-UP WINDOW - Norman wheels around to the window. A
hairy hand shoots out. Norman drops some money into it.

> VOICE
> Next yindow prease.

NEXT WINDOW - another arm shoves out a greasy bag and
Cokes. Suddenly, the arm jerks back.

> CASEY
> Well, Jumpin' Jesus! What the hell
> are you doing, Norman?

NORMAN'S P.O.V. - a gap-toothed, thirty-year-old woman
holds the bag. It's CASEY BURNAND, his sister.

                        NORMAN
            Oh my God.

                        CASEY
            Hell, I heard you might be showing
            up. This is just great.

                        KAROLINE
            Aren't you going to introduce me?
This is the hardest thing Norman has ever done.

                        NORMAN
            Karoline, I'd like you to meet
            Casey . . . My sister . . . She's
            older than me.

                        CASEY
            Thank you, Norman for that
            wonderful introduction.

                        KAROLINE
            Before he tells you, I'm older than
            him too.
CASEY - yells over her shoulder.

                        CASEY
            Hey everyone, come here and meet my
            kid brother.
NORMAN & KAROLINE'S P.O.V. - Krishna, Jesus, Inbong,
Rajiv all wave.

NORMAN - sinks into his seat.

                                        CUT TO:

INT. KAROLINE'S TOYOTA - DAY

Karoline and Norman are parked in the Burger King
parking lot, waiting for Casey.

                        NORMAN
            Don't tell them about us. Let me do
            that my own way.

                        KAROLINE
            If that's what you want.

KAROLINE - makes a show of taking off her tiny wedding
band and moving it to the opposite hand.
CASEY - jumps in the back seat.

>   CASEY
>   We're in luck, Ramji took over for
>   me.

NORMAN - hits the accelerator.

>   CUT TO:

EXT. HIGHWAY - DAY

Karoline's Toyota flies by a sign reading, 'Buick City.'
Flint, Michigan is Norman's home town. It stands in
stark contrast to Grosse Point. It's a blue-and no-
collar town.

INSIDE - Casey squeezes herself up between Norman and
Karoline.

>   CASEY
>   Snatched us some Whoppers!

CASEY - sticks a handful of greasy burgers between them.

>   CASEY *(CONT'D)*
>   It's all right, they're rejects. No
>   one misses them.

>   KAROLINE
>   I'm a vegetarian.

CASEY - digs her thumb between the buns and flings the
saucers of pretend meat out the window.

SCREECH - A car, going in the other direction, slams on
its breaks and blows its horn.

THE PATTY - impacts with the car leaving a huge stain.

KAROLINE P.O.V. - Casey's greasy hand offers the empty,
old bun.

>   NORMAN JR.
>   Casey, forget about the Whoppers!

KAROLINE - feels she has no choice but to accept.

>   KAROLINE
>   Casey, would you tell Norman that
>   it's perfectly natural to think
>   your own parents are different.

>   CASEY
>   Oh right, there's something I have
>   to warn you about before we get
>   home. You have to ask permission to
>   go to the bathroom at night. Okay?

KAROLINE - wants to question this but instead.

                        KAROLINE
          Okay.

                        CASEY
          See there?

CASEY - points out the window.

THEIR P.O.V. - The car flies past a decrepit factory.
The American dream gone to hell. Weeds flow from
neglected storm drains. Deserted trucks and fork lifts
rot on the grounds of the old sweatshop.

                        CASEY *(CONT'D)*
          In order to go to the bathroom on
          the assembly line, you have to ask
          permission. Our father is the one
          who grants permission.

                        NORMAN JR.
          He does more than that.

                        CASEY
          To understand our father, you must
          see the logic in installing this
          quaint little custom at home. In
          order to go to the bathroom at
          night, you'll have to first
          yell out, "I Have To Go To The
          Bathroom."

KAROLINE - attempts to sound upbeat.

                        KAROLINE
          I'll bet a lot of families do that.
CASEY - sticks out a prehistoric bag of French fries . . .

                        CASEY
          How 'bout some golden fries?

                                        CUT TO:

EXT. BURNAND HOUSE - DAY

They pull up in front.

NORMAN'S P.O.V. - His childhood home. Built in the
twenties when working-class men took pride in their
personal little kingdoms.

But now the neighborhood is dying. In a final attempt to
cover the decay, cheap lengths of siding have been
added. Here and there a piece of tin has slipped,
showing the proud, rotting workmanship underneath.

Nearby sits a Buick Roadmaster. A 1950s Chrome-
mobile. From the sad-faced dented grill, the faded two-
tone paint flows back through its baroque architecture
to the massive jagged fins and cathedral tail lights.
The car is like the neighborhood, a shell of its former
glory.

KAROLINE - offers an encouraging smile.

                                        CUT TO:

INT. BURNAND LIVING ROOM - DAY

The place is the product of minds that were children
during the Depression - nothing is too fancy or without
purpose.
NORMAN's P.O.V. - The living room is hung with balloons
and a hand-printed banner that reads, "Happy Retirement."

FLUSH - a doddering toilet down the hall lets go. The
whole house seems to rumble as the load travels through
the iron pipes. Finally silence.

CASEY - charges in in process of zipping up. She grabs
an armful of Hamm's beer and a bag of yellow popcorn.

                    CASEY
          So, how long have you been having
          this fling?

                    KAROLINE
          We've been dating, on-and-off for
          almost two years.

                    CASEY
          Two years! My marriage lasted only
          three weeks. What's the secret?

                    NORMAN JR.
          Don't bring them home to meet the
          family.

KAROLINE - politely laughs. Then there is an uneasy beat
as Casey seems to be studying Karoline. Karoline takes
it upon herself to end it.

                    KAROLINE
          Why don't I freshen up.

                    CASEY
          You need to go to the bathroom?

                    KAROLINE
          Yes.

                                    CASEY
              Well?

                                    KAROLINE
              Well what?

                                    CASEY
              Well?

                                    KAROLINE
              Oh. I have to go to the bathroom.

                                    CASEY
              Permission granted. Down the hall
              and to the right.

KAROLINE - grabs her shoulder bag and exits.

                                    CASEY *(CONT'D)*
              Nice person.

CASEY - yanks on the TV. She immediately becomes riveted
to a Looney-Toon cartoon. She begins laughing so hard a
piece of popcorn comes out of her nose.

BATHROOM - Karoline really doesn't have to use the
bathroom. Instead, she leans against the sink, considers
the floor for a moment, then coldly draws herself
together, closes her eyes, and dreams of some far away
place.

SUBMITTING A SCRIPT
TO HOLLYWOOD PRODUCTION COMPANIES

Screenwriters, unlike playwrights, need an agent. If you send a script to a sit-com, television drama, studio, film company, or producer, 99 percent of the time you'll get it back, unopened. Hollywood requires agent submissions of scripts to protect itself from plagiarism lawsuits. There are only so many stories out there, and if they've pumped millions into a movie and you just happen to submit a script that's similar, they don't want to waste their time and money defending themselves.

NONAGENT SUBMISSIONS

Only the smallest of film companies and producers will read scripts that are not agent submitted. You can find a list of these smaller companies in the book *Writer's Market,* which is available at most book stores, or you can write:

    Writer's Digest Books
    F & W Publications

1507 Dana Ave.
Cincinnati, OH 45207

Rarely do major television shows accept scripts not submitted by an agent, but occasionally there is an exception. An updated list of television shows and their production companies (and phone numbers) can be found in the TV market list within the monthly *WGA Journal*. There too will be information on the rare shows that do accept nonagent submissions.

When you submit a nonagent submitted script, the production company may ask you to sign a *release*. A release is a short contract that protects the production company from a plagiarism lawsuit. It simply states that the writer will not sue. If the company is reputable, signing such a release is usually not a problem.

GETTING A SCREENWRITING AGENT

You find a Hollywood agent much the same way you get a playwriting agent. First you need a wonderful script, one the agent will read and say, "I can make money off this," and then you need to start submitting it to as many agents as possible. You can get an up-to-date list of agents by writing the WGA. For a small charge, they'll send you a tightly typed list of about one hundred agencies, but that's all they can do. The WGA offers no assistance in finding, selecting, or recommending agents.

When that WGA list of agents arrives, it'll include agencies that have anywhere from one to fifty agents working for them. You'll have a better chance of being read if you address your query to an individual agent rather than the whole agency. One trick is to find the new, young, beginning agent within a larger agency. If you sweet talk the secretary, she or he may give you a name. The younger, newer agents are usually looking for writers and just might be willing to read your work. More established agents have a clientele of writers and are seldom interested in taking on a beginner. You'll also want to choose agents who are located in Los Angeles. Agents in other parts of the country can be good, but Los Angeles–based agents will more than likely be better connected.

There are a few important differences between playwriting agents and screenwriting agents. First, unlike some playwriting agents, all screenwriting agents allow simultaneous submissions. You can send scripts to as many agents as you want, all at the same time. Second, a screenwriting agent's fee is always 10 percent. If an agent demands up-front money, a reader's fee, or more than 10 percent, you should assume that the agent is unscrupulous.

TAKING MEETINGS AND PITCHING

If a producer likes your work, she will ask you in for a *meet and greet*. She may also ask you to *pitch* (orally present story ideas) other movie ideas you're working on or want to write. In most cases you want to give a medium or full-length pitch.[5] Here is an example of how a pitch might go. The producer offers you a Diet Coke, you sit in her office, the phone rings every few minutes, and you talk about common friends, what you've done, and nothing in particular. Then the producer asks, "So what else have you got?" It's time to pitch. Presentation is important. You want to tell the producer a succinct, interesting story. Be excited about your story idea, yet tell it so that it can be easily followed. Here is an example of one writer's pitch that worked.

PRODUCER
(On the phone) Sally, hold my calls. Thanks.

WRITER
All right, this movie is called Johnny Hawk. We come up on a Porsche. In the passenger seat is Johnny (Johnny Depp). The driver, a woman who's not good enough for him - too many Abraham Lincoln moles. He says "Shall we do it?" She agrees, starts up the car, and drives into a huge, gated estate. Inside we find the library and the girl's old fart father behind a tank of a desk. He asks his daughter to step outside, he wants to have a private word with Johnny. Once she leaves, he says "You're not going to marry my daughter." Johnny argues, "I've asked her to marry me, she loves me." The old man takes twenty thousand dollars out of the desk and spreads it out in front of Johnny. "You're not going to marry my daughter." Johnny's totally insulted, "She's old enough, we don't need your permission." Another twenty thousand is added to the pile. Johnny is more righteous, "How dare you, sir! You can't buy love!" The old man shoves another heap of bills onto the pile. "You're not going to marry my daughter." Johnny looks at the mountain of bills, glances out to the cobblestone drive, thinks a moment and says, "throw in the Porsche." Cut to, the autumn leaves flying as Johnny Hawk pulls out of town in the Porsche.

(The phone rings. The PRODUCER answers. The WRITER waits five minutes.)

WRITER *(CONT'D)*
This is a movie about a handsome kid who's got the perfect con . . . he goes into a town, finds the richest girl, forces her to fall in love with him, makes sure the parents hate him and gets paid off not to marry into the family.

---

[5] For an example of a short pitch and for more information on pitching see chapter 9.

> (The phone rings. The
> PRODUCER answers. The WRITER·
> waits two minutes.)

                    WRITER *(CONT'D)*
He's in the islands, enjoying his loot. Pool bar –
Oprah's on television. Suddenly he sees a composite
picture of himself and Oprah interviewing his last
"love" victims. They're all happy that they knew him,
for they all learned about men and love through him.
But they want his nuts. He realizes the game is up, and
decides to pull one last major con before retirement.
He has to find the one place on Earth where the women
aren't that attractive, their fathers are wealthy, and
no one watches Oprah. The answer - Yale.

Let's stop the pitch here. Notice that the writer is following formula exactly. He
started with an event—Johnny Hawk being paid off not to marry. He quickly
moved on to the disturbance—Johnny finding himself on television, and then
the end of act 1 moved on to the major decision—Johnny goes to Yale to find
one last con. In most cases, you should stop at this point. You don't want to tell
the whole story if the producer is not interested. If·they show interest, then be
prepared to pitch the rest.

                    WRITER *(CONT'D)*
At Yale he finds the equivalent of Ross Perot's
daughter. He starts the con . . . it's working
perfectly. She's madly in love with him. At dinner
parties, he begins to turn the family against him--
he makes a pass at the mother, the brother, and the
downstairs maid. But there's a problem--he keeps seeing
a pretty graduate student who seems to be following him.
He finally confronts her and she admits that she saw him
on Oprah. But she doesn't want to turn him in. Instead
she wants to write her graduate thesis on the mating
habits of the American Male with Johnny as the star
specimen. He agrees. The con continues, just as
beautifully, with the grad student posing as his sister.

> (The phone rings. The
> PRODUCER answers. The WRITER
> waits one minute.)

                    WRITER *(CONT'D)*
But Johnny is beginning to fall in love for the first
time in his life with none other than the winsome grad
student. He tries to tell her how he feels, but all he
can manage are his trite, old lines. The payoff day

arrives. But Ross says, "you're an S.O.B., son, I'm an S.O.B . . . welcome to the family. Oh, you let my baby girl down, I'll kill you." Guards are assigned to make sure Johnny won't run, his bank account is emptied, and his pretty Porsche impounded.

> (The phone rings. The
> PRODUCER answers. The WRITER
> waits ten minutes.)

                WRITER *(CONT'D)*

There's nothing Johnny can do but go through with the nuptials. After one last attempt to tell his grad student sweetheart how he feels, he apologizes for his actions and heads for the church. It's a huge church, thousands of people are there. He walks out in front of the crowd, there are TV cameras and klieg lights, and then Oprah Winfrey struts out, turns to the cameras and says, "Ladies and gentleman, we caught him!" From the back of the auditorium, Ross Perot gives Johnny the finger. Johnny faces the music.

> (The phone rings. The
> PRODUCER answers. The WRITER
> waits nine minutes.)

                WRITER *(CONT'D)*

Two hours later, Johnny finds himself penniless, carless, and dateless as he attempts to hitchhike out of town. He's cold and tired, when a small VW bug pulls up. It's the graduate student. And for the first time, he's able to express his love. "Love is infatuation with knowledge. If you know someone, know all of their idiosyncrasies and shortcomings, and you're still infatuated, then you're in love." The grad student admits that she, too, must be in love. They ride off into the sunset together.[6]

Pitching is an art. Many Hollywood writers are less successful than they might be because they are not good verbal storytellers. Work on your pitching, tell stories to friends, rehearse your pitches, and always be ready to tell a good story.

SELLING MOVIE RIGHTS TO HOLLYWOOD

Evelyn Waugh commented on Hollywood, "Each book purchased for motion pictures has some individual quality, good or bad, that has made it remarkable.

---

[6] Copyright, Bill Streib

It is the work of a great array of highly paid and incompatible writers to distinguish this quality, separate it and obliterate it." If you should be so lucky as to sell the movie rights to one of your plays, remember three things:

1. When the play is produced, never sign a contract that gives television or movie rights to a theatre or an individual other than yourself. Television and movie rights belong to the playwright alone.

2. Insist that the movie production company pay you to do the adaptation from stage to screen. If you don't, some other writer will be paid and you'll lose what little creative control you have.

3. Always get an agent or an entertainment lawyer to represent you. When money is at stake, most agents will rush to sign you.

SITCOMS

There's a saying in Hollywood, "If you can write funny, you'll die a wealthy person." Humor is something you're born with. You don't decide today you're going to write comedy. Comedy is elusive; either you have the gift or you don't. Often writers find they're funny by accident. The first play I wrote was a serious father and son drama, my own personal version of *Death of a Salesman*. During its first reading at the Circle Rep in New York the audience began to laugh, little titters at first, later guffaws. I sat in the back, horrified. They were laughing at my work of art, my great American father/son story. When it was over, someone turned to me and said, "You meant this to be a dark comedy, didn't you?" I was smart enough to answer, "Yes." That's how I found out I could write comedy.

If you have the comic gene and want to write for sitcoms, then the most common way to break into the industry is by writing spec scripts.

Choose a strong sitcom, one with good ratings that will be around for several years, and write a "spec" audition episode. The key is to study the show, watch many episodes, and make sure you have the story structure and characters down. You want to write an episode using the standard characters of that sitcom and not one dependent on outside characters of your own creation. For example, you don't want to write about one character's long-lost mother coming for a one-time visit (staff writers may do this, but they aren't auditioning for a job). You want to prove you can come up with creative, wonderful stories that use only the standard characters. Stay within the strict confines of that particular sitcom and you'll prove you understand and can write for that particular show.

To write a sitcom, you'll first need a scenario (just like a play) that contains a brief outline of what will happen in each scene. Following is an example of one sitcom writer's outline for an episode of the *Fresh Prince Of Bel Air*. It contains the title, a pitch line or log line that tells the story in one or two sentences, and a step outline.

Fresh Prince Of Bel Air

Title: BUT IT'S NOT THE SAME . . .
Pitch Line: Uncle Philip's membership in a private all-male club almost costs him his marriage when Vivian tries to join.
Step Outline:

COLD Opening[7]	Philip is jubilant to learn that he has been accepted into a very exclusive private club. Vivian notes that it's an all-male club. Philip does not have a problem with that. Vivian does.
I-1	*LIVING ROOM* Philip can't understand why Vivian isn't thrilled for him. He asks his entire family to be at the special honors dinner where he will be inducted. Vivian protests. Philip argues that this hasn't anything to do with prejudice.
I-2	*PRIVATE CLUB* Vivian, Hilary, and Ashley try to enter the private club; they are kicked out of the building.
I-3	*Kitchen* Vivian organizes a nonviolent, sit-down protest. Philip begs her not to embarrass him in front of his friends.
Act Break	*PRIVATE CLUB* Vivian, Hilary, and their friends crash the club. The police are called.
II-1	*HOME* Philip returns after bailing out the family. A moral debate ensues. Vivian argues that there is nothing wrong with keeping someone out of a club because the members don't like them, but you can't keep them out because of their race, gender, or beliefs. Philip asserts that it's not the same, but in the end is left questioning his own beliefs.
II-2	*KITCHEN* Father, snubbed by the kids, leaves for his honors dinner alone. Vivian comes in and asks why everyone isn't ready for the ceremony. She insists that they will not be prejudiced against the club and will attend.
II-3	*PRIVATE CLUB - Acceptance dinner* Philip is shocked to see his family enter. He stands to give his acceptance speech, but finds that he can't; instead he resigns.
II-4	*HOME* Philip joins the lawsuit to change the club's charter.

---

[7] A cold opening is the same as a teaser. It's a scene that takes place before the opening credits.

SITCOM FORMAT

When you have the story worked out, you'll need a copy of an actual script from the show so you can study its particular format. Two Los Angeles book stores sell sitcom, hour-length, and movie scripts.

Script City
8033 Sunset
Box 1500
Los Angeles, California 90046
(213) 871-0707

Book City Collectibles
66231 Hollywood Blvd.
Hollywood, California 90028
(213) 466-0120

Use the actual script as a template, minus the cast of characters page, guest list, list of sets, and list of revisions (these are done only for production). Here is an example of a basic three-camera sitcom format. But remember, all sitcom formats are slightly different.

1.
(A)

COACH

"Art Imitates Football"

by

Bill Streib

A
—

FADE IN:

INT. HAYDEN'S CABIN - NIGHT

IT'S SATURDAY NIGHT. CHRISTINE IS DRESSED TO THE NINES.

CHRISTINE

Hayden, we're going to be late for

Kelly's play.

HAYDEN DRAGS IN, UNCOMFORTABLE IN HIS SUIT. HE FIDGETS WITH THE TIE. SHE ADJUSTS IT.

HAYDEN

(WHINING) Wouldn't you rather watch

the Vikings game on the 'giganto

screen' at Dead Bob's?

CHRISTINE

Dead what?

HAYDEN

Remember Bob's Bar? Well, Bob died,

now they call it Dead Bob's.

CHRISTINE

Isn't that the place they have the

'Scream Till You Bleed' contest?

HAYDEN

You're just jealous 'cause you

didn't win.

CHRISTINE PICKS UP A PAMPHLET.

CHRISTINE

Hayden, doesn't this sound more

exciting, *(READING)* "The-

Alternative theatre, devoted to

ritual and the exploration of the

dark side of the human condition,

presents *Peter Pan*.

HAYDEN

Oh yeah, I feel warm all over.

THE PHONE RINGS.

HAYDEN *(CONT'D)*

That's Luther and Dauber

calling to ask us to do

something fun.

HE ANSWERS THE PHONE.

HAYDEN *(CONT'D)*

(INTO PHONE) Whatever-it-is-I-can't-

do-it-'cause-I-got-to-see-a-dumb-

(CONTINUED)

                                                                        3.
                                                                        (A)

                              HAYDEN (CONTINUED)

              play-that-Kel . . .(BEAT) . . . *ly.*

              Hi! . . .Oh I'm sorry to hear that

              . . . Well, I guess we'll just have

              to find something else to do. Bye.

    HAYDEN DOES A LITTLE END ZONE DANCE.

                              HAYDEN *(CONT'D)*

              The play's been called off!

                              CHRISTINE

              You're kidding!

                              HAYDEN

              They had a small problem in the

              invisible flying system. They have

              to cancel it until they fix the hole

              in the stage floor and Peter Pan

              gets out of the body cast. Isn't

              that wonderful!

                              CHRISTINE

              Hayden, that's tragic.

                              HAYDEN

              (THRILLED) I mean tragic.

    CHRISTINE WALKS OVER AND TAKES OUT TWO WINE GLASSES AND A CANDLE.

                              CHRISTINE

              (SEDUCTIVE) Since we're all dressed

              up with nowhere to . . .

TEMPLATE

A sitcom format template is included in Appendix E.

BREAKING INTO SITCOMS

Once you've written that first spec script, your work has only begun. You need to treat it just like a play. Test the script, have readings, rewrite, and only when it's ready, begin submitting to agents.

You'll also need to write more scripts. It takes most writers from five to thirty spec scripts before they begin to get the hang of sitcom writing and agents start paying attention. Breaking into sitcoms takes a long-term commitment.

When you're good enough, you'll have to move to Hollywood. Agents are seldom interested in television writers who don't live within a short drive of the major studios. If you're lucky, after years of work, one of your scripts might get you in for a pitch meeting or you may sell one and start your career.

Sitcom writing is difficult to break into. In any given season perhaps fifty sitcoms are in production (both network and syndication). Each show averages six to nine writers. This adds up to only about 350 staff positions. Add to this individual episodes that are written by outside writers, and that still adds up to fewer than five hundred sitcom writers.

SITCOM SCHOOLS

Unlike playwriting or screenwriting, there are few classes and no college degrees in sitcom writing. Warner Brothers offers a sitcom workshop in Los Angeles and other major cities, but competition is strong to get in. If you are funny and want to write for sitcoms you need to learn by doing, with little help out there to guide you.

YOUR OWN SITCOM OR TELEVISION SHOW

If you have an idea for a new original sitcom or television show you have, unfortunately, little chance of selling it unless you have a track record. Networks seldom listen to beginners or outsiders. Become a top-notch writer, work your way up from staff writer to story editor to producer, and only then will the doors open and someone listen to your new idea.

HOUR-LENGTH SHOWS

Playwrights break into television hour-length shows much the same way as they do sitcoms. The only major difference is that hour-length shows use screenplay format and are generally split into five acts (the intermission kind). Again, you want to study the show, watch many episodes, order scripts and study the format. Before writing, you will also want to write a scenario that contains a brief outline of what will happen in each act. Here is an example of one writer's outline for an episode of *Star Trek:*

Star Trek

Title: Beverly's Baby

Log Line: The *Enterprise* discovers a heavily damaged Ferengi vessel. A deal has gone wrong. The only Ferengi still alive is a young pregnant woman. When a frantic Beverly cannot save her life, she transfers the still viable fetus into her own womb.

Step Outline:

Teaser	The *Enterprise* answers a distress call. It's a listing Ferengi ship. A deal has apparently gone wrong and all onboard are dead, save one. A woman, barely alive and visibly pregnant.
Act 1	Dr. Crusher desperately tries to save the woman, but all tactics fail. She can keep the female's vital functions going for mere minutes; the baby is also going to die. In a last ditch effort, Dr. Crusher decides to carry the baby to term in her own womb.
Act 2	The transfer works but, to keep the baby alive, Dr. Crusher ingests massive amounts of Ferengi hormones, becoming ill in the process. Suddenly, she's craving worms. Picard decides to visit the base of departure of the destroyed Ferengi ship.
Act 3	Time is running out for Dr. Crusher. Her ears and teeth are growing. She has started to lie and make questionable deals with crew members. Knowing that her life is in danger, Picard orders that the child be delivered.
Act 4	Dr. Crusher is given a successful caesarian. The child is premature, but alive. They arrive at the Ferengi-based plant. When an elderly Ferengi couple ask how much Beverly wants for the baby, she is outraged and refuses to give the child up.
Act 5	Even Picard cannot convince Beverly to turn over the baby. She's been through too much, she's bonded and she must find a worthy home for the child. In the end, Picard must make a deal with the Ferengi. At great cost, he strikes a bargain for information regarding any prospects for the child. The crew is astonished when the same aging couple comes aboard and admits to being the child's grandparents. They were assuming Beverly would be mercenary, and they only wanted their grandchild. They are truly caring, and Beverly is touched and relieved.

MADE-FOR-TV MOVIES

Most made-for-TV movies and movie-of-the-weeks (MOWs) are written by Hollywood insiders who have years of experience and are trusted by the networks. If you have an idea that you think would make a good made-for-TV movie, it's best to write it as a regular movie. Don't limit your market. Write it as a movie and then, if someone should be interested in making it for television, the transition will be easy.

SOAP OPERAS

The rarest of all television writers are soap opera writers. Perhaps only one hundred such writers are currently working. All soaps are written by staff writers. Each show has a group of writers who meet with the head writer and decide where the show's many different story lines are heading, and then episodes are divvied up. The head writer then rewrites each episode to make sure continuity is maintained. Most of these writers got their jobs by being successful writers in other fields (for example, playwrights, hour-length television writers).

WORKING WITH A PARTNER

Writing teams are far more popular in screenwriting and television writing than they are in playwriting. If you decide to work with a partner, make sure you pick a partner who is better than you. You don't want to work with a writer who has less talent, less experience, or less desire.

ADAPTING NOVELS TO MOVIES

If you find a novel, short story, or play you think would make a good movie, you must first receive written permission from the author before you start the adaptation, unless of course the work is in public domain, that is, the author has been dead for more than fifty years). If the author is agreeable, you'll need a lawyer and a contract.

If it's a popular novel you wish to adapt, you must first understand that almost all publishers send the galleys to film companies long before the book is published. This means that, by the time the novel makes it to your local bookstore, almost every film company has already considered it. If you do find that rare overlooked novel that would make a good movie, make sure you have the rights and a contract and always give the original work and author credit on your title page.

TRUE-LIFE STORIES

If you want to write a screenplay based on real events and characters, remember that, just as with novels, more than likely some Hollywood studio has already considered it. If the characters and events were widely reported in the papers, such as Amy Fisher, Waco, and Tailhook, then it's considered a public story, and you can usually write about the incident without obtaining permission (though Hollywood production companies always protect themselves from lawsuits by buying the rights to an individual's story). If the events were less well known or based on an individual's life who is not in the public eye, then written permission from the individual will be needed before you can write and sell the screenplay. One way to get around this is to write a story that you base on the events but change just enough to protect the innocent and allow for, as Nixon would have said, "plausible deniability." Needless to say, the lives and stories of people who are long dead are fair game for screenplays.

FILM SCHOOLS

One way writers break into the industry is by attending film schools. These schools offer master of fine arts (MFA) degrees in screenwriting. Attending one of the top film schools can open many doors, but it's hard to get in. For example, UCLA has more than three hundred applicants each year, but only accepts twenty. All film schools will want to look at a sample of your writing. If you use an adaptation as a sample script, graduate writing programs will be unimpressed. They want original screenplays (plays and short stories), not adaptations. The top film schools are the University of California, Los Angeles (UCLA), the University of Southern California (USC), and the American Film Institute (AFI), which are in Los Angeles. The other top schools are New York University (NYU), and Columbia, both in Manhattan. You can get a list of film schools by going to your library and finding the American Film Institute, *Guide to College Film Programs,* or you can look on the Web at http://www.westernet.net/%7Eedgar/fsc/fsc4.html.

THE PLAYWRIGHT VS. THE SCREENWRITER

Screenwriting is not the easy way out. It still takes years of work. If your goal is to make money, no matter what the cost, screenwriting is for you. If your goal is to have your own work of art produced, you'll have a much greater chance as a playwright. If you're interested in television or movie writing, your chance of success will be greatly improved if you are living in the Los Angeles area, but don't move until you're ready. Start the process by writing plays. Playwriting will teach you the basics of character, structure, and dialogue. When you've had a few plays produced and have won some awards, the transition to screenwriter or television writer will be much easier.

FURTHER READING

If you want to know more about screenwriting, the following books will be of help:

> *Screenwriting 434,* Lew Hunter (Perigee Books)
>
> *Screenwriting,* Richard Walter (Penguin USA)
>
> *Screenplay,* Syd Field (Dell)
>
> *Formatting Your Screenplay,* Rich Reichman (Paragon House)

BECOMING A PLAYWRIGHT

You become a playwright by writing. Too often we enjoy *acting* like playwrights more than *being* playwrights. Several years ago, I met a twenty-year-old student who proudly announced that, because he loved the theatre, he had written

> *When I hear someone talking about loving the theatre, I turn aside and look for a place to throw up.*
>
> Jerzy Grotowski

seven full-length plays. Seven plays at only twenty years of age! I was impressed, even jealous. As our conversation progressed, he told me that of the seven plays he had "written," three were still in the outline stage. He had worked out the synopses of two in his head, and the other two he had abandoned writing until he was "emotionally ready." In truth, he was a playwright who had never written a play. Too many people who call themselves writers never have time to write, or have never written.

We attended a playwriting seminar in which the speaker asked all the students to stand up if they were playwrights. Half the class stood. Then he demanded that the rest of the class stand and proclaim that they too were playwrights. We wish it were that easy! You proclaim yourself a playwright by writing, finishing, marketing, and staging plays. It requires hard work and years of discipline to *become* a playwright.

Why do playwrights stop writing? Usually it's because the final reward is too small. The amount of time and energy it takes to write a play is never worth the money. If you divide the time it took to create a play by the royalties you receive, it's seldom more than minimum wage. When lack of money forces playwrights to turn to screenwriting, they celebrate that first real check. Only later do they realize what they've lost, as their dominant thought becomes "What will sell?" and not "What is truth?"

Rejection is a way of life for a playwright. Years ago, I conducted an experiment. I took what I thought was my best play and did a mass mailing of one thousand queries. Of the thousand submissions, five hundred disappeared into space, never to be heard from again—they didn't even send back the SASP. Four hundred theatres sent rejection letters, some arriving almost two years after the mailing. One hundred theatres wanted to see the script. Of those, fifty rejected it outright, forty were not interested but wanted to see my next play. Ten considered the play for production. Of the ten, four lost interest (mostly after public readings), and six scheduled the play for production. Of the six, one theatre went bankrupt and another changed artistic directors, canceling the production. This left a total of four productions from a mailing of *one thousand!* All playwrights have drawers full of rejection letters, but every now and then it's not a rejection. Sometimes it's a check, or an option, or a letter asking permission to produce. You must be able to fight through the clouds of rejections in order to enjoy the moments of success. If you can face this dim picture and still have the desire to write a play, then perhaps there's hope.

Years ago, I was waiting on tables (as many playwrights do), when several theatre patrons came in for an after-show drink and snack. I noticed that they were holding the playbill for my play that was open a few miles away. They went on and on about how much they liked it—so much, that I decided to speak up:

"You liked the *Kabuki Medea?*"

"Yes! Very much. Wonderful play!"

"Thank you. I wrote that play."

You should have seen the look on their faces! They thought I was some sort of nut. They sat there in stunned silence. It just wasn't possible. The playwright couldn't be their waiter! They never said another word to me. They ate like we did when I was a child and my father was going through his mid-life crisis. We never knew what crazy thing was going to come out of his mouth. One minute he'd be normal and then suddenly he'd start talking about chucking it all, moving to Spain, and raising pet deer. He might as well have said, "I think I'll write a play"; we would've looked at him much the same.

People don't really want the playwright around. Too often they believe that a playwright can only be taken seriously if he lives in a distant, lofty land and has a ponytail. No one wants to know that most playwrights are normal people who have problems, struggle with balancing a checkbook, and usually stumble, only by chance, onto a brilliant idea. They just don't want to hear that most playwrights are waiters who are thankful for those brief moments of insight into a character or story, not because it makes the play better, but because they can stop writing for the day, go to work, and for once feel like they actually got something done.

Playwrights had nothing to do with starting the rumor that writing is a lonely profession. This was forced upon us by the world of directors, producers, and audiences who think that one script must be better because it came from two thousand miles away, while another script must be horrible because it was written by that guy down the block who hasn't got sense enough to wear a jacket when it's about to rain (this is known as "local playwright syndrome"). Playwrights work alone because the art simply is misunderstood by the masses. It's a difficult and painstaking art that appears to the audience to be easy and spontaneous. Few understand that one page of dialogue comes only after days of skillful work and sleepless nights.

I was at a party recently when I had a strange and interesting conversation with a woman. She asked what I did.

"I write plays."

"You'd like to have a play on Broadway?"

"Yes, that's a dream of mine."

"So you can get lots of money and do what you want to do."

I stopped and gave her a questioning look. "But I want to write plays."

"So you can get money and do what you want to do."

"But I don't need money to do what I want to do, I write plays."

She never understood. The conversation ended where it began. Perhaps playwrights aren't normal people. Perhaps we have a different set of goals, or perhaps it's as simple as the statement "I want to write plays."

Years ago, I had a write-up about one of my successes in my hometown paper. I thought it would be nice to have one of my plays produced in the town where I had grown up. So I sent a script to the community theatre, with a nice cover letter reminding everyone who I was. Months passed, nothing happened. I left messages, none were returned. Another letter and six months later, I called to find out what was taking so long. Finally, I got through to the head of the play selection committee. It turned out to be my old high school English teacher. I managed a D in her class twenty years before. She hadn't read the script and told me she wasn't going to. When I asked why, she answered, "I read about you in the paper and frankly, I don't believe it." They never produced the play, I never had my homecoming, but I learned an important lesson that is the key to success in playwriting: The surest way to become a playwright is to outlive the people who say you're not. You outlive them by writing wonderful, powerful, and interesting characters and plots that stand the test of time.

MORE TERMS EVERY PLAYWRIGHT SHOULD KNOW

Anticlimax: When the conflicting forces in a play fail to come to a confrontation or to arrive at a conclusive decision. An example would be Chekhov's *The Cherry Orchard*.

Aside: This is a rather old device that allows a character to make direct comments (supposedly not heard by the other characters on stage) to the audience. It's considered outdated and no longer used. (The only exceptions might be farce, musical comedies, or absurdist plays.)

Blackout: A term used when a playwright wants to indicate an instantaneous darkness on the stage. This is sometimes used to achieve bigger laughs when a scene ends on a joke or humorous moment. It also can be used to heighten the drama at the end of a scene. If there were a major revelation on the last line of a scene, a playwright might use a blackout.

Denouement: The solution or unraveling of the plot. The final outcome of the play. A liberal translation of the French "untying of the last knot." Usually comes after the climax and before the conclusion.

Deus ex Machina: (The god from the machine) From the ancient Greek theatre, this was a machine that lowered the god from above. Once on stage, the god would resolve the characters' problems and set everything right. Today, deus ex machina often means a play that has an unimaginative, sudden ending that may set everything right, but lacks believability. Sometimes they are known as "acts of God." An act of God is a massive coincidence that is too unbelievable for the audience to accept (this now only works in comedies).

Dramatic Irony: This occurs when the audience perceives a double edge (a second ironic meaning) to the scene that the characters do not perceive.

Episodic Plot: A story in which cause and effect is not central to the plot. For example, Brecht's *Mother Courage* has twelve scenes that are largely independent of each other. The events in one scene do not cause the events of the next. Sitcoms are episodic because each episode can stand alone without depending on other episodes for clarity or motivation.

Fish-out-of-Water Story: A story that puts your protagonist into a new or alien environment.

Fourth Wall: On a traditional proscenium arch theatre, this is the imaginary wall between the actors and the audience. Breaking the fourth wall occurs when an actor speaks directly to the audience.

Kitchen Sink Realism: A realistic play that usually deals with family problems and personal relationships. These plays work out a personal relationship and often lead to a lasting understanding. Often these plays take place in a kitchen (hence the label).

Legitimate Drama: The term comes from eighteenth-century England when theatres had to hold a license from the king in order to perform legitimately. Today the term denotes a live stage performance rather than movies or television.

MacGuffin: A MacGuffin is a dramatic trick. Alfred Hitchcock coined the term, which means a thing or event that causes the story to move forward but doesn't have anything to do with the story. An example would be found in the movie *North by Northwest*. The MacGuffin is that Cary Grant's character, a businessman, is mistaken for a spy. The mistake has nothing to do with the story other than starting the proverbial ball rolling.

Motifs: The underlying poetic themes and verbal metaphors of the play.

Nom de Plume: A fancy way to say pen name. If you use a nom de plume, make sure that your agent, postman, and the Dramatists Guild are aware of it. Also, be sure to include the name on your answering machine. You don't want to lose an important message because they think it's a wrong number.

Obligatory Scene: This is the expected clash between adversaries. It's what the audience believes will be the outcome of the action. The obligatory scene is an expected scene or conflict that the playwright sets up, and therefore has an obligation to pay off. It's the major showdown (also called scene-a-faire).

Pathos: When a character is forced to accept a fate that no action of hers initiated. (From the Greek word for "enduring.")

Peripety: An Aristotelian critical term that means reversal of fortune. It is the point in the play where an unexpected change in direction occurs. The most common example is *Oedipus*. When it becomes clear that Oedipus is tracking down himself, the peripety, or reversal, in the story occurs.

Pinter Pause: A long pause. Named for the playwright Harold Pinter whose plays often contain long pauses in the dialogue. Many critics believe that what happens during these long pauses is more important than what is said.

Problem Play: A play that identifies a problem (for example, a problem with society, relations, or political morals), but often doesn't give the audience a solution.

Red Herring: This is a story device that leads the audience to think the play is going one way when it's really heading in another direction. It is a false setup in which the audience is warned of coming events and problems that never appear. It's a smoke screen.

Soliloquy: An outdated device that allows the playwright to reveal the inner-most thoughts and desires of a character by allowing the character to speak to himself. It's seldom, if ever, used on the modern stage. (The only exception might be in farce, musical comedies, or absurdist plays.)

Spine: The play's message. What the play teaches or conveys. The action, characters, and plot(s) all contribute to the spine.

Stichomythia: A form of dialogue in which characters alternate single lines, phrases, and words to build the emotional tension. For example, see Beckett's *Waiting For Godot*.

Superobjective: Constantin Stanislavski is famous for this term. It's the over-all purpose that carries a character though the story. It's the character's driv-ing force. For example, according to Stanislavski, Hamlet's superobjective is "to find God."

Through Line: The major action of a play.

Tragedy of the Common Man: This phrase is often used to describe plays that adhere to the basic principles of tragedy but aren't about kings and gods. For example: *Death of a Salesman*.

Tragicomedy: This is a play having both comic and tragic elements. This can be accomplished by having one serious plot and a second comic plot occurring in the same story; or the playwright can try to balance both elements within the same story, finding the tragic elements of a comic situation and comic elements of the tragic situation. An example of the first would be *Romeo and Juliet,* in which Shakespeare has the comic musician scenes (often cut) separate from the main plot. Another example (Shakespeare is full of them) is *Hamlet*'s gravedigger scene, in which the comedy is mixed into a serious tale.

Villian Defeats Himself: In this type of play or movie the protagonist is evil. The audience rejoices in watching the "bad guy" slowly step backward into hell. An example of a movie in which the villain defeats himself is *White Heat* with James Cagney.

APPENDIX B

REFERENCE BOOKS A PLAYWRIGHT SHOULD OWN

The Synonym Finder, by Rodale Press.

The Elements of Style, by Strunk and White. Macmillan, New York.

Word Wise, A Dictionary of English Idioms, by John O. E. Clark. Henry Holt and Company, New York.

Slang and Euphemism, by Richard A. Spears, New American Library.

Kind Words, A Thesaurus of Euphemisms, by Judith S. Neaman and Carole G. Silver. McGraw-Hill.

The Baby Name Personality Survey, by Bruce Lansky and Barry Sinrod. Meadowbrook Press, New York.

Stage Writers Handbook, by Dana Singer. Theatre Communications Group.

APPENDIX C

FURTHER READING

Although this is in no way a comprehensive bibliography, these are books that all playwrights should read.

Aristotle, *Poetics*.

Brook, Peter, *The Empty Space*. New York: Atheneum, 1968.

Cole, Toby (ed.), *Playwrights on Playwriting*. New York: Hill and Wang.

Egri, Lajos, *The Art of Dramatic Writing*. New York: Simon and Schuster, 1946.

Lawson, John Howard, *Theory and Technique of Playwriting*. New York: Hill and Wang, 1960.

Kerr, Walter, *How Not to Write a Play*. New York: Simon and Schuster, 1955.

Langner, Lawrence, *The Play's the Thing*. New York: G. P. Putnam's Sons, 1960.

Smiley, Sam, *Playwriting: The Structure of Action*. Englewood Cliffs, New Jersey: Prentice-Hall, Inc., 1971.

Baker, George Pierce, *Dramatic Technique*. Boston: Houghton Mifflin Company, 1919.

Archer, William, *Play-making, A Manual Of Craftmanship*. New York: Dover Books, 1960.

PLAYWRITING PROGRAMS

The university systems in the United States and Canada are rare in that they have professional training programs for playwrights. It all started in 1947 when George Pierce Baker offered a playwriting workshop at Harvard. Today, hundreds of playwriting classes are offered all over the United States. A list of graduate and undergraduate programs can be found in *The Playwright's Companion* (1996 edition to the present). A detailed list of playwriting schools, degrees, programs, and classes is found in *The Student's Guide to Playwriting Opportunities* published by:

> Theatre Directories
> American Theatre Works, Inc.
> P.O. Box 519
> Dorset, VT 05251
> (802) 867-2223

Several major universities offer master of fine arts (MFA) degrees in playwriting. These degrees, although they offer no guarantees of success, do offer a playwright two to three years of intense study and a potential for career contacts. The top playwriting MFAs are offered by:

BRANDEIS UNIVERSITY
Department of Theatre Arts
Brandeis University
Alham, MA 02254-9110
http://www.brandeis.edu/

BROWN UNIVERSITY
Department of Theatre & Dance
Box 1897 Brown University
Providence, RI 02912
http://www.brown.edu/

CARNEGIE-MELLON UNIVERSITY
Department of Drama
College of Fine Arts 106
Carnegie-Mellon University
Pittsburgh, PA 15213
http://www.cmu.edu/

COLUMBIA UNIVERSITY
Hammerstein Center/Theatre
School of the Arts
Columbia University
New York, NY 10027
http://www.columbia.edu/

INDIANA UNIVERSITY
Department of Theatre and Drama
Theatre 200
Indiana University
Bloomington, IN 47405
http://www-iub.indiana.edu/

NEW YORK UNIVERSITY
Tish School of Arts
721 Broadway, 7th floor
New York, NY 10003
http://www.nyu.edu/

OHIO STATE UNIVERSITY
Department of Theatre
Ohio Stage University
1849 Cannon Dr.
1089 Drake Union
Columbus, OH 43210
http://www.acs.ohio-state.edu/

RUTGERS UNIVERSITY
Theatre Arts Department
Levin Theatre, Douglass Campus
Rutgers University, PO Box 270
New Brunswick, NJ 08903
http://www.rutgers.edu/

SOUTHERN ILLINOIS UNIVERSITY
Department of Theatre
Southern Illinois University
Carbondale, IL 62901-6608
http://www.siu.edu/siu.html

TEMPLE UNIVERSITY
Temple Theatres
13th & Harris Street
Philadelphia, PA 19122
http://www.temple.edu/

UNIVERSITY OF IOWA
Department of Theatre Arts
University of Iowa
Iowa City, Iowa 52242
http://www.uiowa.edu/

UNIVERSITY OF MASSACHUSETTS
Department of Theatre
Room 112 Fine Arts Center
University of Massachusetts
Amherst, MA 01003
http://www.umass.edu/

UNIVERSITY OF NEVADA AT LAS
VEGAS
Department of Theatre
4504 Maryland Parkway
Las Vegas, NV 89154
http://www.nscee.edu/unlv/UNLV
_Home_Page/OpenFolder.html

UNIVERSITY OF SOUTHERN
CALIFORNIA
School of Theatre
University of Southern California
Los Angeles, CA 90089-0791
http://cwis.usc.edu/

UNIVERSITY OF TEXAS AT AUSTIN
Department of Theatre and Dance
College of Fine Arts
University of Texas at Austin
Austin, TX 78712
http://www.utexas.edu/

YALE UNIVERSITY
Yale University School of Drama
P.O. Box 1903-A Yale Station
New Haven, CT 06520
http://www.yale.edu/

APPENDIX E

TEMPLATES

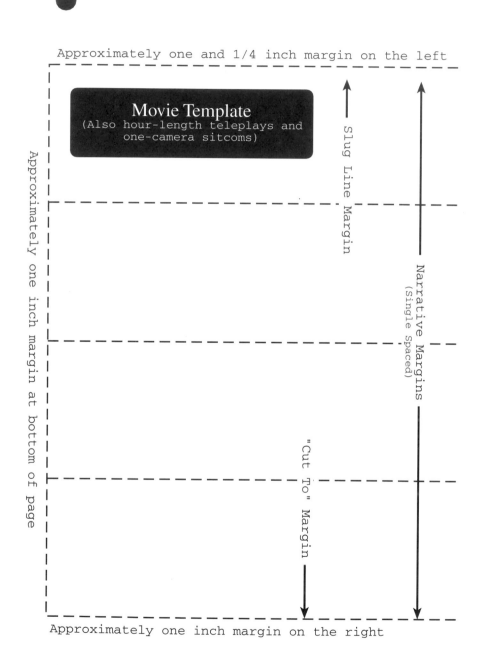

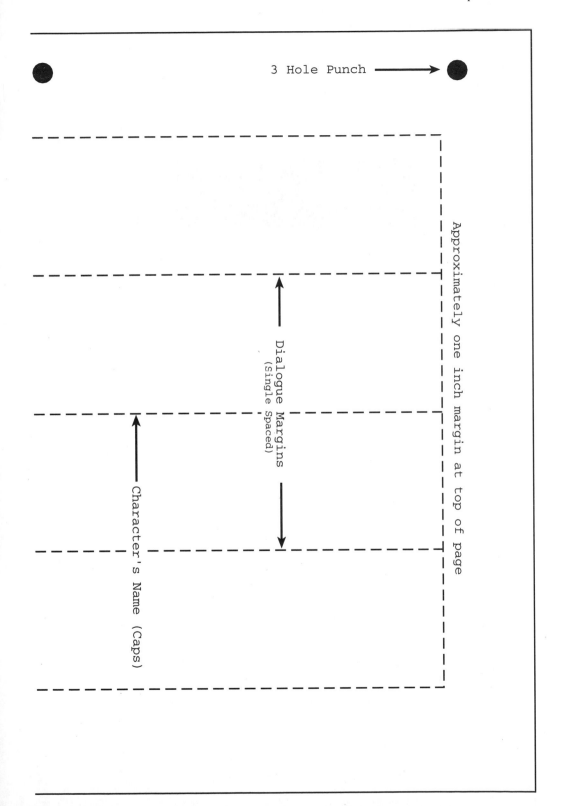

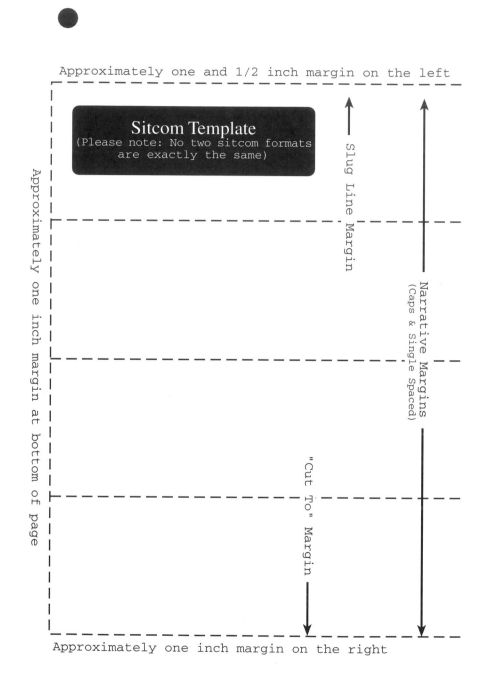

Approximately one and 1/2 inch margin on the left

Sitcom Template
(Please note: No two sitcom formats
are exactly the same)

Slug Line Margin

Narrative Margins
(Caps & Single Spaced)

Approximately one inch margin at bottom of page

"Cut To" Margin

Approximately one inch margin on the right

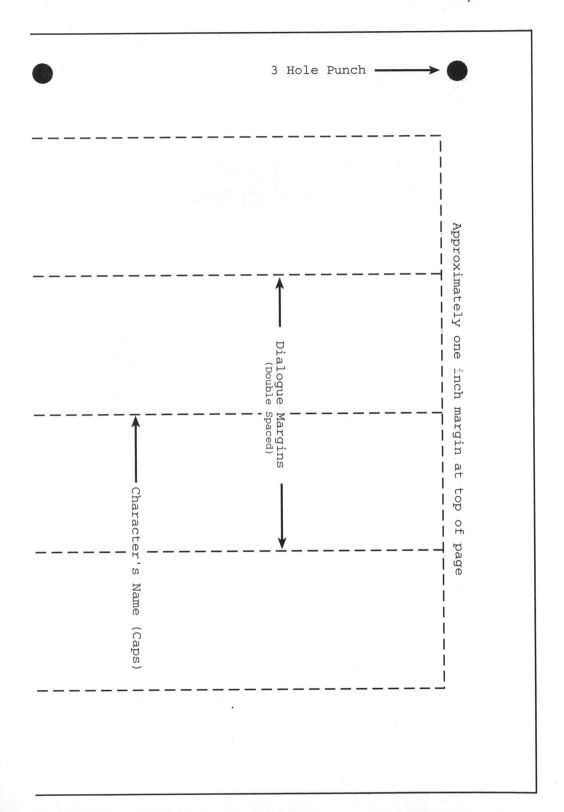

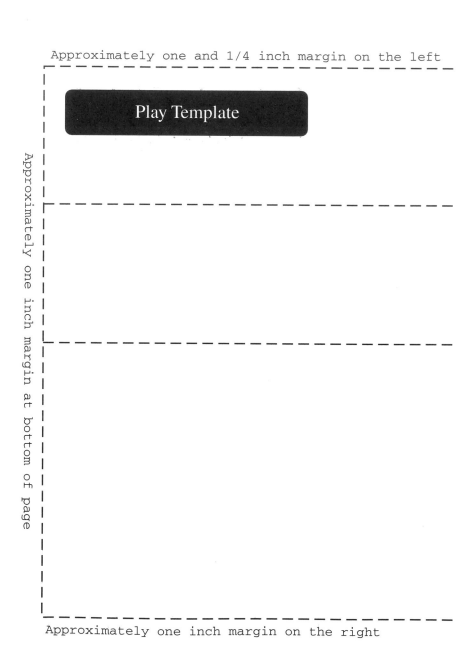

Approximately one and 1/4 inch margin on the left

Play Template

Approximately one inch margin at bottom of page

Approximately one inch margin on the right

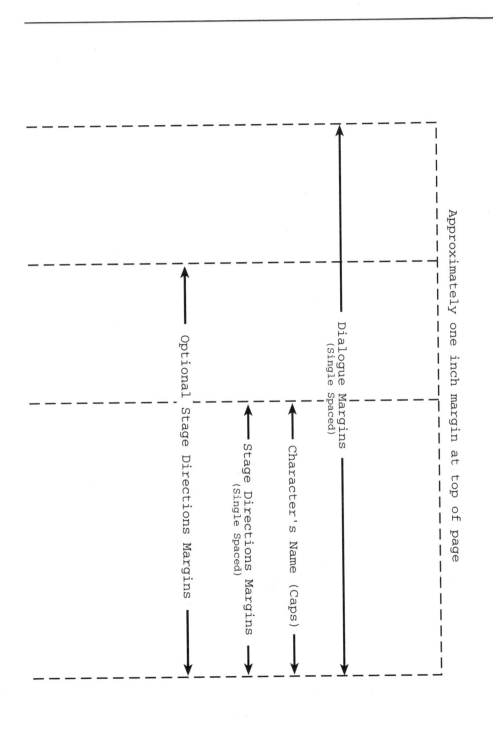

COMPUTER PROGRAMS

Many computer programs can help playwrights and screenwriters format, keep records, make scene cards, even build a story. They can be expensive, and are usually geared toward screenwriting, but they can easily extrapolate to playwriting.

STORYBUILDING SOFTWARE

These programs let you input information about your story and characters and then ask you questions about plot, themes, character development, and structure. In a sense, they "pick your brain" about your play idea. They can help some writers speed up the creative process by offering ideas, phrases, conflicts, and situations that may enable a playwright to free-associate. A few such programs are:

Software	Type	Company	Phone
Collaborator	IBM/MAC	Collaborator Systems	(818) 980-2943
Dramatica	IBM/MAC	Screenplay Systems	(818) 842-7819
Fictionmaster	IBM/MAC	Write Pro	(914) 843-7819
1st Aid For Writers	IBM/MAC	Write Pro	(914) 843-7819
Storyline Pro	IBM/MAC	Truby's Writer's Studio	(800) 33Truby
Writer's Block	IBM	Ashley Wilde Software	(714) 583-9153
Plots Unlimited	IBM/MAC	Ashley Wilde Software	(714) 583-1553
Creative Whack Pack	IBM/MAC	Creative Think	(415) 321-6775
Ideafisher	IBM/MAC	IdeaFisher Systems	(800) 289-4332
Inspiration	IBM/MAC	Inspiration Software	(503) 245-9011
Storyvision	IBM	Story Vision	(310) 392-5090

SUBMISSION RECORD SOFTWARE

The following are two computer programs designed to help a writer keep track of submissions.

Software	Type	Company	Phone
Writer's Record Keeper	IBM	Creative Professional's	(402) 393-8070
Green Turtle	IBM	Green Turtle	(205) 928-2852

FORMATTING SOFTWARE

These programs are designed to help writers format screenplays and plays:

Software	Type	Company	Phone
Final Draft	MAC	Mac Toolkit	(310) 395-4242
Moviemaster	IBM	Comprehensive Video	(201) 767-7990
Script Thing	IBM	Scriptperfection	(619) 270-7515
Script Perfection	IBM	Scriptperfection	(619) 270-7515
Scriptware	IBM	Cinivision	(303) 786-7799
Scriptor	IBM/MAC	Screenplay Systems	(818) 843-7819
Side By Side	IBM/MAC	Audio Easy	(800) 272-8232
Superscript Pro	IBM	Inherit The Earth	(310) 559-3814
PlayWrite	MAC	PlayWrite Systems	(818) 355-0648
Scriptwriting Tools	MAC	Morley & Associates	(612) 884-3991

SCENE CARD SOFTWARE

These programs create and arrange scene cards:

Software	Type	Company	Phone
Story Vision	IBM	Story Vision	(310) 392-7550
Corkboard	MAC	Mac Toolkit	(310) 395-4242

COMPUTER STORES FOR WRITERS

The following stores specialize in computer software for writers:

The Writers' Computer Store
3001 Bridgeway Ave.
Sausalito, CA 94965-1495
Phone: 415-332-7005 Fax: 415-332-7037

The Writers' Computer Store
11317 Santa Monica Blvd.
Los Angeles, CA 90025-3118
Phone: 310-479-7774
http://writerscomputer.com/

Bulloch Entertainment	Toronto	(416) 923-9255
New Media	Los Angeles	(213) 935-5300
Software Supermarket	Los Angeles	(310) 473-9550
Village Computers	New York	(212) 254-9000

You can also send for catalogs:

The Write Stuff Catalog
21115 Devonshire St. #182-153
Chatsworth, CA 91311
(818) 773-6460

WEB SITES FOR PLAYWRIGHTS
AND SCREENWRITERS

RESOURCES FOR SCREENWRITERS AND PLAYWRIGHTS
>   http://www.inkspot.com/~ohi/www/screen.html
>   This site contains information on children's theatre, workshops, film studios, playwriting and screenwriting seminars, tips from the pros, news, movie and theatre databases, and just about anything a playwright or screenwriter should want to know.

RESOURCES FOR SCREENWRITERS AND PLAYWRIGHTS
>   http://www.interlog.com/%7Eohi/www/screen.html

THEATRE CENTRAL
>   http://www.theatre-central.com/
>   This web site contains journals, discussion forums, and columns.

DRAMA DEPARTMENT AT GOLDSMITH COLLEGE, UNIVERSITY OF LONDON
>   http:/www.gold.ac.uk/pub/tgp/.
>   Playwrights may list their plays on this British service if they have had at least one previous production and will appeal to audiences outside the originating country. The information on this database includes cast, subject matter, general information, and text.)

DRAMATIC EXCHANGE
>   http://www.dramex.org/htmlplays.html
>   This web site will list information on any original play. Its service includes synopsis, cast, length, text, and instructions for contacting the playwright.)

PLAYWRITING SEMINARS
>   http://www.fpa.pdx.edu/depts/fpa/playwriting/seminar.html

>   DRAMATISTS SOURCE BOOK
>   http://www.vcu.edu/artweb/playwriting/sourcebook.html

NEW DRAMATISTS
http://www.itp.tsoa.nyu.edu/%7Ediana/ndintro.html

AMERICAN THEATRE MAGAZINE
http://www.vcu.edu/artweb/playwriting/americantheatre.html

COMPREHENSIVE INDEX OF U.S. COLLEGE THEATRE PROGRAMS
http://dolphin.upenn.edu/~intuiton/guide/newguide.html

RESOURCES FOR PLAYWRIGHTS
http://www.teleport.com/cdeemer/Playwrights.html

THEATER COMPANIES
http://www.yahoo.com/Arts/Drama/Theater_Companies/

PLAYS & PLAYWRIGHTS
http://home.earthlink.net/~omniverse/elactheatre/library/plays.htm

GENERAL LINKS TO THEATRE, ACTING AND PRODUCTIONS SITES
http://www.execpc.com/%7Eblankda/acting1.html#theatres

THEATRE LIBRARY (THEATRE LINKS, SEARCH ENGINES, NEWGROUPS
AND MORE)
http://home.earthlink.net/~omniverse/elactheatre/library/
links.htm#writing(dramatic)

POETICS BY ARISTOTLE (full text)
gopher://gopher.vt.edu:10010/02/39/19

GENERAL WRITING RESOURCES
http://www.teleport.com/~cdeemer/General.html

ELEMENTS OF STYLE by Strunk & White
http://www.columbia.edu/acis/bartleby/strunk/

SAMUEL FRENCH THEATRE & FILM BOOK SHOPS
http://HollywoodNetwork.com/hn/shopping/bookstore/sfbook.html

U.S. COPYRIGHT OFFICE GENERAL INFORMATION
http://lcweb.loc.gov/copyright/

REGISTERING DRAMATIC WORKS WITH THE U.S. COPYRIGHT OFFICE
http://home.earthlink.net/~omniverse/elactheatre/library/misc/
copyrite.htm

MORE COPYRIGHT INFORMATION LINKS
http://www.yahoo.com/Government/Law/Intellectual_Property/
Copyrights

10 BIG MYTHS ABOUT COPYRIGHT EXPLAINED
http://www.clari.net/brad/copymyths.html

WRITERS GUILD OF AMERICA, WEST
http://www.wga.org/wga.cgi

INTERNET SCREENWRITERS NETWORK
http://www.hollywoodnetwork.com/hn/writing/screennet.html

RESOURCES FOR SCREENWRITERS
http://www.teleport.com/~cdeemer/Screenwriters.html

SCREENWRITER'S ONLINE CHAT
http://www.tcf.ua.edu/chat/

FILM SCHOOLS
http://www.lather.com/fsc/fsc4.html

INDEX